REFORMING THE WORLD MONETARY SYSTEM: FRITZ MACHLUP AND THE BELLAGIO GROUP

Financial History

Forthcoming Titles

REFORMING THE WORLD MONETARY SYSTEM: FRITZ MACHLUP AND THE BELLAGIO GROUP

BY

Carol M. Connell

LONDON AND NEW YORK

First published 2013 by Pickering & Chatto (Publishers) Limited

Published 2016 by Routledge
2 Park Square, Milton Park, Abingdon, Oxfordshire OX14 4RN
711 Third Avenue, New York, NY 10017, USA

First issued in paperback 2015

Routledge is an imprint of the Taylor & Francis Group, an informa business

BRITISH LIBRARY CATALOGUING IN PUBLICATION DATA

Connell, Carol Matheson, 1948–
Reforming the world monetary system: Fritz Machlup and the Bellagio Group.
– (Financial history)
1. Machlup, Fritz, 1902–1983 – Influence. 2. Monetary reformers. 3.
International finance. 4. Economic policy – Decision making. 5. Economic
history – 1945–1971. 6. Economic history – 1971–1990.
I. Title II. Series
332.4'566-dc23

ISBN-13: 978-1-138-66468-5 (pbk)
ISBN-13: 978-1-8489-3360-6 (hbk)
Typeset by Pickering & Chatto (Publishers) Limited

CONTENTS

ACKNOWLEDGEMENTS

This study was made possible by a fellowship research grant from the Earhart Foundation. I am deeply grateful for the comments and suggestions made by members of the Colloquium on Market Institutions and Economic Processes at New York University where some of my ideas were first presented, and for the generous invitation of Bruce Caldwell to present at a workshop at the Center for the History of Political Economy at Duke University.

The scenarios argument presented here was first made in the *Journal of Management History*, 17:1 (2011), pp. 50–65; framing in the *PSL Quarterly Review*, 64:257 (2011), pp. 143–66; and confidence in the *Journal of the History of Economic Thought*, 34:3 (2012). My interest in the work of Fritz Machlup originated in research on his student, the growth theorist Edith Penrose, which first appeared in the *Journal of Management History*, 13:3 (2007), pp. 228–39.

LIST OF FIGURES AND TABLES

INTRODUCTION

At a time of financial crisis and loss of confidence in the international financial system not unlike the global financial crisis of 2008 in spirit if not specifics, a team of academics, policymakers, bankers and corporate leaders sought to reform the system and build support for their reforms. Drawing on archival and published sources, I have attempted to create a picture of the personalities, issues, debates and compromises that led to the adoption of flexible exchange rates and a modified Triffin Plan with special drawing rights in the International Monetary Fund (IMF). The work focuses on the contribution of the Bellagio Group of non-governmental, academic economists to an understanding of the problems and an exploration of alternative solutions.

Led by economist Fritz Machlup, the Bellagio Group was engaged in a grand experiment. Machlup called it a 'test' to find out whether this group could identify the differences in factual and normative assumptions that might explain the differences in prescriptions for solving the problems of the international monetary system. By design, the selection of the members of this study group would include the foremost protagonists of the most widely discussed monetary plans, distinguished scholars in the field of international finance and renowned teachers.

Contemporary policymakers and students of public policy and macroeconomics will find in Machlup's approach an analogue to the current Group of Twenty Finance Ministers and Central Bank Governors (G20), engaged in creating a framework for strong, sustainable and balanced growth, while putting out the fires of global and regional financial crisis. Strategists will see in the exploration of underlying assumptions, as well as the selection of experts with different specialties, diverse backgrounds and divergent plans for reform, a cross-functional team masterfully facilitated by economist and business leader Fritz Machlup. Machlup used the tools that have become associated with strategy – framing, scoping, scenarios, exploration of assumptions, collaboration, the iterative exploration of alternatives and their implications for execution (including institutions and operational concerns).

While non-strategists and some strategy consultants may believe that the objective of strategy and strategists is to promote a particular interpretation of a problem and a particular solution, at its heart it is not. When the external environment is complex and dynamic, situation analysis must acknowledge the potential for political as well as economic change. This would have been the case in the 1960s, given the conflicting political and economic issues behind economic integration of Europe and world monetary crisis management. It is true today.

The invitation of academics to join the Bellagio Group was no less strategic. Most of the academic economists had played an active public policy role before academia. All represented the nations of the Group of Ten, which had assumed greater importance within the IMF after the General Arrangements to Borrow put them on the hook to bail out nations suffering serious balance of payments deficits. Many members of the Bellagio Group were also working towards European integration.

The Bellagio Group worked closely with the chair and deputies of the Group of Ten – from Dr Otmar Emminger to Emile van Lennep and Rinaldo Ossola, and a hundred others who would become prominent in national and global government and politics. Again, the decision was strategic. Despite its description as a study group, Machlup and co-leaders Robert Triffin and William Fellner sought to have impact on the private discussions and policy recommendations of the Group of Ten. Timing was, if not everything, a significant aspect of their strategy: Bellagio Group meetings and output were timed to coincide with, even slightly precede, the meetings and output of the Group of Ten and the IMF.

Largely missing from contemporary scholarship on Machlup is a study of his work with the members of the Bellagio Group and their collaboration on issues confronting international monetary reform in the 1960s and 1970s through twenty-two conferences under the Bellagio Group umbrella and five under the aegis of the Bürgenstock Group. The Bellagio Group was the de facto forerunner of the current Group of Thirty, chaired by Jean-Claude Trichet. The mandate of the Group of Thirty is broad, covering exchange rate systems and currency arrangements, international capital markets and capital flows, the role and operations of international financial institutions, central banking and financial supervision, international trade and trade policy and comparative studies in macroeconomics, product and labour markets. The G20 mandate appears to be more closely aligned to the Bellagio Group's interests. Certainly, the problems confronting the G20 include those unresolved in the 1960s and 1970s – the shared responsibilities of mutually interdependent surplus and deficit countries, the role of the IMF, modifications to institutions and operational requirements to ensure compliance.

Research Questions and Original Hypotheses

The research presented in this book was driven by four questions:

What were the international payments problems that stimulated academics and policymakers to recommend changes to the gold exchange standard? What were the origins of these problems?

For each of the four major policy proposals, who were the advocates, and what were the assumptions and values? What were the anticipated macroeconomic effects? The four major policy proposals advocated by clusters of Bellagio Group members are: the semi-automatic gold standard by which each participating country would fix the gold value of its monetary unit and guarantee to maintain that value, with the result that countries following this standard would enjoy fixed rates of exchange; flexible exchange rates; multiple currency reserves and a new mega-central bank with centralized reserves.

What was the impact of Bellagio's proposals on public policy, then and now?

What was the legacy of Bellagio's members on the international trade and finance scholarship from 1960 to the present?

Preliminary hypotheses point to the relevance of this study to contemporary problems of exchange rates and trade deficits.

Hypothesis 1: The international payments problems that stimulated changes to the gold exchange standard had roots in macroeconomic issues of savings, investment, trade and growth, issues as important to economists and public policy leaders dealing with post-WWII economies as they are to us today.

Hypothesis 2: The choice of exchange regime has a profound influence on stability and growth.

Hypothesis 3: The Bellagio Group members went on to become active members in public policy in the US and abroad and shaped international trade and monetary policy.

Hypothesis 4: Study of Bellagio Group members and their students reveals a significant impact on international trade and finance scholarship from the 1960s to the present.

Methodology

Taking a historico-biographical approach, the books draws on the Register of the Fritz Machlup Papers at the Hoover Institution and the Robert Triffin Papers at Yale University, as well as on the published works of Machlup, Triffin, Fellner and their contemporaries. Many economists, inside and outside the Bellagio Group, struggled with the same issues. My purpose here was to give them voice. This is a group story.

The Organization of the Book

Chapter 1, A Crisis in Confidence, examines the tensions that were already in place when the Bretton-Woods Agreement was signed linking the dollar to gold, identifies the major players and the issues, their perspective on reserve currencies, the Group of Ten countries and their growing influence on world growth. The chapter sets the stage for the series of debates that absorbed academics and policymakers from 1963 to 1977.

Chapter 2 is an introduction to Fritz Machlup, his research and methodology. Machlup began his academic career in monetary economics; hence Chapter 2 begins with his dissertation on the gold standard in Austria and his later reflections on the meaning of this work. The chapter draws attention to the model he developed for assessing the impact of change on economic systems. Machlup believed this model was key to an understanding of balance of payments problems. Machlup published in many other areas of economics – from patents and knowledge to productivity and innovation – while he was working on monetary issues. The chapter also puts some focus on these areas.

Chapter 3 is an introduction to Robert Triffin. Triffin, a fellow émigré and friend of Machlup since the 1950s, was deeply engaged in European integration issues as well as in the broader problems of international monetary system reform. The chapter provides a brief summary of Triffin's work for the Federal Reserve and IMF before launching into his work for the European Commission and his numerous papers on overall system reform. The chapter explores the importance of confidence to the thinking of Machlup and Triffin.

Chapter 4 is an introduction to William Fellner. A long-time friend of Triffin and Machlup, and a colleague of Triffin at Yale, Fellner began writing on inflation, taxation, government regulation and economic growth, particularly the importance of productivity and innovation, beginning in 1942 and throughout the post-war period. The chapter reviews Fellner's writings on these issues, as well as his contributions to monetary system reform. Fellner's thinking on system reform is compared with that of Machlup and Triffin as expressed in their joint publication *Maintaining and Restoring Balance in International Payments*. Some focus is put on Fellner's concept of credibility.

Chapter 5, Why Economists Disagree, provides a brief review of the framing literature. The chapter covers the first four Bellagio conferences and how Machlup framed the problems confronting the world monetary system.

The Bellagio Group discussions stimulated further publication and discussion of reserve currency and exchange rate solutions to liquidity and payments adjustment problems. Chapter 6 covers a variety of multiple reserve currency plans introduced in the early 1960s to reduce dependence on a single currency linked to gold as well as to increase liquidity. The plans covered in this chapter include one that was actually introduced into use – the European Payments Union (EPU) unit of account. The chapter compares these plans and examines the lessons we can draw today from the European unit of account.

Chapter 7 examines some of the major arguments for variations on flexible and fixed exchange rates made by the Bellagio Group economists and by their contemporaries. Variations include both gold-based and non-gold-based fixed rates, like the optimum currency area theory of Robert Mundell brought to life in the ECU, as well as the band proposal of Egon Sohmen, among other variations on managed and unmanaged floating. An important conclusion emerges from this review of the literature: Many of the economists drawn into the fixed versus flexible debate had been writing on adjustment and liquidity issues since the Great Depression and through World War II.

Chapter 8 explores the growing importance of the deputies of the Group of Ten, those countries committed to bailing out IMF members in financial crisis. For the deputies, the focus of multiple currency reserve plans has shifted to payments adjustment and to the relative responsibilities of deficit and surplus countries. The Bellagio Group is brought in to orchestrate the first Joint Meetings of Academics and Officials focused on these issues, leading to the publication of *Maintaining and Restoring Balance in International Payments* in 1966.

Chapter 9 deals with the evolving role of the Bellagio Group from informal study group to social interest non-governmental organization (NGO). In a series of conferences through 1977, the Bellagio Group economists, working with the deputies of the Group of Ten, would operationalize special drawing rights. They would help the mostly European deputies build a European viewpoint on major issues confronting the IMF in settings outside the main body, where participants could talk freely.

Beginning in the late 1960s, when some degree of exchange rate flexibility was becoming more acceptable, the Bellagio Group took its model of scenario-based discussion and publication to a new audience of corporate economists and private bankers. A series of five conferences were held. After a review of the scenario analysis literature, Chapter 10 explores the conference discussions and the publication of *Approaches to Greater Flexibility of Exchange Rates: The Bürgenstock Papers*.

While the last Bellagio Group meeting was held in Basle in 1977, there would soon be a successor. Chapter 11 examines the Group of Thirty, formed in 1978 and drawing on many of the same members with the same core competence in monetary economics. The mandate and operations of the Bellagio Group and the Group of Thirty are compared.

How did contemporaries evaluate the contributions of the Bellagio Group? What have economic historians had to say? How did the Group's leaders assess their role in monetary reform? Chapter 12 answers these questions and discusses the requirement for a new Bellagio Group to deal with unresolved issues.

The Bellagio Group's leaders and members were teachers and mentors with extensive influence on scholarship in many fields. Chapter 13 examines a few of these student/teacher and student/mentor relationships. Equally importantly, this chapter speaks to the importance of mentors even when the advisee pursues a different intellectual path.

The final chapter draws a set of conclusions about the Bellagio Group's contributions and lessons for today.

1 A CRISIS IN CONFIDENCE

Introduction

Nearly a half-century before the financial crisis of 2008–9, there was another time (conservatively, from 1959, when Triffin first presented his analysis to a Congressional committee, to 1977, the end of the Bellagio Group conferences, which is the period covered in this book) when reforming the world monetary system was on everyone's lips. Many academics and policymakers were formulating plans for its reconstruction before illiquidity, speculation and loss of confidence brought the system to a predicted ruin. Not since the Great Depression was the fear of a total financial meltdown so real.

In his statement before the US Congress, economist Robert Triffin articulated the problem that would become known as the 'Triffin Paradox'. That is to say, as the global economy expanded, the United States – as the marginal supplier of the world's reserve currency – could continue to supply reserve assets to foreigners by running a current account deficit and issuing dollar-denominated obligations to fund it. If the United States ever stopped running balance of payments deficits and supplying reserves, the resulting shortage of liquidity would pull the global economy into a contracting spiral. Nevertheless, Triffin warned that if the deficits continued, excess global liquidity risked fuelling inflation. Moreover, the build-up in dollar-denominated liabilities might cause foreigners to doubt whether the United States could maintain gold convertibility or might be forced to devalue, thus undermining confidence in both the dollar and the monetary system depending on the dollar. Triffin would call for a radical reform of the system in *Gold and the Dollar Crisis*.[1] US President John F. Kennedy would urge members of his cabinet to act on Triffin's proposals.[2] Fred Bergsten of the US National Security Council and the Brookings Institution would call *Gold and the Dollar Crisis* 'the most influential book ever written on the international monetary system'.[3]

We know in the end that flexible exchange rates prevailed and that the underlying system was not reformed. We know also that Triffin believed that the outcome was the result of Fritz Machlup's influence on influential policymakers and academics who had strong policymaking ties – policymakers like Otmar Emminger of Germany, Robert Roosa of the United States and Andre de Lattre and Giscard d'Estaing of France.[4] Contemporary literature, much of it written by insiders to the reform debates, supports Triffin's perspective on Machlup's influence and that of the group he led, the thirty-two non-governmental economists. This group would become known as the Bellagio Group, for the Rockefeller resort on Lake Como where members frequently convened. This brand name, as it were, is also given to a series of conferences that included the original Bellagio Group members but also finance and treasury officials from the industrialized nations, corporate economists and strategists and private bankers. In an age before television programmes needed academic experts to interpret current events, how did Machlup and the Bellagio Group develop their outreach and exert an influence on the monetary system of today? Former historian of the International Monetary Fund Margaret DeVries wrote, 'In 1963–64, a group of 32 academic economists and public officials identified three basic problems of the Bretton Woods system: liquidity, adjustment and confidence in reserve media. For the next decade, discussions of the system's shortcomings centred around these three problems.'[5] In the economic literature, liquidity and confidence were and are two related, even intertwined factors, influencing how economists and policymakers felt about the third factor – the likelihood and speed of payments adjustment.

This chapter reviews the critical balance of payments problems facing the world after World War II. Then, using 2012 as an example, it discusses surpluses and deficits in balance of payments in terms of the impact on trade and employment. Perceived in this context, the contributions of trade economists to new thinking about balance of payments theory, comparative advantage, effective tariff and protection theory, optimum policy combinations and exchange rate regimes are discussed. Finally, the chapter puts the Bellagio Group in context and summarizes monetary system events and actions through the Jamaica Accord of 1976.

Balance of Payments Problems in the 1960s

From 1946 to 1973, exchange rate policy was dominated by the Bretton Woods system. It differed from the prior period's gold-exchange standard in three ways. Instead of pegged exchange rates, Bretton Woods established adjustable exchange rates to eliminate balance of payments deficits, subject to the existence of what was known as 'fundamental disequilibrium' (although the term was associated with crisis and countries sought to avoid sending a message of crisis to their trading partners). Capital controls were permitted in order to curb potentially volatile international capital flows. The International Monetary Fund was created with the mandate to monitor national economic policies, extend balance of payments financing to countries at risk, sanction governments responsible for policies that destabilized the international system, and compensate countries that were adversely affected.[6] In practice, despite the adjustable peg, parity changes were rare. Exchange controls substituted for the absence of an adjustment mechanism until the restoration of current account convertibility in 1958.

Under the Bretton Woods system, the universally accepted reserve asset for international payments was gold, but gold supplies were limited and new gold stores were under the control of countries (fundamentally South Africa and Russia) where gold was mined. Hence, US dollars and British pounds sterling (the latter only after 1958) were established by the Bretton Woods Agreement as substitute currencies for international payments, although convertible to gold upon request. The dollar was also a medium for the financing of foreign trade through the Eurodollar market, which permitted high interest-bearing US dollar-denominated short-term deposits at foreign banks or foreign branches of American banks that were not subject to US bank reserve requirements. The Eurodollar market was actively promoted in Britain as a way to continue Britain's international financial leadership role. According to Gianni Toniolo, most central banks at this point (early 1960s) took a positive attitude towards the Eurocurrency market because it provided them with a flexible, high-yield investment outlet and temporary cover for liquidity imbalances, and they used the Eurocurrency market (Bank for International Settlements, Bank of Italy) for this purpose.[7] The central banks' attitude of benign neglect of the Eurodollar market began to change in 1967–8 following international monetary events that accelerated the pace of short-term capital flows – the 1967 War in the Middle East, the sterling devaluation of 1967, the gold crisis of March 1968 and the French franc crisis later in the same year. Having grown to a huge size, the Eurocurrency market was heavily dependent on monetary policies in the USA, as concern spread about the War in Vietnam and President Lyndon Johnson's Great Society programme.

From 1958 to 1968, a whole series of agreements, regimes rules and institutions were needed to ensure the Bretton Woods financial system worked. Institutions included the International Monetary Fund, Working Party 3 of the Organisation for Economic Co-operation and Development, and the Bank for International Settlements, which was tasked with problems of money and exchange. Agreements and regime rules included swap agreements between central banks; the London gold pool; the General Arrangements to Borrow; and the institution of special drawing rights in the IMF. The London gold pool (consisting of the United States, Germany, United Kingdom, France, Italy, Belgium, Netherlands and Switzerland) was created to regulate and protect the price of gold on world markets. The gold pool broke down under the outflow of gold reserves and France withdrew from the agreement. The devaluation of the British pound, followed by a run on gold and an attack on the pound sterling, led to the March 1968 gold crisis, which Charles Coombs of the New York Federal Reserve Bank said to Federal Reserve Chairman William McChesney Martin was 'a crisis more dangerous than any since 1931'. Thereafter a two-tiered market system was enforced, calling for an official exchange standard of $35, along with open market transactions. While the USA pledged to suspend gold sales to governments to trade in private markets, and gold pool members said they would not sell to private persons, some participants converted currency reserves into gold and sold it at higher rates. The system proved unsustainable and would collapse in 1971, when West Germany left the Bretton Woods system, and the United States abolished direct convertibility of the dollar.

Nevertheless, maintaining the system's viability for as long as possible was highly desirable given the high rate of growth in international trade. To support such trade required the creation of increasing international liquidity, primarily in the form of central bank reserves. Insufficient means of international payments would obviously reduce trade and therefore output growth and therefore employment. Full employment and growth required trade liberalization. Individual countries would proceed with a programme of trade liberalization only if they felt comfortable with a level of reserves believed to be capable of cushioning the domestic economy from international monetary shocks.[8] Hence, the provision of international liquidity largely depended on the US balance of payments deficit, although managing the size of those deficits was critical to confidence in the international currency. This had not been a problem given the dollar shortage that prevailed through much of the 1950s, when the USA ran balance of payments surpluses. The problem began to manifest when US purchases from Japan and Western Europe, as well as the country's overseas investments and military expenditures, led to larger US balance of payments deficits.[9]

The USA and Europe shared a common fear: the balance of payments effects of short-term money flows (increasingly those through the Eurodollar market, as well as the ability of central bankers to cash in dollars for gold at any time). Both sides of the Atlantic feared that the ratio of dollar liabilities to American-held gold might one day increase to a level that causes a loss of foreign confidence in the dollar and a run to the US Treasury gold window.

American policymakers saw loss of confidence as a threat to national economic well-being and foreign policy. Presidents Dwight Eisenhower, John F. Kennedy and Lyndon Johnson considered US payments deficits a problem as critical to US security as the nuclear threat. Kennedy calculated that the US payments deficit in 1962 was equal to the cost of maintaining US troops in Europe, and weighed the advantages of eliminating the deficit by recalling the troops or by negotiating with the French as the USA had done with Germany to pay for the troops via US armaments purchases, thus allowing the USA to use the cash received to retire the deficit.[10] Cold War Presidents were concerned that the Soviet Union might pursue an alliance with Germany or that France might pursue an alliance with Germany, pushing the USA out of European affairs.

European policymakers feared restrictions on or termination of all sales of gold by the US monetary authorities; restrictions on international payments through the introduction of foreign exchange controls and prohibitions of capital transfers; import restrictions of all sorts; the blocking of deposits of foreign nationals; the end of convertibility; elimination of key currencies from the official reserves of central banks and consequently a drastic reduction in 'liquidity' everywhere; and, ultimately, reductions in production and employment resulting from import restrictions and export reduction. Many high-level French officials believed that the international monetary system was rigged in favour of the Americans. Charles de Gaulle criticized America's 'exorbitant privilege' and threatened to liquidate the French government's dollar balance. France was at that time a large creditor of the US Treasury.[11] France's ambassador to the USA Hervé Alphand had told de Gaulle that Kennedy was receiving all kinds of dangerous advice on monetary policy from his advisers. Controls and a gold embargo were being considered. Europe was already deeply engaged in building an external monetary policy to end dependency on the USA and the US dollar as the pivotal international currency, which involved reforming the international monetary system to base it on a neutral, non-dollar standard.[12]

For all practical purposes, fixing Bretton Woods without actually reforming it would boost confidence and enhance trade. Hence the plethora of minimalist, exchange rate-oriented approaches and, ultimately, the victory of floating rates. As Barry Eichengreen and Harold James have argued, 'a consensus on the need for monetary and financial reform is likely to develop when such reform is seen as essential for the defence of the global trading system'.[13] The energy of economists from the Group of Ten countries around exchange rate solutions can be partially explained by the Group of Ten's responsibility for macroeconomic policy under the IMF. As important a factor was the continued pressure towards European integration and particularly intra-Europe trade at this time. The six members of the European Coal and Steel Community (France, Belgium, Luxembourg, West Germany, the Netherlands and Italy) pursued regional integration of the goods markets with the European Economic Community (EEC), but left macroeconomic policymaking in the hands of the member states. However, the balance of payments chapter of the Rome Treaty signed in 1957 required member states to adopt economic policies that would ensure balance of payments equilibrium.[14] In the exploration of alternative solutions to problems with the Bretton Woods financial system, governments needed to decide whether they wanted to have an independent monetary policy, which required a flexible exchange rate, or to forego an autonomous monetary policy in the interests of having a stable and predictable exchange rate. In the spirit of Carsten Hefeker (1996) and Jeffry Frieden (1994), what might be called an interest-group approach to exchange rate policy preferences, given capital mobility, would suggest that large export-competing traded goods producers like Germany would be open to flexible rates.[15] At the same time, countries like France and England, as well as banks and firms that were heavily involved in international trade and investment and cared deeply about the predictability of the exchange rate, were in favour of fixed exchange rates anchored by gold. Italy, a weak state with weak institutions, looked to European integration to impose greater fiscal and monetary discipline.[16] Economic integration was important to small open economies like Belgium and the Netherlands, both of which also pursued a stable exchange rate policy. Integration was avidly pursued by democratic regimes (social democrats in Germany; Christian democrats in Italy, Belgium and the Netherlands). During the 1960s, French official position was polarized between two views on reform: those advocating a return to gold and a policy of hoarding gold as an insurance and bargaining resource to diminish US power in Europe (exemplified by Jacques Rueff, Maurice Couve de Murville and Charles de Gaulle), and those seeing the solution in developing a European monetary personality with a common or parallel currency and a composite reserve unit to replace the dollar (exemplified by Triffin, Andre de Lattre and Giscard d'Estaing).

How Balance of Payments Deficits Affect Trade, Employment and Growth

When we think about the problems affecting the world economy or national economies in 1960 versus 2012, we may not consider the interdependencies at play that may make a singular focus on payments adjustment or more jobs or decreased government spending irrational. As early as 1945, for a conference organized by the Twentieth Century Fund with help from Machlup, then at the University of Buffalo, and Paul Homan of Cornell University and managing editor of the *American Economic Review*, Machlup would write, 'Can anything be said about the preference of our society for the particular goals, about the probable choice that would be made among them, if they can only be attained alternatively? ... We cannot choose between "more employment" and "more income" without knowing how much we have to forego of the one in order to secure more of the other.'[17] The temperaments of decision makers and the impossibility of getting reliable estimates of the cost of stability in terms of progress – and progress in terms of stability – account for the differences of opinion, according to Machlup. Homan also supported this view, 'Economists who attempt to give answers to questions of future policy designed to cope with future developments must necessarily start from some set of reasonable assumptions.'[18]

In 2012, we are faced with the same problem – choosing between one and the other objective, knowing that there are interdependencies that affect the cost. At the end of 2011, the US current account balance, that is the sum of the balance of trade (exports minus imports of goods and services), net factor income (such as interest and dividends) and net transfer payments (such as foreign aid), stood at minus $583.6 billion, nevertheless significantly below 2006 when the balance was minus $800.6 billion, the highest it had ever been. Given that US imports exceed exports by $200 billion, the United States has amassed trillions of dollars of foreign debt to finance continued purchases and debt servicing, leaving itself vulnerable to sudden changes in the sentiment of global investors. For every country selling less than it buys abroad, there are unemployment consequences in the home country. Making less (and servicing less in the home country) means fewer jobs. US unemployment stands at 8.2 per cent. It has been coming down annually since it stood at 9.7 per cent in 2010, but it has been stuck at 8.2 for most of 2012. True, people who are unemployed are importing less, but they are making less, contributing to the trade imbalance. Unless exports are increasing dramatically, there is a paradox of thrift that kicks in, making a vice of personal saving. True, a depreciation of the dollar would make the price of US goods and services more attractive, as well as the USA as a location for foreign direct investment enterprise. But there are lags that would make any potential gains long in coming as the standard of living in the home country adjusts downward, and would not compensate for lower-cost goods and services abroad where the standard of living remains lower still. Because the system is inherently bilateral, there are gainers as well as losers. For every country in deficit, there is a trading partner in surplus. While the USA is in deficit, China, a major US trading and investment partner, has a current account balance that is in surplus, accounting for 2.8 per cent of gross domestic product (GDP). As of 2012, China – and Japan – each hold $1 trillion in US treasury certificates (US debt).[19] How does the confidence problem affect debt holders? A serious confidence problem could (again) lower the credit rating of the USA, raise the cost of borrowing, and cause investors to call in their loans or sell their investments and flee to safer investments elsewhere in the world, putting the cycle on continuous spin.

Europe today has its own version of the deficit and liquidity problems that confronted the world in the early 1960s. In 'Global Imbalances and the Financial Crisis: Products of Common Causes' (2009), Maurice Obstfeld and Kenneth Rogoff linked the US and European situations to economic policies of the 2000s and the transmission of these policies through the financial markets, affecting borrower and lender alike.[20] The answers to the chronic deficit problem – inflate your way out of debt, grow your way out of debt, or hunker down, make the payment adjustments and restrict domestic spending – were the answers that governments and central bankers evaluated in the early 1960s. They faced these choices drawing on experiences of the Great Depression and unfathomable unemployment and of the devastation of Europe in World War II, significant war inflation, struggles for recovery and its fifty-year economic miracle of growth. As Homan wrote, 'the deep and prolonged depression ... called into question not merely the adequacy of existing means of combating depressions but indeed the basic conceptions which underlay them ... The war blotted the problem from sight – for the time being. Unemployment disappeared. But the spectre remains ... Can the means be found to ensure that, at some later period, there will not develop another depression ... And looking into a more distant future, are the means at hand to keep people fully employed in a world which ... will remain at peace?'[21] The vital problems the USA faced in the post-war world were twofold, according to Alvin Hansen. The first: 'What role are we prepared to play in cooperation with other countries to solve the great economic problems that concern the world family of nations?' The second question: 'Shall we be able to maintain full employment in the United States? ... We cannot afford to overlook the threat to the stability of any international arrangements, whether political or economic, that would arise if this great country experienced a recurrence of deep depression and prolonged mass unemployment.'[22] Hansen wrote, 'The great depression beginning in 1929 must be set down as one of the most profoundly explosive events in all world history. It has shattered the old patterns of man's thinking in a thousand ways, and particularly in respect to economic institutions and economy policy.'[23]

An Explosion of Innovative Thinking in Economics

In the 1960s, Peter Kenen was working on a modification of the Hecksher-Ohlin theory of competitive advantage, demonstrating that international differences in skills affect the pattern of trade in manufactured goods.[24] Harry Johnson, building on James Meade's *Trade and Welfare*, analysed the welfare effects of tariffs, subsidies and the alternative effects of tariffs in the presence of domestic distortions.[25] Building on work initiated by Jacob Viner in the 1950s on the 'trade creation' and 'trade diversion' effects of customs unions, Jaroslav Vanek studied the effects of a customs union on the welfare of participating countries and the rest of the world.[26] Many economists took on a theory of effective protection looking at the effects of commercial policy on patterns of world trade and specialization. Johnson (1965, 1968) and Max Corden (1966) distinguished between nominal tariffs of traded commodities and effective tariffs, rates of protection afforded to particular production processes.[27] The investigation of the tariff structure of major industrialized countries showed that tariffs provided escalated protection, higher for finished goods, lower or non-existent for raw materials. The industrialized countries were getting the raw materials for their manufactures from underdeveloped countries, which were seriously disadvantaged by the tariff structure, inhibiting economic growth in these countries. Johnson (1965) and Bela Belassa (1967, 1968) worked on this issue,[28] finding that restrictions of the export of manufactures and processed goods from less-developed countries locked them into a dependence on primary products and impeded their economic development, a perspective introduced by Raul Prebisch (1961). Also engaged in this issue were economists Edith Penrose and Stephen Hymer, whose work is discussed in Chapter 13.

Among the economists generating significant public attention with a solution to the problems of Bretton Woods was Jacques Rueff, a monetary economist and adviser to Charles de Gaulle, who argued that the current gold exchange regime should be replaced by a pure gold standard, holding that international deviation from the gold standard had caused the global financial meltdown in 1933. He had first gained de Gaulle's trust in 1958–9 when Rueff's austerity plan to stabilize the French economy succeeded in its aims. Privately, Rueff did not believe that US deficits were caused by Cold War commitments, but by the USA's practice of financing its external deficit by increasing its IOUs or international liabilities rather than by losing gold. He argued for a rise in the price of gold sufficient for the USA to repay what it owed to foreign central banks. He argued further that other participating nations should fix the gold value of their currencies. No central bank should be permitted to lend to the USA or to any other debtor country the currency against which it had already created credit in the domestic economy. In a study of the French position from 1960 to 1968, Michael Bordo, Dominique Simard and Eugene White (1994) established that, while the French did promote and support a currency standard tied to gold, they used proposals to return to an orthodox gold standard as well as conversions of its dollar reserves into gold as tactical threats to induce the United States to initiate the reform of the international monetary system towards a more symmetrical and cooperative gold-exchange standard regime.[29] A similar but earlier case for use of tactical threats by the French was made by economist Paul Einzig. He painted a darker picture of the 'ambitious and destructive policy pursued by the French in the sphere of International Finance', using gold purchases in New York and the repatriation of dollar balances to pressure the USA to refrain from revising Germany's war debts in 1930.[30]

Michael Heilperin was a professor at the Graduate Institute of International Studies in Geneva, the home of Ludwig von Mises from 1935 to 1940, where in the Misean tradition, education favoured the return of an international gold standard. Like Mises and Rueff, Heilperin saw no alternative than to raise the price of gold to take account of the extended inflation created by excessive issuance of US dollars in the period from the mid-1950s to the early 1960s. He departed from the Misean ideal of a fully automated gold standard to propose a managed form of gold standard, just as the pre-1914 gold standard had been a system of managed, gold-linked currencies. All advanced industrialized economies starting with the Atlantic community must purposively create a gold standard. Implementation would require unified international management. The first phase of introducing a gold standard would require paying all future external deficits on current account in gold. The spread of US dollar liabilities held in foreign central banks would be halted by prohibiting additional accumulation of dollar reserves. In the second phase, the price of gold would be doubled to $70/ounce (for the reasons outlined by Rueff). However, the exact price change would be a matter of international agreement. The USA must over an agreed period then pay off all of its foreign liabilities in gold, and all countries must formally agree to make their currencies fully convertible into gold, while permitting free trading and free private ownership of gold. Later Heilperin modified his gold standard approach to call it a semi-automatic gold standard.

Sir Roy Harrod of Oxford University was a specialist in international economics and policy and biographer of Keynes. By the early 1950s, Harrod was predicting the kind of crisis that befell the Bretton Woods Agreement twenty years later: gold supplies could not keep pace with world trade. Harrod created several plans that were designed to bolster the Bretton Woods Agreement from the threat of collapse given the US external payments imbalance, but his favourite plan involved an increase in the price of gold. Gold would not so much act as a currency standard as it would an official reserve. Unlike Rueff and Heilperin, Harrod did not propose to eliminate existing dollar (and sterling) balances from official monetary reserves. Instead, Harrod wanted to maintain the dollar-gold exchange standard and supplement international reserves by raising the dollar price of gold. Harrod estimated that the price of gold should be doubled, thereby raising world gold reserves by $40 billion. Bretton Woods member countries would then be able to expand domestic credit in pursuit of higher growth and full employment. Without raising gold reserves, Harrod foresaw that the development of world trade would be impeded by a shortage in international liquidity, encouraging policymakers to maintain tighter, deflationary monetary policies, increasing the likelihood that such policies would be transmitted internationally.

Along with Xenophon Zolotas, head of the central bank of Greece, some European economists including Friedrich Lutz of Switzerland, as well as some US policymakers including Assistant Secretary of the Treasury for Monetary Affairs Robert Roosa, were more than happy to exchange the dominant reserve currency position for a basket of multinational currencies backed by gold.

The creation of a world central bank to multiply the capacity of the world monetary system by creating international reserves and making individuals banks shock-proof was the basis for the Keynes Plan, which called for the creation of an International Clearing Union and a new international currency. The IMF would be the lender of last resort under plans introduced by Triffin. Still others, led by Milton Friedman and including Machlup, Johnson and William Fellner, sought to eliminate gold completely (Machlup wanted to reduce the price of gold to drive it out of hoarding and into central banks) and set exchange rates free to float.

While proposed exchange rate regimes differed, most were variants of intellectual currents that were prominent during the economic downturn of 1929–33 and the creation of the Bretton Woods financial order: Keynesianism, Austrian economics and the Chicago school. Multiple reserve currencies and centralized reserves regimes required some degree of international cooperation and management, ideas close to Keynes who saw the advantage of 'managed money' versus rigorous adherence to a gold standard for national well-being.[31] The Austrians were fundamentally committed to a monetary system based in gold. In his 1965 essay 'The Gold Problem', Ludwig von Mises reflected, 'the gold standard alone makes the determination of money's purchasing power independent of the ambitions and machinations of governments, of dictators, of political parties, and of pressure groups.'[32] The Chicagoans saw 'exchange rate flexibility as a way to reconcile otherwise conflicting objectives, including the necessity for far reaching international coordination of internal monetary and fiscal policy in order for any country separately to follow a stable internal monetary policy'.[33] Under exchange rate flexibility, as Friedman expressed it, 'Inflation and deflation in any one country will then affect other countries primarily in so far as it affects the real income position of the initial country; there will be little or no effect through purely monetary channels'.[34]

While there were many plans, Table 1.2 lists four dominant policy themes – semi-automatic gold standard; multiple currencies; centralized reserves; and flexible exchange rates – and their advocates.

In addition to economic innovations, scholars from many disciplines were working the concepts of framing (which appears in Fellner's work in the 1960s; framing is discussed in Chapter 5), scenario exploration (the term is used by Otmar Emminger of the Deutsche Bundesbank to depict Machlup's work; scenario exploration is discussed in Chapter 10), and strategy. Economists of the 1950s led industry and firm theory studies. In the 1960s and 1970s, they found themselves on the planning teams of major corporations and government agencies (hence Emminger's suggestion to Machlup that he expand the audience for the discussion of monetary reform to include a larger corporate audience).

Group of Ten and IMF Studies Launched; Machlup, Triffin and Fellner Respond

At the Annual Meeting of the World Monetary Fund in Washington, DC on 2 October 1963, then Secretary of the Treasury and Governor of the International Monetary Fund Douglas Dillon announced at a press conference the launching of two studies on 'the outlook for the functioning of the international monetary system', one to be undertaken by government economists of the Group of Ten, the other study to be made by International Monetary Fund economists. At the press conference, the New York Times reporter Edwin Dale (later spokesperson for David Stockman of the US Budget Department) asked Secretary Dillon whether the Group of Ten intended to hold hearings, and particularly whether individual economists outside the governments would be heard.[35] The answer was no, accompanied by a remark about academic economists having had their say to no result. Machlup, along with Fellner and Triffin, felt challenged to embark on their own study, involving economists of widely divergent views and with no problem or proposal considered 'out of bounds'.[36] Hence the idea for a series of alternative conferences was born.

More than a one-off initiative of academics, the impact of conferences planned by Machlup, Fellner and Triffin would be greatly enhanced by the augmented workload and growing importance of the deputies of the Group of Ten industrializing countries who had financed a prospective bailout of IMF member countries in payments deficit or crisis.

Among deputies who would be crucial to the reform effort were Robert Roosa, Otmar Emminger and Andre de Lattre. Roosa was undersecretary of the Treasury for Monetary Affairs under President Kennedy, and stayed in the job through 1964 under President Johnson. He had been vice president of the Federal Reserve Bank of New York after World War II. He was also the chair of the deputies of the Group of Ten. He would shortly relinquish this post to Emminger. In *Monetary Reform for the World Economy*, Roosa argued that the last twenty years after World War II had been a time of 'more creative change and innovation' than in any previous period, yet critics 'predict imminent crisis unless further reforms are initiated at once'.[37] He hastened to say that he did not share that assessment, but added 'I do think the time has come for reappraisal'.[38] Nevertheless, 'The continuation of [US] deficits, substantial losses of gold by one country ... maintaining the gold anchor needed for a stable monetary system, and the development of inflationary conditions throughout much of Europe, all combined to create an atmosphere of uneasiness in which appeals for reform flourished ... One of the first requirements ... was that the United States brings its accounts back to balance ... in its own interest and in the interest of world stability'.[39]

Emminger accepted the role of chair of the deputies of the Group of Ten, after Roosa stepped down. He was a director of the Deutsche Bundesbank and had been with the bank since 1953. From 1953 to 1959 he was West Germany's executive director in the International Monetary Fund, and consistently played a leading role in the monetary committee of the European Common Market. He found that political intrusions had made his task as chair difficult to an unbelievable degree, and advised Triffin that there was not much chance for early progress towards rational reform or evolution, not because the experts are slow but because politics had entered the picture. We get a glimpse of his thoughts about the need for reform from the essay 'D-Mark in the Conflict between Internal and External Equilibrium, 1948–75', wherein he states, 'The conventional view that the United States was the main source of worldwide inflation up to 1973 is largely correct as concerns the origin of destabilizing foreign-exchange flows. The deficit on US official reserve transactions during the decade 1960–69 amounted to $11 billion ... This vast outflow of dollars caused a corresponding creation of central bank money in the recipient countries, with a multiplier effect on the money supply ... The United States emerged from World War II with extremely high liquidity and a structurally low interest level. In a number of European countries, the opposite applied; the shortage of liquidity was most severe in Germany'.[40]

French Finance Minister Andre de Lattre was the first to use the expression 'exorbitant privilege' of US largesse with no attempt to keep balance of payments in check. In *Politique Economique de la France depuis 1945*, de Lattre criticized US foreign direct investment, which he attributed to a lack of long-term capital available domestically as well as to a desire to shape the economic choices of the host country.[41] A tough critic of the General Arrangements to Borrow and the Ossola Committee's work on the creation of reserve assets, de Lattre was nonetheless impressed by Triffin, Zolatas, Machlup and the group of economists working with him on monetary reform.

The Bellagio Group Conferences in Historical Context – The Timeline of the Monetary Reform Efforts

The story of the Bellagio Group conferences begins in 1963 and ends in 1977. As will be clear in Chapters 2–4, 6 and 7, thinking and publishing about post-Depression, post-World War II problems by the economists of the Bellagio Group and their peers has a long, rich history. The immediate events that stimulated their thinking about exchange rate and policy options appear below.

Table 1.1: Summary Chronology of Monetary System Events, 1944–77

1944	Bretton Woods conference – Bretton Woods system of pegged exchange rates.
1947	International Monetary Fund established.
1953	ECOSOC report on 'The Adequacy of Monetary Reserves' defined adequacy.
1959	Robert Triffin introduces the Triffin Paradox, the plan for centralized reserves under the IMF, and an international reserve unit.
1960	Short-term capital movements put pressure on gold reserves; some monetary experts propose expanding world liquidity. Others propose multiple reserve currencies, raising or lowering the price of gold, or freely floating exchange rates.
1961	London Gold Pool formed to keep gold price fluctuations within a reasonable range.
1962	US Federal Reserve introduces 'swap' facilities (central banks would provide each other with credit lines).
	General Arrangements to Borrow enlarge fund resources by $6 billion to deal with payments imbalances, liquidity crises.
1963	Central bankers contest liquidity need, request focus on adjustment.
	Governor of the IMF Douglas Dillon launches Group of Ten and IMF study groups on monetary reform.
1964	Three more Bellagio Group conferences are held. The group's final report is issued.

Group of Ten and IMF reports are published. Group of Ten report suggests OECD's Working Party 3 focus on faster adjustment of payments imbalances. Study group of the creation of reserve assets formed with Rinaldo Ossola as chair.

At the IMF Annual Meeting in Tokyo, deputies of the Group of Ten ask to explore reserve creation.

1964　Fritz Machlup invites Otmar Emminger, chair of the deputies of the Group of Ten, to a meeting to see why Group of Ten and Bellagio Group reports diverge.

1965　President Charles de Gaulle and Giscard d'Estaing, finance minister, call for a return to the gold standard.

Robert Roosa, US Treasury, proposes a composite reserve unit (CRU).

Giscard d'Estaing proposes a French version of the CRU plan.

Report of the Ossola committee on the creation of reserve assets published.

Otmar Emminger, chair of the deputies of the Group of Ten, asks the Bellagio Group to work with the deputies on payments adjustment and reserve asset plans.

1966　Meetings of officials and academics become frequent as deputies of the Group of Ten, largely a European group, become more important to the effort and want to separate themselves from the Fund as a whole.

1967　Emminger/Deputies Report on Special Drawing Rights is approved at the IMF Annual Meeting in Rio.

1968　London Gold Pool collapses. Pound devalued. Gold two-tier system instituted.

Joint Meeting of Officials and Academics held in Bologna to discuss devaluation of the pound, 'gold rush', adjustment.

1969　Report on Special Drawing Rights becomes part of the IMF by-laws.

First Bürgenstock conference of bankers, corporate executives and academics held to discuss floating exchange rate alternatives.

1970　First SDRs created and allocated.

1971　Last of five Bürgenstock conferences held in Tarrytown, NY.

United States suspends convertibility of dollar into gold – Bretton Woods system collapses.

Germany floats.

Smithsonian Agreement signed by Group of Ten countries, who agree to appreciate their currencies against the dollar.

1972　European Community countries adopt 2.25 per cent band against the dollar.

1973　Managed floating adopted (currencies float daily, but central banks intervene by buying and selling currencies).

1974　Committee of Twenty on Reform of the International Monetary System sets guidelines for managed floating.

1976　Jamaica Accord legitimizes managed floating.

1977　Last Joint Meeting of Officials and Academics held in Basle.

Conclusions

Chapter 1 focused on the relationship of balance of contemporary payments deficits to trade, confidence and stability – issues important to the policymakers, central bankers and academic economists engaged in monetary reform. Then as now, descriptions of the issues were political as well as economic, and issues were international, regional and interrelated. How to deal precisely with the interrelationship would become a problem for policymakers and for academics working on new theories to optimize the policy mix. Policymakers were divided on the issue of how big a crisis they were dealing with. Some believed there was no crisis and maintaining the status quo was the appropriate response. Others, particularly the academic economists, experimented with a number of possible solutions. Trained as trade economists, they rose to the challenge to innovate economic policy or theory to solve a problem they understood to have real impact on trade and growth.

Several movements conspired to bring economists and policymakers together. Among them was the growing importance of the Group of Ten countries and their deputies and their desire to find and own solutions to the adjustment and liquidity problems confronting the system. They had committed $6 billion in crisis and payments imbalance protection to the IMF. They were responsible for the 1962 version of a bailout. They wanted to be sure this money was not squandered by a USA unwilling to restrain its spending – and an IMF lacking the peer review and penalties to restrain a member organization. They wanted support from outside the IMF, and they found it in the Bellagio Group.

European integration was ongoing during the period, and this complicated the world situation. Many of the actors on that stage were also policymakers on the world stage. Others were among the economists of the Bellagio Group. Like most of these economists, Machlup had been working and publishing in the area of monetary reform for many years. Chapter 2 introduces us to his life and thought.

Table 1.2: Exchange Rate Policies and their Advocates

Setting	Fundamental Postulates	Advocates
Semi-Automatic Gold Standard	Raise the price of gold sufficiently to allow the removal (redemption) of all reserve currencies from the system, leaving only gold as the reserve asset.	Pierre Dieterlen Albert Hahn Sir Roy Harrod Michael Heilperin Fritz Machlup (decrease in price of gold) Jacques Rueff Walter Salant
Centralized International Reserves	Criteria and procedures developed by and implemented to regulate the growth of world reserves in a way that avoids world inflation and deflation so that volume and allocation of resources meet current conditions.	Edward Bernstein A. C. L. Day Sir Roy Harrod Alexandre Lamfalussy Robert Triffin Pierre Uri

Setting	Fundamental Postulates	Advocates
Multiple Currencies	The monetary authorities of reserve currency countries will coordinate their policies to ensure no abrupt and destabilizing changes are made in the composition of reserve holdings and also raise the foreign-exchange component of their reserves when it is generally agreed such a change is needed to alter the growth rate of gross reserve/monetary gold stocks.	Edward Bernstein Friedrich Lutz Robert Roosa Burton Malkiel Xenophon Zolotas
Flexible Exchange Rates	Changes of a flexible exchange rate will provide an effective equilibrating mechanism by generating market forces which tend to increase export revenues and decrease import expenditures of countries whose foreign receipts have been decreasing and/or payments increasing, and inversely for countries whose receipts have been increasing and/or payments decreasing.	Milton Friedman Gottfried Haberler Albert Hahn George N Halm Harry G. Johnson Friedrich Lutz Fritz Machlup Egon Sohmen

Source: Author's own research.

2 FRITZ MACHLUP, HIS RESEARCH AND METHODOLOGY

Introduction

Born 1902, Fritz Machlup's lifelong interest in monetary economics and methodology were shaped by the Europe of his university days (1920–3), as well as by his specifically Austrian roots. In his 1980 career retrospective, 'My Early Work on International Monetary Problems', Machlup paints a picture of pre- and post-World War I Europe. The Europe of 1914 had ten currencies, all with fixed gold parities and fixed exchange rates. The Europe of 1920 had twenty-seven paper currencies, none with a gold parity, none with fixed exchange rates and several of them in various stages of inflation or hyperinflation.[1] Monetary experts were raising questions about the best techniques for stabilization and perhaps a return to the gold standard.

This chapter focuses on Fritz Machlup's body of work in monetary economics from 1923 to 1962, particularly his early writings on the gold standard; the theory of foreign exchanges, trade and devaluation; opportunity costs; frameworks for organizing and assessing change in payments balance and exchange rate policies, including his distinctive writing on issues of payments adjustment, liquidity and confidence; through to his 1962 *Plans for Reform of the International Monetary System*. Because Machlup, much like William Fellner, pursued so many areas of economics – from patents to the production of knowledge to the theory of the firm – and published prolifically in these areas, the chapter also gives some focus to these areas.

Early Writings on the Gold-Exchange Standard

Machlup's 1923 University of Vienna dissertation on the gold-exchange standard, *Die Goldkernwahrung*, was supervised by Ludwig von Mises and published in 1925. It was followed by *Die neuen Wahrungen in Europa* in 1927, a book in which he described the adoption of the gold-exchange standard by one country after another, as well as by his work on the transfer problem (1930), the price of gold (1941) and the theory of foreign exchanges (1939), all three of which were reprinted in *International Payments, Debts and Gold* (1964).[2] Machlup was the first economist to attribute adjustment and liquidity to a failure of confidence, and to argue that a restoration of confidence would render adjustment and liquidity moot.[3] His former student John Williamson attributes Machlup's belief in the importance of confidence to the role it played in the collapse of the gold-exchange standard during the Great Depression.[4]

Machlup's dissertation provides significant insight into his thinking about balance of payments. Machlup wrote, 'Throughout my book I had a running battle with what was generally called the balance of payments theory of currency depreciation. This was an utterly naïve theory which tried to explain the rising prices of foreign currencies by the deficit in the balance of payments, but failed to see that the deficit was determined by an excess supply of domestic money relative to monetary developments abroad'.[5] Again, quoting from his dissertation, Machlup took what appeared to be a monetarist approach: 'The automatic contraction of the money supply in the course of financing the payments deficit was the very essence of the adjustment process, and to offset this contraction was to prevent the adjustment and to make the deficit chronic'.[6] Machlup would acknowledge that his hard line on deficits and money supply betrayed the university student's lack of experience.

The Theory of Foreign Exchanges, Devaluation and Trade

Machlup's essay 'The Theory of Foreign Exchanges' was written after he had left Austria for the United States and had begun teaching at the University of Buffalo. It was published in two parts, between 1939 and 1940, by *Economica*. Machlup described the work as 'essentially an analysis of market equilibrium, dissecting both supply and demand in the market for foreign currency, first with flexible, then with fixed exchange rates'.[7] Machlup used a simple curve analysis to demonstrate how shifts of supply and demand curves may be caused by monetary changes. 'For example, an excess supply of domestic money caused by a rise in the stock of money or a decline in the demand for it, would shift the demand curve to the left. Hence, the curve analysis which I proposed may also be used in an exposition of the monetary approach to exchange rate and balance of payments analysis'.[8]

Machlup's essay proceeded methodically from assumptions where curves are given, and unchanged to assumptions where they shift in more or less determinate directions, and finally to assumptions where one can hardly know anything about either the shapes or the shifts of the curves, and, hence, about the most likely outcomes of specific changes and possible repercussions and adjustments. His desire was not to examine the past, but to produce an ex ante theory, linking exchange rates with trade. To synchronize transactions in the exchange and commodities markets, he assumed all contracts were for future delivery.

Machlup further assumed that all offers and bids in the foreign exchange market were exclusively those of commodity traders, the exporters offering foreign currency for sale and the importers bidding for foreign currency. On these assumptions, a surplus or deficit in the balance of trade is impossible and complete adjustment is achieved instantaneously without the possibility of a time lag.[9] If incomes are given and unchanged, the elasticities of supply and demand curves in the exchange market are indispensable variables in the analysis of the effects of changes in tastes, production costs, tariffs and other trade barriers. His first task was to explain how these elasticities were derived, his next and subsequent steps to introduce new conditions while maintaining all of the previous assumptions – long-term capital movements, unilateral transfers, sales and purchases of services to and from foreign residents, movements of gold and foreign balances under the gold standard or any system with pegged exchange rates. The final section of his essay deals with exchange speculation and interest rates.

Again, in 'The Theory of Foreign Exchanges', Machlup refuted those economists who argued that currency devaluation has a negative impact on the terms of trade: 'A rise in the price of foreign currency makes imported commodities more expensive in terms of dollars (assumed here to be the domestic currency) and exported commodities cheaper in terms of the foreign currency. A fall in the price of foreign currency makes imported commodities cheaper in terms of dollars and exported commodities more expensive in terms of the foreign currency.'[10]

In 'Elasticity Pessimism in International Trade', Machlup argued that analysts who make the assumption that currency depreciation lowers the prices of export goods to foreigners, and therefore depreciation is a good thing, are only half right and are missing the full logic of depreciation. They assume wrongly that domestic prices remain unchanged although the volume of exports in increased, making the implicit assumption that the elasticity of supply of these export goods is infinite.[11]

Opportunity Costs

While Machlup completed his dissertation under Ludwig von Mises, his teacher (indeed Mises's teacher as well as Gottfried Haberler's and Joseph Schumpeter's) was Friedrich von Wieser. Wieser built on Carl Menger's view of subjective value, coining the term 'marginal utility' and developing the idea of 'alternative cost' (later known as 'opportunity cost'). His notion of alternative cost suggests that cost depends on the value of an alternative opportunity lost when the resources were used for the chosen commodity. Although opportunity cost can be hard to quantify, its effect is universal and very real on the individual level. In a 1980 interview with the *Austrian Economics Newsletter*, Machlup would credit a definition of 'cost theory', specifically that 'cost is foregone utility, or what was later called opportunity cost'.[12] Wieser's later works, beginning with *Social Economics* (1914), were an ambitious attempt to transcend economic theory and apply his ideas to real human society. The principle behind the economic concept of opportunity cost applies to all decisions, not just economic ones. In *Human Action* (1949) Mises would offer the same characterization: 'costs are equal to the value attached to the satisfaction which one must forego in order to attain the end aimed at', and later 'Costs are the value attached to the most valuable want-satisfaction which remains unsatisfied'.[13] In Schumpeter, entrepreneurs, for whom innovations represent an opportunity to change not only the technology and products, but also influence the structure of demand, conditions of the formation costs and prices, and connect opportunity cost with the pursuit of productive opportunity.[14] Haberler (1930) would recast David Ricardo's theory of comparative advantage in terms of the opportunity cost of specializing in one commodity versus another. Machlup would apply this reasoning to the economic effects of public policy choices in a capitalist system.[15]

For Machlup, opportunity cost marries all five of the major contributions to economics he identified with the Austrian School, namely subjectivism, individualism, preferences, marginalism and time. Machlup would say, 'Opportunity cost refers to the next best alternative foregone in an act of choice. From the Austrian perspective, only individuals make choices and, hence, cost is always personal and "subjective". Since choices only relate to possibilities that the individual still views as open to him in the future (whether that future is a moment from now or a month from now), the opportunities are those the individual imagines in his mind, as he sees and evaluates them'.[16] Machlup's exploration of alternative opportunities using scenarios can be traced to Eugen von Bohm-Bawerk.[17]

Is the discussion of opportunity cost economizing applicable to enterprise outside the firm, even to public policy? According to James Buchanan (1969), yes – given a choice-influenced conception of cost, the consequences of economic choice may be borne by the decision maker or by others on whom costs may sometimes be shifted.[18] Machlup would frame the discussion of changes to the gold-exchange standard under the Bretton Woods system in terms of opportunity costs. In his paper 'Eight Questions on Gold: A Review', Machlup (1941) argued that the US-imported gold reserves do not represent a sacrifice of wealth or income despite the fact that:

> The huge quantities of gold which we have purchased are a rather useless asset. We have neither an industrial use for them nor a monetary use in domestic circulation nor a monetary use in the sense that we may ever intend to have sufficient import surpluses to use substantial portions of the gold in international payments. If this is correct, has it not been utterly foolish to buy all this gold? Not if the gold has cost us little or nothing and if the purchase has had desirable secondary effects.[19]

Among these 'secondary effects' is a contribution to national income that has resulted indirectly from gold purchases, even though the gold as such is of no direct use to the USA. If foreign nations use the dollars received for the gold to purchase American products, income is created in the United States.[20] An opportunity cost arises when gold purchases finance foreign purchases of American securities, which are then resold to the USA against US product purchases when unused capacity and unemployment are low. Even then, potential costs must be weighed against political costs:

> But why should we fool ourselves with an analysis which neglects all political considerations? Are not the British purchases even in serious bottleneck situations of such a nature that we do not mind foregoing new 1942 model automobiles and several other things which may constitute the opportunity cost of our aid to Britain? We are in fact quite glad that the British have still some American securities-at one time acquired with the help of our gold purchases-because we have an easier political problem if we repurchase American securities than if we have to buy British government obligations.[21]

Certainly, Machlup's contemporaries acknowledged that he was the first economist to frame the discussion of balance of payments problems in terms of payments adjustment, liquidity and confidence.[22] Importantly, each potential solution to the adjustment problem or the liquidity or confidence problem would have an opportunity cost (a more or less negative impact on the two remaining problems). Machlup would use a partial equilibrium adjustment model as a framework for group discussion, where a specific exchange rate regime would be proposed as a disequilibrating change and the equilibrating impacts on adjustment, liquidity and confidence evaluated in terms of fundamental postulates, operations and institutions needed to implement the regime. He admits: 'In view of the layman's idea that a trade deficit is always a "disequilibrium" of the balance of payments, it is important to comprehend that explaining the deficit means to show it as an adjustment, or an equilibrating change, following an antecedent disequilibrating change, for example increased government spending, expansionary monetary policy, devaluation of trading partner's currency, receipt of foreign investment, etc.'.[23]

Using a Partial Equilibrium Model to Account for Changes in Payments Balance, Trade and Exchange Rate Policy Regimes

A key problem for Machlup, as for Mises, Hayek and others in the Austrian tradition, was how economic actors adapt to unanticipated change. Machlup's unconventional version of marginalism produces a process story appropriate for analysing adjustment to exogenous change using a four-step partial equilibrium adjustment model. Just as adaptation to change and measuring change were important to Machlup, so was a third and related idea, verification, which he defined as a procedure designed to find out whether a set of data about a class of phenomena is obtainable and, then, whether the data can be reconciled with a particular set of hypothetical generalizations about these phenomena. Machlup argued that the purpose of the model, which he called the 'machine', is not to put the assumptions of economic theory to empirical test, but rather the predicted results that are deduced from them.[24] Machlup's 'fixed part of the machine' is strikingly similar to Imre Lakatos' 'hard core' of scientific research programmes.[25] Here, the purpose of the model is to provide an 'invisible hand', a genetic explanation of a process, involving social (rather than natural) phenomena, that unfolds in time. The story provides a plausible mechanism whereby the displaced activities of individuals aiming at particular ends, and not at the phenomenon in question, nevertheless result in the occurrence of the phenomenon.[26] In Machlup's model, the input is an 'assumed' change that causes other things to happen, and the output is the 'deduced' or predicted change. Both assumed and deduced change can be empirically verified by observed data. The machine with all its parts furnishes the connection between the assumed cause, the input, and the deduced effect, the outcome. The machine consists of many parts, all of which represent assumptions or hypotheses of different degrees of generality. The so-called fundamental assumptions are a fixed part of the machine; they make the machine what it is; they cannot be changed without changing the character of the machine. All other parts are exchangeable.[27]

The exchangeable parts of Machlup's model are a series of adjusting changes (neoclassical partial equilibrium positions) caused by a sequence of individual actions and reactions that must be explained or accounted for in terms of the knowledge, preferences and expectations of the individuals doing the acting. Hence, the knowledge, preferences and expectations of the actors must provide sufficient cause for their actions and seem reasonable and understandable in common sense terms.[28] In the conferences Machlup would organize around balance of payments problems and exchange rate regimes, causal connections between disturbing changes (change in exchange rate regime) and adjusting changes (payments balance/imbalance, liquidity increase/decrease, confidence increase/decrease) would be essential to the discussion of alternative exchange rate scenarios.

In an article for Banca Nazionale de Lavoro called 'My Work on International Monetary Problems, 1940 – 1964', Machlup (1982) positioned this model squarely in the middle of 'discussions of dollar shortage, payments balance, trade balance, exchange rates and so forth' where the terms 'equilibrium' and 'disequilibrium' were bandied about as though they were good or bad and clearly visible from the data. He wrote:

> To disabuse students of such views, I felt it necessary to write an article on 'Equilibrium and Disequilibrium: Misplaced Concreteness and Disguised Politics' ....
> The chief purpose of the essay [was] to show the dangers to clear analysis that may

arise from the failure to notice the differences between analytical, descriptive and evaluative equilibrium concepts. But it went beyond making such distinctions and attempted to show that in descriptions of factual situations and in judgements of positive and negative values the pair of terms was redundant, confusing or both, whereas in abstract economic analysis it was an important methodological device, a mental tool helpful in suggesting 'a causal nexus between different events or changes.'[29]

Because the layman's idea of a trade deficit is always a 'disequilibrium' of the balance of payments, Machlup wanted to show the deficit as an adjustment or equilibrating change, following an antecedent disequilibrating change, for example, increased government spending, expansionary monetary policy, devaluation of a trading partner's currency, receipt of foreign investment, or any one of a number of possible actions.[30]

Confidence as Cause and Effect

Machlup was also among the first economists to attribute adjustment and liquidity issues to a failure of confidence and to argue that a restoration of confidence would render adjustment and liquidity moot. His former student John Williamson attributed Machlup's belief in the importance of confidence to the role it had played in the collapse of the gold-exchange standard during the Great Depression.[31] For Machlup, the French (and German) focus on payments adjustment had a simple explanation: for many years the United States had spent, lent and invested abroad more than it had received, and had paid for it partly in dollars, which the monetary authorities of many nations were prepared (some of them reluctantly) to hold in their monetary reserves. Some of the foreign spending and investing in the United States had been for purposes of which the French government did not approve, particularly the war in Vietnam and the takeover of foreign firms, including industrial concerns in France. It followed then that the French would regard adjustment as the most urgent requirement. However, Machlup argued, would discontinuance of the Vietnam war and the US takeovers in Europe erase the payments deficit of the United States, or instead lead to offsetting changes in other items of the balance, such as reductions in American exports or imports (as could well happen if spending and investing abroad were replaced by increased spending and investing at home)?[32] A second feature in the French position had been the downgrading of all plans for the creation of new reserves and borrowing facilities. The affluence of the Bank of France that followed the devaluation of 1958 made it hard for the French to appreciate any talk about a present or imminent shortage of reserves in the world. If some nations had been unable to get a share of this abundance or even to avoid payments deficits, they evidently have not been 'living right.'[33]

To the American argument that the creation of a new reserve asset was needed only to take the place of the annual additions to foreign dollar reserves necessitated by the payments deficits of the United States, the French reply was that the deficit must be stopped and that a plan for the creation of international liquidity would only delay serious efforts to achieve payments adjustment. While Machlup argued that the French position was understandable, he saw the problem differently: the American difficulties in achieving balance are not in fact connected with the absence of an arrangement that provides safeguards against future contingencies. 'Such contingencies, as I see them (or fear them) are less likely to arise from inadequate liquidity than from inadequate confidence'.[34]

The American position, as Machlup saw it, rested on two optimistic suppositions: 1) that the payments deficits could and would be eliminated in short order; and 2) that the dollar was as good as gold and would remain so even if the deficit should last for another few years. Granting these assumptions, the problems of adjustment and confidence are not so troublesome, and the provision of liquidity is the first order of business. The liberalization of foreign trade since 1950 and the return to convertibility in 1956 – both so important for the growth of world trade and prosperity – were possible only thanks to the ample provision of liquidity to the countries concerned. If the deficit of the United States is now eliminated and nothing takes its place, the annual increments to reserves will be confined to acquisitions of gold by monetary authorities. Little can be expected from this source if the present private demand for gold continues. But if aggregate reserves fail to increase, several more countries will suffer deficits in their international payments. To stop losses in their reserves, countries may adopt illiberal commercial policies and place new restrictions on convertibility. World trade and finance would then be halted, and may be reversed. To avoid this, the nations must agree on a method of creating adequate annual increments in world liquidity with no time to lose.

Machlup saw the weakness of the American position in its assumptions. The American attitude regarding the problem of confidence was understandable given its debtor position: one can hardly expect a debtor, in a situation regarded as precarious by some of his creditors, to propose and urge that measures be taken to safeguard against a loss of confidence in his ability to pay, hence the US government's refusal to recognize that the confidence in the dollar is or may be shaken. Machlup argues that it is wrong to assume that confidence can be safeguarded by refusals to talk about safeguards or that the balance of payments of the United States and confidence in the dollar are separate problems: 'I do not refer to the simple connection between the two, namely, the recognition that a prolonged deficit will "eventually" shake the confidence in the dollar. Instead I refer to a generally overlooked connection, namely, the fact that a weakening of the confidence – private, not official – in the dollar has for the past few years caused the deficit in the balance of payments. To seek adjustment without confidence is probably hopeless'.[35]

Changes in the confidence in the convertibility of the gold and foreign exchange value of a currency are usually reflected in changes in the flow of private short-term capital. Given that short-term capital also moves in response to interest rate differentials, it is not always possible to disentangle the two factors; nevertheless, from 1951 to 1966 the movements were so dramatic that there could be no question about their cause. From 1951 to 1959, private short-term capital had moved into the United States every year except 1954; the flow was reversed in 1960 and there followed substantial outflows for five years.[36] For this reversal in the flow of funds, Machlup argued, there is no other explanation than a decline in confidence in the unrestricted convertibility of the dollar at fixed exchange rates and a fixed gold equivalent. But to look only at movement of short-term capital is to underestimate the actual effect of the decline in confidence. Long-term capital is, as a rule, guided by many more factors than are significant for the flow of short-term funds, but expectations regarding the future convertibility and stability of the dollar are certainly not insignificant.[37]

Machlup concluded, 'I submit that a system of securing confidence would all of itself restore balance in the payments position of the United States. For, if there are no longer any doubts in the unlimited convertibility of private dollar holdings (by US citizens as well as foreigners) at rates that do not involve any loss (or foregone gain) to the holder, the redirection in the flow of private capital will wipe out the American deficit to be financed by official settlements'.[38]

Arguing that there were many systems that could secure confidence, Machlup broke them into four types: 1) collective international guarantees; 2) exchanging all official holdings or official excess holdings of dollars against debts ('reserve units') of an international agency; 3) 'locking in' fixed amounts or proportions of dollars in the official reserves of the financially most developed countries; and 4) making gold less desirable as an asset to hold than dollars, by providing for a slowly declining price of gold (perhaps through gradually increasing seignorage charges). Machlup argued that making gold less desirable by decreasing its price would strengthen the dollar not only as the currency in which to trade, invest, hold savings deposits and hold working balances, but also as official reserve currency. In fact, one of the objectives that could be realized with any of the four systems of securing confidence described above was to reduce the dollar from its present position as unlimited reserve currency. Doing this would exclude or minimize the possibility of financing a payments deficit of the United States by voluntary or involuntary loans from central banks of other countries.

To what extent did the world surplus of reserves add to confidence? Machlup argued it was not a final amount but annual additions to reserves that had a positive impact on confidence. Using the example of his wife's desire to add annually to her wardrobe, Machlup argued that the central banker does not care whether his reserve ratio (to his liabilities or to the total money supply) is 47 or 74 per cent, he cares that his reserves increase, however modestly, and do not decrease.[39] 'Let us repeat: it cannot be reasonably said of any particular amount of reserves, either in a particular country or in a group of countries, that it is needed or adequate, but it can be said convincingly that an *increase* in reserves will be needed or adequate to prevent restrictions on foreign trade and payments. Emphasis on the size of reserves is mistaken; emphasis on additions to reserves is justified.'[40] Machlup argued that justification of additions to reserves is a matter of politics, because in countries suffering losses in foreign reserves, the authorities will sooner or later adopt policies that restrict international trade and capital movements. One way to avoid the restriction is to avoid the causes (or pretexts) for their imposition, that is, deficits in the balances of international payments; but, Machlup argued, the easiest way to avoid or reduce deficits and avoid restrictive policies is to provide for annual additions in official reserves.[41]

How much of an increase in aggregate monetary reserves will be needed to reduce the size of the deficits and the number of deficit countries sufficiently to avert restrictions on trade and capital movements will depend on the distribution of the deficits and on the political propensities of various countries to impose restrictions. These propensities are shaped by the beliefs of the people in charge of policymaking; and these beliefs, in turn, are derived from rational theories, irrational myths and traditional principles or prejudices.[42]

Some countries may patiently put up with higher interest rates, some with effective wage stops, and some even with unemployment when confronted with a deficit in their balance of payments; an 'adequate' increase is therefore not a quantitative measurement but a matter of political judgement.

'Plans for Reform of the International Monetary System'

First published in 1962, 'Plans for Reform of the International Monetary System' is a lengthy essay, significantly updated and republished in Machlup's *International Monetary Economics* in 1964. Some thirty-seven new plans or variants of old plans for the reform of the international monetary system were being published 'at an extraordinary rate'.[43] In his introduction to the essay, Machlup identified major themes running through the plans and through contemporary discussions of the plans by advocates and adversaries.

Among these themes is the attitude of bankers, central bankers and national politicians towards the establishment of centralized reserves. There were fears of loss of independence, aversion to central control, suspicion of neglect of local needs, a mistrust of power and the potential for mismanagement in the hands of a central authority. These were the same fears, Machlup attested, that preceded the establishment of a central bank in the industrialized countries. These fears kept central bankers from embracing the international central bank suggested by the Keynes Plan (and also one of the variants of the Triffin Plan), as well as the multiple reserve currency plan proposed by the French (and later by the American Edward Bernstein).

Another major theme Machlup discerned is the inclusion of borrowing facilities in the count of world reserves to assess the adequacy of available liquidity. The whole notion of 'international liquidity' is confusing because it treats owned reserves, borrowed reserves and borrowable reserves as though they were the same. This theme would be a source on ongoing debate around the potential for misuse of credit by the USA and other nations in persistent payments deficit.

Machlup knew that policymakers and even some economists might criticize his exploration of multiple plans without making a recommendation. The best solution would depend on the circumstances, including the fit with other measures adopted and objectives accepted. As Machlup wrote, 'Monetary policy, credit and fiscal policy, wage policy investment policy, growth policy, employment policy, counter-cyclical policy, etc. ... are so closely related to one another that it would not be possible to formulate a rational policy concerning the international monetary system irrespective of all other areas of economic policy ... Policies regarding the international monetary system must take account of the measures and intentions of governments of a multitude of nations. The theories entertained by influential monetary experts will, of course, be important, but what is really decisive in the relevant considerations are the notions, the beliefs, the courage and the powers of persuasion of central bankers, ministers of finance, and other leaders of economic policy in the major countries. Consequently, one cannot possibly expect that there will be one particular plan among all plans for the international monetary system that may be singled out and proclaimed as "the best" under any set of conditions.'[44] There is, therefore, no substitute for scenario exploration and the assessment of strategic alternatives in light of divergent circumstances.

There is no substitute for scenario exploration and the assessment of strategic alternatives. There is not one solution appropriate to all situations, but possibly many, one better than other depending on the general environment and the objective to be achieved. Since circumstances and goals change, the best solution today must be reconsidered as circumstances change.

Machlup as Polymath; Comparison with Fellner

Machlup was in many ways so similar to William Fellner in the depth and breadth of his economic writing. Machlup wrote on capitalism and competition, patents and innovation, and the theory of the firm. The point has been made that the Depression and World War II had a profound impact on thinking and policy action. The world going forward would be one of full employment (subject to a tolerable unemployment rate), continued economic growth, innovation to fuel that growth, entrepreneurial firms, the protection of intellectual capital, free trade (with the reduction or elimination of tariffs and non-tariff policies destructive of free markets) and investment. Machlup and Fellner were influenced by these events.

The economics of patent protection has its root in the 1950–1 work of Fritz Machlup with his graduate student Edith Penrose, including 'The Patent Controversy in the Nineteenth Century' and *The Economics of the International Patent System*. Machlup followed in 1958 with the paper 'The Optimum Lag of Imitation Behind Innovation.'[45] Machlup concentrated his analysis on the optimal length of a patent grant, one of the two main dimensions of patent protection (the other being the scope or breadth of protection). In 'Patents and Inventive Effort' (1961), Machlup drew on oligopolistic competition theory to make a cogent argument for research and development outlays by large firms with or without patent protection: 'No firm in competition with a few others can afford to let its rivals steal a march upon it as far as the technological base of its competitive position is concerned. The research and development work is essential for the maintenance of its position. It cannot allow itself to fall seriously behind in the technological race, regardless of whether inventions promise it … patent protection.'[46]

Machlup's contribution to the economics of patent protection has been acknowledged by Griliches, Mansfield, Nordhaus, Stiglitz and Das Gupta, as William Baumol and Dietrich Fischer noted in their introduction to 'Optimal Lags in a Schumpeterian Innovation Process' (1977).[47] Machlup's paper 'The Supply of Inventors and Inventions' (originally published in 1960; later published by the National Bureau of Economic Research (NBER) in 1962) introduced Bill Gates's 'garbage can' model before there was a Bill Gates or a Microsoft:

> Invention is the solution of a technological problem; but it is possible that in the course of solving a problem or as a result of solving it new problems are raised. Thus, an invention may fulfill a task and at the same time create more tasks. To be sure, not all inventions are of this sort. The solution of an old problem may leave less to be done, one item of the agenda having been checked off as completed. We may call such a solution an 'agenda-reducing' invention. If the solution, by raising new problems, leaves more to be done than there had been before, we may call it an 'agenda-increasing' invention or discovery.[48]

The paper was one of many presented at a conference called 'The Rate and Direction of Inventive Activity: Economic and Social Factors', sponsored by the National Bureau of Economic Research and the Committee on Economic Growth of the Social Science Research Council. Machlup's colleague and friend William Fellner presented his paper 'Does the Market Direct the Relative Factor-Saving Effects of Technological Progress?' at the same conference. Fellner was interested in how market incentives – from high wages to high interest rates – influence the inventor's focus on labour-saving or capital-saving inventions. Three other Fellner papers written in 1961 covered the same theme, including 'Two Propositions in the Theory of Induced Innovations', 'How to Accelerate Increases in Production' and 'Appraisal of the Labour-Saving and Capital-Saving Character of Innovations'. The latter was written for another conference, this time sponsored by the International Economic Association.

As Richard Nelson explained in his introduction to the NBER's book of conference presentations, the growing body of research findings on productivity 'had turned the attention of economists interested in economic growth to the process of technological change and improvements in productivity and efficiency'.[49] Nelson saw the cold war and national security interests, as well as an increased focus on competition through new products, as additional compelling reasons why innovation had become so important to growth.

Production and Distribution of Knowledge

In the year before the Bellagio Group conferences began, Fritz Machlup published a pioneering study entitled *The Production and Distribution of Knowledge in the United States* (1962). No stranger to industry studies (he had had many industry studies underway at Johns Hopkins in the 1950s, as well as research into firm growth by his student Edith Penrose), Machlup found that the 'knowledge industry' in 1958 was already 30 per cent of gross national product (GNP) and forecast that the industry would account for 50 per cent of GNP by the late 1970s. His forecast also called for rising demand for knowledge-producing workers and declining demand for productive labour. While 'knowledge had always played a part in economic analysis ... to most economists and for most problems of economics the state of knowledge and its distribution in society are among the data assumed as given'.[50] Given his interest in patents and innovation, it is not surprising that he would find that 'the growth of technical knowledge, and the growth of productivity that may result from it, are certainly important factor in the analysis of economic growth and other economic problems'.[51] For Machlup, producing knowledge was not only a matter of 'discovering, inventing, designing and planning but also disseminating and communicating'.[52] Producing and distributing were essential to making knowledge what it is: messages created, transmitted and received. Given Machlup's approach to knowledge in his life and in the classroom (his penchant for establishing connecting principles), it is impossible not to think of his work on the Bellagio Group and on his relationships with government officials engaged in monetary reform as a knowledge-producing and distributing endeavour. He would plan a deeper study of knowledge to be published in eight volumes. He published three volumes before his death in 1983.

Conclusions

Chapter 1 examined Machlup's early experience in Austria and his writings leading up to the Bellagio Group conferences to understand his thinking about the balance of payments adjustment problem. For Machlup, balance of payments and dollar shortage theorists did not understand that monetary policy and misaligned exchange rates were the disturbing changes causing an adjustment, i.e. reduced monetary reserves. Frameworks and methods that Machlup had developed in the late 1950s for use in his own research and that of his students proved invaluable to an exploration of the effect of policy on outcomes, as Machlup acknowledged in his biographical essays for *Banca Nazionale del Lavoro Quarterly Review*.

Like Fellner, Machlup had broad interests in aspects of national competitiveness on which he continued to publish even as he immersed himself in monetary reform. These issues are not separate and distinct from monetary reform, but are heavily influenced by issues like capital flows, availability of talent and investment.

Like Triffin, he published on every aspect of monetary reform. A friend since the early 1950s, Robert Triffin would later identify Machlup's methodology as key to his achievements and to his particular strength as an organizer. Chapter 3 examines Triffin's body of work and points of tangency with Machlup.

3 ROBERT TRIFFIN AND THE TRIFFIN PLAN

Introduction

Born in Belgium in 1911 and educated at the Catholic University of Louvain, Triffin left for the USA in 1935 to pursue an MA at Harvard University. He returned briefly to Belgium, where his decision to go back to the USA to become the first Belgian to earn a PhD at Harvard put him at odds with Léon H. Dupriez, head of the economic research institute at Louvain (along with Fernard Baudhuin and Paul van Zeeland), where Triffin had been a research assistant. Yet his decision to return to the USA in 1939 was propitious, because the Nazis invaded Belgium in 1940.[1] This just-in-time escape from an authoritarian regime is a life experience he shared with Machlup and Fellner.

In his brief biography in the *Banca Nazionale del Lavoro Quarterly Review*, Triffin acknowledged Joseph Schumpeter, his dissertation adviser, as a major influence on his understanding of pure economic theory.[2] He studied fiscal policy from a Keynesian perspective with John Williamson (whose national key currencies perspective Triffin would not share) and Alvin Hansen (whose perspective on 'fundamental disequilibrium' Triffin would embrace). Like Hansen, Triffin believed that a country's balance of payments position might arise from significant internal imbalances (deep recession, low output, high unemployment), which could outweigh balance of payments considerations and point towards major policy changes.[3]

From 1942 to 1946, Triffin was chief of the Latin American section of the Board of the Federal Reserve System and one of the US 'money doctors' who argued against a passive monetary policy geared externally to respond automatically to changes in the balance of payments, and instead argued for activist monetary policies that *insulated* the national economy from international disruptions.[4] From 1946 to 1949, Triffin played various roles at the International Monetary Fund, first as Director of Exchange Control Division, then Observer, later as US representative to the Intra-European Payments Committee of the Organisation for European Economic Co-operation (which became the Organisation for Economic Co-operation and Development) from 1948 to 1951, and also served as US alternate representative to the European Payments Unit from 1950 to 1951. He became a professor of economics at Yale University in 1951, where he remained until 1977.[5]

Triffin met Machlup in the summer of 1952 at the Merrill Center for Economics, owned by Amherst College. Both had been invited by Willard Thorp, an economist who had helped draft the Marshall Plan, now a trustee and acting president of Amherst who ran Merrill's annual conferences on the beach at Southampton, Long Island.[6] They found they had a lot in common, including 'the conviction that the first order of priority was the dismantling of the pervasive bilateral shackles that were then strangling and distorting world trade and payments, but we advocated two very different solutions to this common objective'.[7] It was at the Merrill Center that Triffin first saw Machlup's method of 'smoking out the reasons explaining why we could logically argue for such different means to reach our common objective'.[8] Machlup would never attempt to convince him of his viewpoint or seek agreement. Triffin brought this fact to light in his essay 'The Impact of the Bellagio Group on International Monetary Fund Reform', because 'our Merrill Center discussions anticipated by more than ten years the fundamental technique imparted by Professor Machlup to our Bellagio Group meetings'.[9] Triffin and Machlup continued to communicate frequently by letter exchange in the period leading up to the Bellagio Group conferences. Having established their relationship, Chapter 3 now moves to a discussion of Triffin's thought about international monetary system reform and European integration.

This chapter focuses on Triffin's writing from 1947 to 1962, including his critique of the Bretton Woods system; work for the European Commission and thoughts on a common currency; the Triffin Plan – its critics and Triffin's defence; the relationship between trade, deficits and the developing world; adjustment policy or market mechanism – the differences between his thinking and Machlup's; and finally, how Triffin and Machlup came together on the issue of confidence.

Critique of the Bretton Woods System

Triffin found fault both with the classical gold standard and with the Bretton Woods gold-exchange standard. He in no way trusted the pre-1914 classical gold standard to be self-managing, with payments imbalances settled simply by shipments of gold and central bankers as passive facilitators.[10] The existence of fractional reserve banking requirements (officially at 33 per cent) led to multiplier effects in the credit base, speeding up adjustment but at the same time exaggerating the amount of expansion or contraction and affecting both investment and output. Triffin argued that those nations heaviest hit by adjustment burden were not the big countries with payments imbalances, but the small raw-material-exporting nations that depended on them.[11]

Likewise, Triffin found that the Bretton Woods system's key currency approach was fundamentally unstable, dependent as it was on the degree of confidence held in a currency. Because confidence itself depended on many factors, including the monetary and fiscal policies of national authorities, the use of national currencies as international reserves of national monetary authorities interfered with parity adjustments by reserve currency countries when needed. For that reason, national monies could not sustain their position as liquidity stabilizers or as international media for financing or payments adjustment. Key currency countries will therefore fall from grace and will not provide the basis for a sound international financial order. In 'Europe and the Money Muddle', Triffin had argued that the growth of foreign countries' reserves had taken place in recent years largely as a result of a vast redistribution of net reserves from the United States to the rest of the world, and that such a movement could not continue indefinitely without eventually undermining confidence in the dollar itself.[12] Triffin considered the very survival of the gold-exchange standard to be increasingly precarious, 'because central banks are being called upon to finance debtor countries' policies in which their own governments have no voice, and with which they may profoundly disagree'.[13] He doubted the future mainte-nance of convertibility if 'uncoordinated national decisions and policies' were made by 'several scores of independent national states'. He called for 'A collec-tive organization and effective internationalization of the present gold exchange standard ... if we are to eschew the well-known pitfalls unanimously denounced by economists and sadly demonstrated by events in the early 1930s'.[14]

Triffin and the European Commission

In the late 1950s and 1960s, the balance of payments adjustment and liquidity problems that were raising fears worldwide were also the concerns of the Euro-pean Commission, particularly the concerns of France (a deficit country) and Germany (a surplus country). According to Ivo Maes (2004), Robert Marjolin, in collaboration with Triffin, drew up a proposal for the creation of a European Reserve Fund, which would pool 10 per cent of the international reserves of the member states' central banks.[15] The Fund would provide for different types of loans available to assist countries with balance of payments difficulties and to support economic growth. Marjolin also proposed that the accounts of the Fund would be expressed in a new unit of account. Triffin's work on the European Reserve Fund was important to the European Commission, although the Fund never became a reality, and is clearly a prototype of the Triffin Plan and later the special drawing rights in the International Monetary Fund.

In the second half of the 1960s, Triffin would play a role in the develop-ment of a 'Memorandum on Community Action in the Monetary Domain', a predecessor of the Barre Memorandum aimed at establishing closer ties between European Community countries. The Barre Memorandum (1969) would pro-pose that member states agree to adjust their exchange rates only with prior mutual consent; that fluctuation margins be eliminated; and that a single Euro-pean unit of account be established.

In *Europe and the Money Muddle*, Triffin acknowledged that the requirements for monetary unification were nearly identical to those for free and stable
exchange rates. Participating countries or regions must subordinate their internal
monetary and credit expansion and maintain balance of payments equilibrium.
'The significance of monetary unification, like that of exchange stability in a free
market, is that both exclude the resort to any other corrective techniques except
those of internal fiscal and credit policies'.[16] He saw monetary union as a political rather than an economic problem: 'Monetary unification will thus be desired
insofar as political unification is accepted as an objective, but resisted as long
as such an objective is not yet acceptable to governments and public opinion'.[17]

On the details of a common currency, Triffin dispelled hardship objectives:
'Monetary unification would not require, in any manner, a full unification of
national levels of prices, costs, wages, productivity or living standards. Price differentials would be limited by transportation ... Wages, incomes, living standards and
productivity would nevertheless continue to differ from one country to another'.[18]

The Triffin Dilemma and Triffin Plan

Triffin expanded his analysis and suggestions in 1959 in several articles, and particularly in those published by the *Banca Nazionale del Lavoro Quarterly Review*
(1959) and in his October 1959 Statement to the Joint Economic Committee
of Congress, in which Triffin expounded on what would be called the 'Triffin
Paradox' or 'Triffin Dilemma'.[19] Triffin's 1959 prescription was to replace gold
and foreign currency reserves by gold-guaranteed deposit accounts at the International Monetary Fund. First of all, this would enable the IMF to control the
expansion of world reserves, adjusting them to the non-inflationary requirements of the growth of world trade and production, rather than to the vagaries
of the US balance of payments and the private gold market. To guard against
inflationary abuses of the Fund's lending capacity, Triffin suggested that a quali-
fied vote of two-thirds or more of the total weighted voting power be required
to authorize any IMF lending susceptible of increasing world reserves by more
than 3, 4 or 5 per cent a year.[20] Secondly, Triffin suggested that the expansion of
International Monetary Fund lending capacity be used for three key purposes:
to finance traditional stabilization assistance to deficit countries, subject to the
adoption of agreed readjustment policies; to offset speculative switches from
some currencies into others or into gold; and to accelerate the financing of development in the third world through the purchase of obligations of the World
Bank, its affiliates, and newly emerging regional development banks.[21]

Triffin's later writings placed increasing stress on the inflationary potential
of continuing US deficits and the threat of a gold and dollar crisis. He admitted that he had underestimated the duration and rise of US deficits that foreign

central bankers would be willing to absorb, despite the inflationary growth of world monetary reserves and of the money supply overall in member countries under the traditional system of fractional reserve requirements. Measured in US dollars, the world reserve pool rose from $58 billion in 1959 to $159 billion by the end of 1972 and to $319 billion by the end of 1977, while gold holdings remained practically unchanged and special drawing rights and International Monetary Fund lending contributed barely 10 per cent to the total $262 billion increase of world reserves between 1959 and 1977.[22]

Triffin's prescription for the reform of the system changed somewhat over the twenty-year period, including and especially on the role of gold in the system. Triffin's 1959 proposal would have required all members to hold a certain proportion of their gross monetary reserves in the form of Fund deposits. All would have to agree to accept such deposits in settlement of their international claims without limit, but would also have the right to convert at any time into gold, if they so wished, any deposits accrued to their Fund account in excess of their minimum requirement.[23] He considered a minimum requirement of 20 per cent to be acceptable and achievable mostly through net claims of $2.6 billion already held by members of the Fund and by transfers to the Fund of about one-third, or $5.3 billion, of the $15.8 billion in foreign exchange reserves then in existence. Only a handful of countries – primarily the United States, which held no foreign-exchange reserves – would have had to satisfy their minimum deposit requirements by gold transfers ($3.4 billion, or less than 10 per cent of the $37.9 billion in world monetary gold holdings at the time). Of total gold reserves of $56.2 billion, a minimum of 20 per cent or $11.2 billion would have been held in Fund deposits, but countries could have retained if they wished 61 per cent, or $34.5 billion, in gold and 19 per cent or $10.5 billion in foreign exchange.[24]

While Triffin thought these provisions would be adequate at the time, he advised that safeguards would have to be put in place to maintain the Fund's liquidity both against unforeseen conversions of excess deposits into gold and against the increasing gap between the probable level of world gold stocks and the desirable expansion of overall monetary reserves.[25] Triffin offered a solution to the problem: raise the 20 per cent deposit requirement to a higher ratio of gross monetary reserves or impose higher deposit requirements on the portion of each member's reserves that exceeds the average ratio of world monetary gold to world imports.[26]

Critics of the Triffin Plan and Triffin's Defence

Both inside and outside the Bellagio Group, a plan that required IMF supervision drew fire. Burton Malkiel wrote, 'Triffin has attempted to steer a delicate middle course between two apparently irreconcilable goals' – a full intellectual commitment to an international central bank and emancipation from gold on the one hand and appeasement of Western distrust of supranational organizations on the other.[27] Charles Kindleberger argued, 'Many economists, but few bankers or central bankers, recommended flexible exchange rates as a means of eliminating ... all the problems of adjustment, liquidity and confidence'.[28] He noted that many economists saw the Triffin solution as 'the first-best solution economically', but 'most of them think that it is politically out of the question'.[29]

Outside of the Bellagio Group, the argument against the Triffin Plan was made by Oscar Altman, then at the IMF, who attacked Triffin's assessment of the liquidity needs of growing international trade and argued that demands on an expanded IMF would rest on important exchange guarantees, involve intervention in the money markets of the USA and UK, and require changes in IMF assets from currency and short- to medium-term loans to long-term investment.[30] Leland Yeager faulted the Triffin Plan for focusing on the liquidity problem with its high potential for inflation and no mechanism to resolve balance of payments problems.[31] J. Herbert Furth argued that the Triffin Plan would make its appeal to three kinds of people: nationalists *outside* the reserve currency countries because it promised the end of US and UK financial dominance; to inflationists *inside* the reserve currency countries because it condoned large deficits; and to adherents of central planning because it substituted planning for market forces.[32]

In a report to the Group of Ten on 28 February 1964, Otmar Emminger, chair of the deputies of the Group of Ten and head of the European Monetary Committee, pooh-poohed the need for reform, noting the divergent views expressed from the outset on the health of the international monetary system – from Professor Heilperin's diagnosis of a 'half-century of monetary chaos' to the arguments of Triffin in 1959 and Rueff in 1961 that the world faced a 'first class international crisis if their respective advice were not heeded quickly'. He noted that central bankers held a different view of the system, published as 'Conversations on International Finance' in the *Monthly Review* of the Federal Reserve Bank of New York, namely that 'the international financial system has demonstrated a high degree of flexibility and resilience' and was much better than its reputation in academic circles.[33] Emminger found the Triffin Plan unacceptable because nations were not prepared to hand over so much responsibility and financial power to an international body.

In 'A Brief for the Defense', Triffin summarized the mains points of disagreement between himself and the IMF's Altman: 'The main issue is *not* whether admittedly crude forecasts of future reserve deficiency are "unproven" or even "incorrect"', as Altman seems to argue, 'The main issue is whether the creation – or destruction – of the international monetary liquidity indispensable to the smooth functioning of our international monetary system should be left to such wild gambles as it has been left, with disastrous results, over the past ten years, or even over the past half century'.[34]

Disputing the thesis of colleagues Emile Despres, Charles Kindleberger and Walter Salant (that the United States had become the financial intermediary or central banker for Europe and that American deficits reflect a mutually advantageous and equilibrating function), Triffin contrasted his plan's calls for centralized reserves as a merger of sovereignties for sound expansion of the international economy with the DKS troika for whom the United States as lender of last resort results in a surrender of sovereignty.[35]

Triffin himself found the flexible rates solution to the payments adjustment problem limited for three reasons. Flexible rates ignored monetary (fiscal and credit) policies as a major instrument for readjustment of balance of payments. Flexible rates focused instead on problems of prices, employment and restrictions as the only factors involved in the adjustment process. Finally, flexible rates were inattentive to payments imbalances caused by 'spillover' of purchasing power from countries following expansionist monetary policies towards countries following contractionist policies. Hence, proponents of flexible rates typically rejected arguments for additional reserves or 'cushioning', and equated 'adjustment' with 'correction'.[36]

In 'After the Gold Exchange Standard', Triffin assessed current reform plans, including his own, and compared the Triffin Plan with the Bernstein and Stamp plans: 'I would be less than candid, however, if I left unmentioned the major objections raised against my own plan. They come ... from two opposite ends of the political spectrum. Conservative central bankers are afraid of the inflationary potentialities of a system which would, in fact, endow the Fund with money creating power. Inflationists and monetary nationalists, on the other hand, denounce the harsh discipline which the Fund might impose upon prospective borrowers and the loss of national sovereignties to a world central bank, which they read into my plan'.[37]

He addressed the first objection by repeating, even strengthening his original proposal. As for the second objection, he argued that nothing in his proposals would make the discipline of the Fund on prospective borrowers any harsher, nor would they limit the national sovereignty of any member state any more that it already is. Instead, all Fund members would have an additional outlet for the investment of their reserves. This outlet would combine the attractions of both gold and foreign exchange holdings, i.e. safety against exchange risks together with earning power. Triffin admitted that his proposals never really contemplated the establishment of the fully fledged worldwide central bank or super-central bank, which some commentators have read into them. They would, instead, create a central depository for central bank reserves, now dispersed among national money markets – primarily London and New York – in the form of foreign exchange holdings, and organize a clearing house for settlements among national central banks. Nevertheless, his plan would enable the Fund to intervene more actively to adjust the creation of international liquidity to the needs of an expanding world economy; to offset through appropriate shifts in its investments the dangerous impact of destabilizing capital movements; and to give more adequate support to members whose deficits are either recognized as purely temporary in character or are in the process of being corrected through the implementation of mutually agreed stabilization policies.

Triffin thought his plan might be adopted on a regional rather than on a worldwide basis, possibly by the EEC, as it provided a framework to help develop increasingly closer monetary integration – even up to and including full monetary unification – among countries pursuing long-term objectives of economic integration and political federation. Triffin was sceptical about implementing the plan through the International Monetary Fund. Heavy and complex administrative machinery, the impossibility of maintaining secrecy, and the large number of heterogeneous countries would make rapidity of decision next to impossible. These difficulties require a more realistic organization of international monetary cooperation, and particularly a drastic decentralization of the International Monetary Fund's machinery.

Triffin suggested an alternative scheme: reserves might be deposited with the OECD or EEC, and he went so far as suggesting that the USA and Canada join the EEC:

> The Members of the OECD could distribute their international deposits between the IMF and an OECD monetary organization in rough proportion to their pattern of international trade and payments outside and within OECD. This would help solve or bypass the voting power hurdle mentioned above by keeping a substantial portion of the deposits under the more closely-knit and more workable management of OECD. That would also give vital and powerful support to the development of the closer harmonization of the 'financial and economic policies for growth and stability of these industrialized nations of the world whose economic behavior significantly influences the course of the world economy and the trend of international payments', called for in President Kennedy's Message of February sixth on the balance of payments and gold.[38]

Members of the Monetary Committee of the European Economic Community, whose president Otmar Emminger was also chair of the deputies of the Group of Ten, found fault with Triffin's prescription for change, although not with his diagnosis. Emminger would write that the Triffin Plan would encourage continued US deficits by putting the International Monetary Fund in charge of correcting short-term imbalances. The International Monetary Fund continued to be linked too closely with the USA for European comfort.[39]

Triffin believed his close ties with both the United States and the EEC created problems at times: 'For instance I was told by one of the participants that when President Kennedy urged members of his cabinet to act of my proposals for world monetary reform, he was asked by the Secretary of the Treasury Douglas Dillon whether I was an American or a European. He had seen me in April of that year as a member of the US delegation to the OEEC and was surprised to see me serve, at an annual IMF meeting in September, as member of the European Community delegation. President Kennedy answered jokingly, "Relax, Doug! He is our first Atlantic citizen, and we need more of them"'.[40] In his article 'An Economist's Career: Why? Why? How?' in the *Banca Nazionale del Lavoro Quarterly Review*, he identified the two issues to which his academic research was devoted, 'which I regarded as complementary rather than exclusive to one another: worldwide monetary reform of the crumbling gold convertible dollar exchange standard, and regional monetary cooperation, culminating possibly someday in full monetary – and therefore political – union in various parts of the world'.[41]

The Bellagio Group conferences would give the Triffin Plan new life. The (potential) shortage of liquidity exposed by Triffin in his congressional testimony and in *Gold and the Dollar Crisis* had an important influence on the plan to ensure credit availability in the event of a future financial crisis by creating a new reserve asset – the special drawing rights of the IMF.

The Relationship between Trade, Deficits and the Developing World

There is no question that Triffin understood that trade was the crucible in the relationship between US deficits, protectionism and the impact on developing countries. Presenting to the American Society of International Law at its Annual Meeting in 1962, Triffin offered his wholehearted support to the Trade Expansion Act of 1962 against protectionism: 'What is at stake is not a mere trade bargain, but a long overdue adaptation of outworn and narrowly nationalistic policy instruments and institutions to the most obvious requirements of rational policymaking in an interdependent world'.[42] Even as early as 1960, three-fifths to two-thirds of imported goods in 1960 were not produced at all in the United States. They required raw materials unavailable in the USA in the quantities needed, and at a much higher cost. As Triffin saw it, 'The real impact of our protective tariffs is not to create jobs. It is to shift jobs around, away from our most efficient industries and towards our least efficient ones ... increase their production costs beyond what they would be otherwise, and they prevent us from negotiating feasible reductions in foreign tariffs and restrictions against our exports'.[43]

It is interesting that the period 1960 to 1973 saw a relatively high rate of unemployment in the USA, 4.9 per cent on average. Canada too experienced high unemployment of 5.1 per cent, compared with 1.3 per cent in Japan and 2.6

per cent for Europe (consisting of France, Germany, Italy and the UK).[44] Why was this happening? US GDP growth year on year from 1950 to 1973 was 1 per cent, versus France and Italy at 5.1 per cent, and Germany at 6.0 per cent.[45] There would have been significant anxiety over jobs in the USA, prompting protectionism. Recall Machlup's assessment of the decline of productive labour versus knowledge work (growth of services) as early as 1958. He estimated 30 per cent of jobs were knowledge worker jobs in 1958, versus 70 per cent productive labour. Capital-labour ratios are higher for capital-intensive industries or economies. Again, from 1960 to 1973, the capital to labour ratio for the USA was 2.2, for France 4.6, for Germany 6.0, for Japan 11.0.[46] That would suggest that the US industry was still very labour-intensive. Hence, it is reasonable to assume there was some anxiety about jobs, making the Trade Expansion Act was a tough sell.

Drawing on the Depression and World War II experiences, Triffin showed that growth resumed when tariffs were cut. 'The greatest cut in our imports coincided, of course, with the worst depression and the most ferociously protective tariff ever experienced by this country. Our imports were slashed by more than two-thirds between 1929 and 1932 ... our important declined by $3.1 billion but our loss of exports was $3.7 billion ... After WWII, the US slashed tariffs to one-third and imports expanded to $14.5 billion; exports rose to $20 billion'.[47] Triffin compared the US experience with that of post-war Europe. 'The most spectacular evidence of liberal trading policies, however, is that of post-war Europe. The great depression and the second World War had produced the most restrictive trading system imaginable ... The major achievement of the Organisation for European Economic Co-operation (OEEC) lay in the progressive dismantling of these so-called "quantitative" restrictions'.[48] The OEEC's success prompted the creation of the European Economic Community and the European Free Trade Area (EFTA), and also prompted members of the EFTA to join the European Economic Community. Internal trade between community members increased 73 per cent between 1959 and 1962, more than twice the growth of the USA.[49]

Within the common market, there would be one tariff mutually agreed upon by the members and governing their relations with the rest of the world. 'A country encountering balance of payments difficulties in its relations with the rest of the world will no longer be able to protect itself through independent tariff or trade restrictions ... Finally, the removal of trade barriers will, of necessity, involve a growing harmonization of other measures having a powerful impact on the pattern of trade'.[50] Was Europe a role model for the rest of the world? Or was Europe enjoying the benefits end of the 'balance' of trade? Triffin would return to this theme again in 1987 and 1991, after attempts to reform the monetary system ended in a whimper.

In his 1991 article 'The IMS (International Monetary System – or Scandal?) and the EMS (European Monetary System – or Success?)', Triffin acknowledged the progress made by the EMS to perform the essential function of an exchange rate system, that is, to stabilize real exchange rates within the European Community at competitive levels consonant with desirable capital movements from its more developed to its less developed participating countries.

Adjustment Policy or Market Mechanism: Areas of Agreement and Disagreement between Triffin and Machlup

Triffin acknowledged that he had put more emphasis on the appropriateness of financing some balance of payments disequilibria rather than on the prompt adjustment Machlup recommended in his writings. Nevertheless, Triffin would argue in 1987 and 1991, when adjustment seemed to have been left out of the reform, that 'officials need far more preaching about the need for adjustment than about the need for financing'.[51]

They differed as well on exchange rate flexibility. According to Triffin, 'For countries professing to avoid inflation as well as unemployment, the need to alter exchange rates among themselves arises only from the occasional failure of these preferred policies'.[52] Machlup would support the so-called 'band' proposal, allowing countries to adjust their exchange rates by a limited per cent within a 12-month period. Triffin thought these shifts difficult to control and pointed to cases in Mexico, Australia, New Zealand, Italy and even Canada as examples of successful floating.

On the issue of gold, Triffin and Machlup agreed on the need to phase gold out of the system. In their work on special drawing rights (special reserve assets), they would also seek to phase out reserve currencies.

Importantly, they both saw stability as essential to a viable system.

Revisiting their points of concurrence in 1991, Triffin acknowledged that he and Machlup were in total agreement about the ideal system: 1) the adoption of a single reserve instrument, international reserve deposits in the IMF; 2) growth of reserves in the range of 3–5 per cent through similar growth IMF loans and investments; and 3) earmarking of loans and investments for high priority objectives, including development in less capitalized countries.[53]

How Triffin and Machlup Came Together Intellectually: Confidence, Not Liquidity

I argue here that the issue that drew Triffin and Machlup together was that of confidence. And of the two issues, liquidity and adjustment, both found the adjustment issue a safer and more secure route to confidence.

The confidence issue as cause or effect has a long history in the monetary theory literature, where confidence is linked to expectations and uncertainty, originating in the notion of unintended consequences. In 'Money as a Substitute for Confidence', Franz Ritzmann (1999) identified two early divergent views of confidence that he associates with contemporaries Henry Thornton and David Ricardo.[54] The former is psychological –value derives from subjective confidence in the reliability of one's fellow men, social institutions and established rules of behaviour. The latter is objectivist and not interested in the demand side. For the objectivist, the value of money is regulated by the mechanics of the quantity theory, occasionally distorted by irregular and transitory aberrations in velocity of money. We see these two sides of the confidence coin in Fritz Machlup and Robert Triffin. Machlup followed the psychological school, and for him psychological expectations are based on interpretations of reality or future reality – an internal or Thorntonian view. Triffin – for whom dispositional expectations are based on specific actions or the results of actions (data, not feelings) – held an external or Ricardian view.

Dequech (1999) argued that the degree of confidence is a function of uncertainty perception and uncertainty aversion. Uncertainty perception depends on the level of knowledge about the existence of uncertainty itself and upon the institutional factors that increase or decrease uncertainty. Uncertainty aversion relates to Keynes's 'animal spirits', which are influenced by the institutional environment in which an individual operates'.[55] In 1936, Keynes applied his concepts of uncertainty and confidence to the theory of economic fluctuations: 'Our desire to hold money as a store of wealth is a barometer of the degree of our distrust of our own calculations and conventions regarding the future. The possession of actual money lulls our disquietude and the premium which we require to make us part with our money is the measure of the degree of our disquietude'.[56] For Machlup, individuals control how much uncertainty they can tolerate for how long through market mechanisms; for Triffin, publicly accountable institutions can circumscribe uncertainty and restore confidence.

Confidence is part of the frame we have come to consider important to financial markets, but it was not always as important to international organizations capturing data on international capital flows like the Bank for International Settlements (BIS), or data on money supply and interest rates like the IMF, because it was not susceptible to data collection. Following Sheila Dow (2008), the frame or framing refers to the way in which something is presented and thus perceived. It depends on our role in society (academics versus policymakers, for example). Different disciplines frame the subject matter in their own characteristic ways (economics versus sociology, for example), but even within disciplines there can be framing differences, ranging from differences in the meaning of terms to theoretical differences, to differences in policy recommendations.[57] This method of framing follows from logical positivism, which requires that scientific statements be testable against facts.

Much of the framing literature surveyed has been focused on group action and hence is particularly relevant to this analysis of the influence of Robert Triffin and Fritz Machlup. Especially noteworthy are Thomas Nelson, Zoe Oxley and Rosalee Clawson (1997), whose research goes deep into the psychological mechanisms by which framing influences political attitudes, including support for the hypothesis that framing effects are stronger (not weaker) among respondents with a sophisticated understanding of the issues. For the sophisticated, framing appears to activate existing beliefs and cognitions (making participants particularly aware of their arguments) rather than changing beliefs.[58] The authors suggest that it is not framing alone but the social, interactive process itself that is important to mobilization and collective action. In public policy, Alex Mintz and Steven Redd (2003) identified subtypes and variations of framing as manipulation, including evaluative, wherein the frame operates as an anchor in the assessment of the environment, and productive, wherein the frame serves to produce an intended outcome.[59] Again, framing as evaluative and productive manipulation – guided thinking about issues in terms of outcomes – is especially relevant to this analysis.

Triffin would convince Machlup as well as the Bellagio Group members that special reserve assets would solve the confidence problem by providing additional liquidity, as well as finance the adjustment problem in the short term.

Conclusions

Triffin was single-mindedly committed to monetary system issues both European and international during the period covered by this book. While Triffin believed that his impact was limited to European integration, his plans for a European Reserve Fund and his active campaign for an international reserve unit led to the creation of the special reserve unit or special drawing rights in the IMF. It is interesting that Triffin thought the OECD might have been a substitute organization for reserve creation and allocation. He was ready to explore this alternative when conversations around the Triffin Plan were rejected by the European Monetary Committee. Triffin saw the European monetary unification experience as a lesson for the world, and so it has become.

Although Triffin never accepted the idea of an automatic mechanism, and Machlup did not trust policymakers to restrain themselves from interfering with the system, Triffin and Machlup shared many common beliefs about the requirements of a viable monetary system. Chapter 3 introduces the third co-leader of the Bellagio Group, the economist William Fellner.

4 WILLIAM FELLNER AND THE INTERSECTION OF MACRO AND MICROECONOMICS

Born in Budapest in 1905, William John Fellner was a colleague of Robert Triffin and like Triffin a mutual friend of John and Marina von Neumann. Marina von Neumann would later recommend Fellner to a seat on the US President's Council of Economic Advisers. Like Fritz Machlup, Fellner inherited a family business and in the same industry: paper. Like Machlup, he was a cartel director. Both Machlup and Fellner were Jewish (although Fellner was raised as a Lutheran). The archives reveal that the Machlup's firm in Austria had been confiscated by the Nazis. The Nazis would reach out to Machlup while he was in Buffalo, his first US assignment, requiring a full accounting of his assets. There is nothing in the published work of Machlup or Fellner to suggest how they felt about this period. Nevertheless, the archives are full of letters Machlup sent to get family members and friends out of Austria. The Fellner letters at the Hoover Institution (other than the letters exchanged with Machlup and Triffin) have not been foldered, so it remains to be seen whether he found himself playing a similar role for family and friends in Hungary.

Fellner earned his doctorate in economics from the University of Berlin in 1929, joined the faculty of the University of California, Berkeley in 1939, and became a US citizen in 1944. Fellner left Berkeley for Yale University, becoming a professor of economics there in 1952 and retiring in 1973. In 1970, he began his association with the American Enterprise Institute as an Adjunct Scholar.[1] The correspondence between Machlup and Fellner began in 1939 (according to the Machlup Archives) and was frequent, professional as well as friendly. They shared their thoughts about John Richard Hicks on income effects (Machlup was writing a review), and recommended contributions to volumes they were editing on income distribution (Fellner) and distribution theory (Machlup). Deeply impressed by the talent of Egon Sohmen, they sought to recommend him for available academic positions.[2]

This chapter examines Fellner's 1942–73 writings on inflation; government regulation, full employment and economic growth; oligopoly and the reaction function; balance of payments, liquidity and flexible exchange rates; and compares his thinking with that of Machlup and Triffin, especially in the volume produced by the trio called *Maintaining and Restoring Balance in International Payments* (1966). While Machlup and Triffin played a larger role in the original Bellagio Group conferences (1963–4), Fellner made a significant contribution to the Joint Conferences of Officials and Academics (1964–77).

In their festschrift for William Fellner, published as *Economic Progress, Private Values and Public Policy* (1977), Bela Belassa and Richard Nelson characterized Fellner as 'one of the most complete economists of his generation in the range of the topics, techniques and perspectives.'[3] Fellner's work ranged from pure theory to policy. Like Machlup, Fellner's economic writings dealt substantially with business, competition, oligarchy, technology and innovation. They dealt as well with inflation, full employment and economic growth as well as balance of payments deficits, liquidity and exchange rate flexibility. Fellner's work demonstrated the same concern with the effects of trade-offs versus having it all that Machlup articulated in his summary to the Twentieth Century Fund's conference, *Financing American Prosperity* (1945). This is the first time we see Machlup engaged in a study with some similarities to the Bellagio Group conferences – many economists with differing outlooks brought together under one roof, their presentations collected for publication and their recommendations summarized by Machlup. Nevertheless, it was the notion of trade-offs, opportunity cost economizing, that was reflected in Machlup's attempt at summary:

> It is often assumed that the objectives 'full employment', 'highest national income', 'stability' and 'growth' are all perfectly compatible with one another. There is, however serious doubt about it – particularly whether it is possible to combine full employment with the highest possible real income for the community, and whether stability is consistent with the greatest growth of productivity ... We cannot choose between 'more employment' and 'more income' without knowing how much we have to forego of the one in order to secure more of the other.[4]

War Inflation and the Lessons from World War II

Like most of the European central bankers who would attend the Joint Conferences of Academics and Officials, Fellner had experienced the burden of inflation caused by borrowing to finance a foreign war. Inflation was an overwhelming concern, solvable by a proportionate tax increase without exemption, as Fellner argued in 'War Finance and Inflation', written in 1942 (the same year his book *Treatise on War Inflation: Present Policies and Future Tendencies in the United States* was published).[5] In 1947, reflecting on the route not taken, Fellner argued that a proportionate income tax of 10 per cent applied to all income without exemption and superimposed upon the prevailing income tax structure, along with borrowing from household and corporate savings, price ceilings and rationing, would have prevented any appreciable inflation potential:

Given such a tax, and given the direct controls necessitated by specific shortages, it would not even have been necessary to use war bond 'drives' as a further means of reducing the demand for goods. However, it would of course have been necessary to prevent such wage increases as might start an inflationary process even in the absence of a pre-existing excess of demand over supply (that is to say, even in the absence of an 'inflation potential').[6]

Even for normal periods, Fellner advocated a flexible tax policy adjustable at quarterly intervals as a means of reducing economic instability, and a 'pay as you go' policy rather than the build-up of government debt. He saw the difficulties standing in the way of such adjustments to be political in nature, necessitating some delegation of power on the part of Congress, possibly to a committee of its own rather than to the executive branch.[7]

Invited to become a member of the Group of Independent Experts on Rising Prices of the Organisation of European Economic Co-operation (OEEC) in 1959, Fellner participated in a study of inflation in Western economies. Other members of the group who participated in the study and co-authored the study report published as *The Problem of Rising Prices* (1961) were: Milton Gilbert, Friedrich Lutz, B. Hansen (Denmark), R. F. Kahn (UK) and P. DeWolff (Netherlands), chair. By 1960, rising prices were a continuing problem. Efforts to understand inflation in terms of the aftermath of the war or the disturbances brought about by the Korean War had failed to offer a plausible explanation. The report analysed the rise in prices in the years 1953–60 in the twenty member or associate countries of the OEEC, and finds the 'median' rise as being between 2 and 3 per cent a year. The report also categorized the reasons that caused prices to rise as excess demand for goods and labour; excessive negotiated wage increases; monopolistic pricing; and special or temporary factors, such as bad harvests, a rise in indirect taxes or relaxations of rent controls. The first two factors, demand and wage increases, were seen as the most important. The study participants made recommendations for policy action, but their conclusions were not unanimous.[8] In a chapter entitled 'Balance of External Payments', the authors acknowledged that balance of payments is outside their study mandate, but they concluded, 'We must emphasize ... that the major cause of balance of payments difficulties in the past decade has been inflation and rising prices'.[9] They affirmed that these difficulties would not have resulted had all countries inflated at the same time, but that is not how the system works. Inflation was uneven and therefore responsible for the balance of payments surpluses and deficits in many countries. The authors concluded that overall price stability would remove a major cause of the disturbances, while 'allowing adjustments of relative prices to take place in response to market forces, particularly in internationally traded goods'.[10] Changes in transactions on capital account offer a large area for correcting imbalances. Government policy and private capital movements must also contribute to balance. 'This stresses the need to have monetary and fiscal policies that result in interest rates among countries that stimulate outflow from surplus countries and capital inflow to deficit countries'.[11]

The group believed that stability of prices should be an object of policy. They recommended, first, a better management of demand: excess demand had risen in the past chiefly because action was not taken promptly and firmly. In future greater use would probably have to be made of fiscal policy, and fiscal instruments would probably have to be rendered more flexible. Second, the majority of the group went on to recommend that governments have a wages policy. Government representatives should attend important wage negotiations to represent the general public's stake in the outcome. Changes were also 'certainly necessary' in the institutional framework of wage negotiation, which in many countries was still strongly marked by pre-war experience. Dissenting views were expressed by Fellner and Lutz, who objected to any government policy setting of wage rates.

Government Regulation, Full Employment and Economic Growth

In *Monetary Policies and Full Employment* (1946), Fellner identified cyclical unemployment as the fundamental problem affecting US economic well-being, for which not guaranteeing full employment but instead using expansionary fiscal and monetary policy at the first sign of a major recession was the solution. These approaches should be scrapped if business investment revives or inflation rises. Fellner advised raising the target unemployment rate from 4 per cent to 5 per cent to deal with the inevitable frictions in the employment market. Fellner also advocated implementing a federally subsidized employment programme to offset the hardship of the 5 per cent target.

Fellner argued that a guarantee of full employment leads to inflation. In his paper, 'Hansen on Full-Employment Policies', Fellner held that the full employment guarantee contemplated by Hansen would create chronic upward pressure on wages and prices, a possibility that Hansen did not consider:

A de facto guaranty of full employment would create conditions in which a chronic upward pressure on prices and wages would have to be anticipated. Any group acting in its own interest would have to proceed on the assumption that the other groups will exert an upward pressure on wages and prices regardless of how the group itself behaves. Consequently, a public-minded (rather than 'narrowly selfish') attitude on the part of any one group would place it at a disadvantage without forestalling the inflationary tendency. This is the prototype of a situation in which people can be made public minded – or 'responsible' from the point of view of the economy as a whole – only by rigid co-ordination, that is to say, by controls.[12]

Fellner's book *Trends and Cycles in Economic Activity: An Introduction to Problems of Economic Growth* (1956) introduced three factors critical to sustainable economic growth: 1) improvements in the productive process – technological advances, population growth, net additions to natural resources – all of which served to offset the classical law of diminishing returns; 2) mobility of resources – adjustments of the internal structure of the economy, including wage, price and interest-rate adjustments; and 3) a flexible supply of money and credit.[13]

Government regulation can eliminate unemployment, but at the expense of business investment, innovation and democratic rule. In 'Rapid Growth as an Objective of Economic Policy' (1960), Fellner argued that the long-run growth of output is linked to population growth, to the growth of the capital stock, and to technological-organizational improvements ('innovations'), and the growth of per capita output and the rise of living standards should be explained by the increase in the capital-labour ratio and by technological-organizational progress; nevertheless, if the level of money wage rates and of prices does not possess unlimited downward flexibility, then it is not possible to count on the 'real balance effect' to ensure full employment. Sure, it is possible to eliminate unemployment via government investment or through deficit-financed transfer payments to consumers, but it is questionable whether the essentials of a decentralized market economy and of its political institutions could be preserved under large-scale programmes of this sort.[14] This is fundamentally the same view that Fellner communicated in *Maintaining and Restoring Balance in International Payments* (1966).

Oligopoly, Tacit Collusion and the Reaction Function

One of the best known of his works, Fellner's *Competition Among the Few* (1949) described the tacit collusion of big firms within the same industry to protect their common interests, control competition and avoid conflict.[15] Fellner's work made a significant contribution to our understanding of industry concentration and isomorphism, and of the impact of large firms on wages, prices and inflation. Psychological interdependence is the theme of Machlup's own work on oligopoly, 'The Characteristics and Classifications of Oligopoly' (1952).

In his book *Towards a Reconstruction of Macroeconomics* (1976), Fellner argued that there is a game of strategy going on between policymakers and the public: they anticipate and act on assumptions about the other's future responses. Further, the public attaches probability judgements to the way the behaviour of the authorities may become influenced by the behaviour of the public itself. Hence, expectations based on presumed future behaviour underscore the importance of credibility. For example, a government policy to combat inflation can be effective only if businesses and workers are convinced that the rising unemployment and declining real output brought on by demand-management strategies will not be followed by a reversal of policy. If government policy lacks credibility, then wages and prices will roll back and an even reduction in real output will be required to control inflation. Although Fellner had reservations about some of the propositions of rational expectations and the emerging monetarist view, he felt that both offered policy guidance superior to the mix of policy solutions known as 'neo-Keynesian fine-tuning', because monetarism focused on a single policy variable, namely the money supply.[16]

Balance of Payments Deficits, Liquidity and Limited Exchange Rate Flexibility

In a presentation made to the Academy of Political Science, Fellner spoke out about 'Budget Deficits and their Consequences' (1963), stating that 'it would be difficult to overstate the worldwide damage done by fiscal orthodoxy during the 1930s. That attitude was, of course, self-defeating, even by its own standards. The effort to keep deficits within narrow limits during the thirties aggravated the deep depression which was plaguing European countries as well as the United States. The European upheavals led to the war and to the emergence of enormous wartime deficits a few years later'.[17]

A fascinating and unorthodox conservative, Fellner was against economists using their arguments to espouse political values. Speaking out about the recessions of 1957–8 and 1960–1, Fellner took on the critics who argued that the 1957 policies should have been less conservative: 'I feel that a critic who develops this argument is thereby expressing a political view in the narrower sense of the term, in that he is quarrelling not with a misconception concerning the significance of budget deficits but with the ranking of political values in a range in which the rankings acceptable to different individuals are observably and legitimately different'.

Returning to the interpretation of deficits, Fellner suggested, 'those given to orthodox misconceptions have on various occasions prevented planned deficits when planned deficits would have been needed to avoid economic contractions (and, incidentally, also to avoid very large unplanned deficits)'.[18] Nevertheless, behind these misconceptions 'there is the poorly articulated view that the economist's "rational fiscal policy" would become linked with decisions reflecting highly controversial political values. In particular, there is the fear that economic advisers often favour programmes involving appreciable risks of inflationary pressures and balance of payments crises such as prepare the ground for ambitious administrative controls'.[19] This paper presented the first of several instances where the focus on value judgements and political viewpoints embedded in seemingly rational arguments sounded very close to Machlup. The same was evident in Fellner's 1972 paper 'The Dollar's Place in the International System', to be discussed below.

Two of Fellner's major papers on deficits, liquidity and flexible exchange rates were written for presentation at joint conferences of officials and academics held to discuss these problems. In Zurich in January 1966, twenty-seven experts (fourteen academics and thirteen officials) spent several days going over the main issues. They agreed that each of the academic economists would prepare a brief paper on a special issue and that Professors Fellner, Machlup and Triffin, who had acted as a steering committee, would present comprehensive papers on the principles of maintaining and restoring balance in international payments. The drafts of some of these papers and a glossary were distributed early in April. A second conference was held in Princeton in April 1966, in conjunction with the Washington meeting of the officials of the Group of Ten. Twenty-five persons (thirteen officials and twelve academics) attended the Princeton conference. Some of the drafts were reviewed and discussed in detail, others only on the main points. The primary purpose of the papers was to be of help to the officials of the governments in their inquiry into the balance of payments problems, so essential in their negotiations on the necessary improvements of the international monetary system. The participants of the symposium agreed that the papers should be made available through publication in the form of a book. The book was *Maintaining and Restoring Balance in International Payments*, published by Princeton University Press in 1966.

So very close to the critical conference topic of adjustment, Fellner's own paper 'Rules of the Game' argued that only continuous consultations among Western monetary authorities, leading to a state of mutual understanding among them, had a hope of greatly reducing the difficulties of payments adjustment. Under the Bretton Woods system, even close cooperation would likely lead to incomplete coordination of the price trends of the individual countries around a general inflationary trend, thus reinforcing those inflationary tendencies already observable.[20] Failure to achieve close collaboration concerning the adjustment process and an internationally acceptable means of payment would aggravate present difficulties: 'For example, insistence on balancing the United States' international accounts at fixed exchange rates and within a short period would presumable lead *either* to appreciably more unemployment than this country had even in its post-war recessions *or* to a significant extension of the scope of discriminatory measures (including exchange control). Both these alternatives being highly unpalatable, failure to achieve systematic collaboration might bring the Bretton Woods era to an end under dramatic circumstances, which it is not enjoyable to contemplate.'[21] Fellner recommended instead letting free-market processes perform more of the equilibrating function.

Fellner offered a new definition of fundamental disequilibrium, based on the practical inability of the countries concerned, to reach an understanding on jointly sufficient demand restraints in deficit countries and demand expansion in surplus countries. He considered it useful and in accordance with the spirit of the charter of the International Monetary Fund to view disequilibria as fundamental in cases where such understanding cannot be achieved, and when it therefore becomes necessary to resort to policies of a structural kind, for example to exchange-rate readjustments. Fellner held these exchange rate readjustments to 'belong among the policies that the countries concerned may decide to adopt'.[22] To avoid discriminatory measures and controls in situations of fundamental disequilibrium, Fellner recommended changing the mix of monetary and fiscal policies on which the governments of deficit and surplus countries have been relying.

Deficit countries that are determined to avoid aggregate-demand restraints can usually move to a tighter monetary policy (implying higher interest rates) coupled with a more expansionary fiscal policy, and surplus countries can move to a policy of easier credit coupled with tighter fiscal policy. For deficit countries this amounts to borrowing, for domestic fiscal expenditure, funds that would otherwise be invested abroad or invested in the domestic economy. While from the vantage point of the surplus countries, the policy recommendation is investment at lower interest rates in deficit countries rather than in surplus countries. Budgetary ease in deficit countries may be brought about by tax reductions and/ or by increased government expenditures; budgetary tightness in the surplus countries by tax increases and/or by a reduction of expenditures.[23]

While Fellner and Machlup tended to separate the 'deficit' and the 'surplus' problems, Machlup tended to use the first rather than the latter as his most frequent example of the imbalances to be financed and remedied. Fellner, like Triffin, spoke throughout of imbalance as a two-way problem. Like Machlup, Fellner leaned towards greater exchange rate flexibility, particularly through a combination of the proposals involving a 'wider band' and a 'crawling peg'. While Fellner advocated a widened band between exchange-rate support limits and avoidance of official intervention within the band, he shied away from unlimited flexibility for fear of occasional destabilizing speculation. In his paper 'On Limited Exchange-Rate Flexibility', which became chapter five in *Maintaining and Restoring Balance in International Payments*, Fellner began with a full restatement of a declaration signed by twenty-seven economists in favour of the band proposal or shiftable parity. Among the twenty-seven were some economists who favoured *more* flexibility, but signed the declaration as a first step. Adding his own thoughts, Fellner argued, 'I do not know how many signers would agree with my view that *within the band* there should be no official intervention at all. The *unmanaged* limited flexibility – that is, the unmanaged "margin flexibility" which I have in mind – has many adherents. However, other adherents of limited flexibility are prepared to *permit* official intervention even at exchange rates that have not hit one of the limits of the band. To me it seems that under such a system of managed limited flexibility it would be very difficult to devise and enforce agreements which would exclude the danger of official actions at cross-purposes'.[24] Fellner advanced this argument again in his paper 'Specific Proposal for Limited Exchange-Rate Flexibility' (1970).[25]

In his paper 'A "Realistic" Note on Threefold Limited Flexibility of Exchange Rates' (1970), one of a collection of papers written by the organizers and participants in the Bürgenstock conferences (1968–70), Fellner recommended a plan for limited flexibility in three ways: 1) limited in extent (falling within the 'widened band' and 'crawling peg' categories); 2) limited to currencies tending upward in relation to the dollar; and 3) limited to a very small number of currencies for which gradual upward flexibility would be put into effect by specific policy decisions. His plan was 'realistic', he believed, because talk of widened band or crawling peg was already widespread, and his recommendation was based on a plan first described for Germany in the 1966–7 Report of the Council of German Economic Experts. In fact, the German mark was introduced as a candidate for Fellner's proposal. In a system of limited exchange rate flexibility, countries running chronic balance of payments surpluses with the United States would avoid the accumulation of large dollar balances, without being able to convert their dollars into gold, by revaluing their currencies upward in relation to the dollar.[26]

In 'The Dollar's Place in the International System: Suggested Criteria for the Appraisal of Emerging Views' (1972), Fellner put on his Machlup hat, quite literally exploring and classifying alternative exchange rate policies, before establishing criteria for appraisal. In fact, the article acknowledged comments during the drafting by Cooper, Machlup and Haberler. What do we expect of a viable system – and what are we likely to get, given central banks are unlikely to abstain from interventions in the market; given exchange rates will adjust but domestic policies may be obstructionist; given the ultimate outcome is a return to some kind of pegged system versus free floating; and given a possible return to convertibility and the perpetuation of a reserve squeeze on the USA? Fellner made a systematic assessment of existing exchange rate policy solutions, but argued for the establishment of a system of exchange rate adjustability combined with protection of the value of foreign dollar reserves. [27]

In 'Controlled Floating and the Confused Issue of Money Illusion' (1973), Fellner addressed the question: Is money illusion responsible for any existing differences between the domestic side-effects of achieving current account objectives under exchange rate flexibility on the one hand, and achieving these objectives under fixed rates on the other? The question is important because it would be unsound to build long-run policy on money illusion.[28] The notion of money illusion is a lack of sufficient realization that one's income depends on prices and inflation as well as on the nominal size of the income. While the concept has been attributed to Keynes, it was also the focus of a book by Irving Fisher, *The Money Illusion* (1928). The money illusion referred to by Fellner is the overhang of dollars, the vestiges of the old system that have remained since the move to controlled floating in 1973; and secondly, allowing a country's exchange rates to adjust downward is a more readily acceptable method to eliminate a trade deficit than is devaluation of the country's money at fixed rates. On the overhang, Fellner recommended consolidation – convertibility into SDRs or limitedly in gold – and the encouragement of private foreign investment in the US to absorb foreign official dollars.[29]

In 'Schools of Thought in the Mainstream of American Economics' (1977), Fellner distinguished between economists who base their analysis on the assumption that a consistent and reasonably steady long-run oriented policy attitude will make the short-run behaviour of market participants fall in line with expected long-run results – provided market forces are allowed to manifest themselves freely enough. Those usually counted among the monetarists tend to be long-run oriented in this sense. Other economists, who have remained very influential, either state or at least imply in their analysis that a direct-policy concern with the results obtained in successive short periods is needed for ensuring a satisfactory long-run outcome of the economic process. Those usually regarded as neo-Keynesians tend to be short-run oriented in this sense. It is the distinction between long- and short-run orientation that comes nearest to qualifying as a distinction between influential schools of thought in the contemporary Western scene.[30]

In Fellner's view, neo-Keynesians tend to base demand management largely on ad hoc adjustments of fiscal (budgetary) variables to the changing economic outlook rather than on regulating money aggregates, which is clearly a matter of short- as against long-run orientation. While the demand-effect of fiscal policies expresses itself mainly or exclusively in the short run, repetitive short-run disturbances could suppress correction in the long-run. What does not fit into the long-run oriented approach is the conception that the fiscal variables need to be adjusted more or less 'currently' to the changing economic outlook. Over time, the cumulative nominal expansionary effect of fiscal policy will be absorbed (offset) increasingly by rising prices, since expansionary fiscal policies raise interest rates and beyond a certain point the private sector will not produce the additional goods for which the additional money incomes are creating demand. A similar problem arises with unemployment.

Confidence, Credibility and Rational Expectations

We do not find in Fellner the confidence language found in Machlup and Triffin. We find in Fellner's papers from the late 1970s onward a well-articulated desire to piece together rationality, expectations and the credibility effect (the latter term coined and defined by Fellner), although the credibility hypothesis also appears in *Towards a Reconstruction of Macroeconomics: Problems of Theory and Policy* (1976) in Fellner's argument that inflation can be curbed through a consistent policy of demand restraint. We find rational expectations in Fellner's early work, in the notion of the economy as a self-regulating system where credible information leads to actionable expectations, but also the belief that rational expectations theory is flawed. In Fellner's 'Rules of the Game' (1966), were countries to share credible information about their surplus and deficit status, their fiscal policies and their intentions with respect to adjustment, were they to collaborate closely, there might be reason to hope that expectations would be rational. This closeness of collaboration puts too great a burden on administrative machinery. Suddenly, what was intended to be minimal support interventions by central banks to limit speculative swings under controlled floating since 1973 threatens to evolve into official intervention and systematic international reform managed by a super-bureaucracy.[31]

In 'The Credibility Effect and Rational Expectations: Implications of the Gramlich Study' (1979), Fellner argued, 'Conclusions derived from analysis incorporating what may be termed the credibility effect overlap with conclusions from analysis commonly associated with the hypothesis of rational expectations. Both hypotheses lead to a critical attitude concerning essential features of the macroeconomic models most frequently used, but the two hypotheses need to be distinguished from each other. In this paper, I ... argue in favour of the hypothesis stressing the credibility effect. My conclusion is that, once one eliminates the unconvincing elements from the rational expectations hypothesis, one is left with the credibility hypothesis as it is here interpreted.'[32] What is the credibility effect, and how does it differ from rational expectations? Fellner's credibility effect maintains that market expectations, and thus the effect of past money wage and price increases and of any observed slack on current money wage and price increases, are significantly influenced by the expected future behaviour of policymakers. Emphasis is placed on the difference between states of the economy in which inconsistent policies lead market participants to form diffuse personal probability distributions with risk allowances playing a large role in their decision making, and states of the economy in which firm and credible policies condition the public's expectations and lead to much more strongly peaked and widely shared personal probability distributions concerning future events.

The rational expectations hypothesis overlaps with that of the credibility effect, because both stress that the public is forming its expectations on the basis of all available information, including information on the probable future actions of policymakers. Fellner believed the overlap is only partial. For example: the views commonly associated with the rational expectations hypothesis suggest that experience has in fact enabled the public to detect a system by which the authorities exert an influence on nominal demand, while the credibility hypothesis suggests that the public can detect such a system only if the authorities play effectively into the hands of the market participants by behaving consistently in an understandable fashion. If policymakers adopt confusing strategies, they risk creating highly volatile market expectations.

Fellner addressed the credibility hypothesis again in 'The Valid Core of Rationality Hypotheses in the Theory of Expectations' (1979). Here he acknowledged that Herbert Stein's characterization of rational expectations fits the credibility hypothesis equally well: 'It is possible to view the credibility hypothesis – [namely] the hypothesis stressing the significance for market expectations of a consistent and credible policy posture – as a member of the same family of hypotheses as that on which rational expectations theory in the usual sense in based. At any rate there exists a substantial overlap'.[33]

The 'Credibility Versus Confidence' work of Edwin LeHeron and Emmanual Carre at the Institute of Political Studies makes a distinction between confidence, which implies mutual understanding, and credibility, which is about behaviour. 'By a strategy of credibility, we mean a central bank that adopts a model of behaviour and then follows it. It says what it does and does what it says'.[34] They attribute the credibility hypothesis to Finn Kydland and Edward Prescott (1977), William Nordhaus (1975), Robert Barro and David Gordon (1983), and Kenneth Rogoff (1985). Fellner took criticism on his credibility hypothesis from James Tobin, Basil Moore and Robert Gordon.

Conclusions

Fellner and Machlup shared a life experience that bonded them, whether or not they ever talked about it. Both had profound experience of war-time inflation in the Austria and Hungary of their early university days. They were already colleagues, actively writing to each other about students and publications in the 1950s. Both wrote on a range of issues related to competitiveness, innovation, productivity, oligopoly and monopoly – issues all related to economic growth. Like Machlup, Fellner continued to write on these issues even as he played a co-leader role in the Bellagio Group conferences and began writing on balance of payments issues. While Fellner's work on balance of payments problems is perhaps not as well known as Machlup's, is it clear that he deeply immersed himself in these issues from the beginning of the 1960s. Both economists were committed to freely floating exchange rates, but in their own writing and in the Bellagio Group conferences they explored myriad possible solutions, given the ultimate decision would be made by the national governments of IMF member nations. Both economists shared a belief that government intervention in market mechanisms was to be avoided. The confidence connection, which links the work of Machlup and Triffin, may have a complement in Fellner's credibility theory.

5 WHY ECONOMISTS DISAGREE: THE ROLE OF FRAMING IN CONSENSUS BUILDING

Introduction

The title of this chapter – 'Why Economists Disagree' – takes its name from Fritz Machlup's speech before the American Philosophical Society on 12 November 1964, five months after the fourth Bellagio Group conference. In his speech, Machlup explained his decision to bring together economists from eleven countries, many of them chosen because they were well-known advocates for divergent, often feuding, schools of thought on the problems and solutions to problems facing the international monetary system in the 1960s, for an 'inquiry into the sources of disagreement on international monetary prescriptions'.[1] Like scientists, Machlup said, 'Economists also have an exact-construct world, created for purely theoretical analysis; but no outsider cares what they do with it or appreciates the broad agreement of the analysts about the theoretical system that constitutes their discipline. The economists' work becomes known only where it deals with the real-life world, in which most things are unknown and almost everything is uncertain'.[2] Machlup was interested in a process whereby participants would collaboratively define the problem they wanted to solve, examine possible solutions in light of the desired outcome, and allow themselves the freedom to consider hybrid or compromise solutions. The group that came to be known as the Bellagio Group met eighteen times between 1964 and 1977 in Bellagio at Lake Como, Washington, DC and Princeton, as well as in nine European centres.

This chapter first provides a brief review of the framing literature, then addresses the establishment of the frame in the Bellagio Group conferences, the selection and identity of the participants and the use of framing at the Bellagio Group conferences. The chapter then draws conclusions and sets the stage for Chapter 6.

The Framing Literature

Contributions to the framing literature have come from sociology, psychology and strategic management, among other social sciences. In sociology, David Snow and Robert Benford (1992) defined a frame as 'an interpretive schemata that signifies and condenses the "world out there" by selectively punctuating and encoding objects, situations, events, experiences, and sequences of action in one's present or past environment'.[3] They focused on framing as the process of deliberate and focused persuasive communication essential for the mobilization of consensus prior to collective action, and as the cognitive process necessary for orienting and sustaining collective action.[4] In psychology, Robert Entman (1993) defined framing as the process of selecting aspects of a perceived reality and making them more salient to promote a particular problem definition, causal interpretation, moral evaluation, and/or treatment recommendation for the item described;[5] while Arnos Tversky and Daniel Kahneman (1981) saw framing as selecting and highlighting some features of reality while omitting others, with the effect that alternative descriptions of a decision problem (different frames) often give rise to different preferences. This occurs because decision makers are normally unaware of alternative frames and of their potential effects on the relative attractiveness of options, although they would wish their preferences to be independent of frame.[6] In strategic management, Paul Nutt (1998) saw framing as important to strategy success by influencing the interpretation of what needs to be done as a guide to the search for strategic alternatives.[7] Research in cognition has also influenced strategic management's response to framing, suggesting that managers use cognitive frames to cope with ambiguous situations.[8] According to Donald Hambrick and Phyllis Mason (1984), frames filter managers' perceptions about what is happening and what action should be taken.[9] Gerard Hodgkinson et al. (1999) investigated the framing bias that arises when trivial changes to the way in which a decision problem is presented, emphasizing either the potential gains or the potential losses, lead to reversals of preference, with decision makers being risk-averse when gains are highlighted and risk-seeking when losses are highlighted.[10] To overcome this bias, decision makers are encouraged to develop more elaborate models of problems, taking into account both the potential gains and losses involved, to ensure that trivial features of the decision context do not unduly influence choice behaviour.

In this context, Machlup emerged as the principal actor, having created a process for evaluative and purposeful framing by which sophisticated thinkers with a preference for a specific strategy to eliminate payments imbalances come to a better understanding of their beliefs and cognitions around three issues which, in the course of moderated dialogue, they come to agree are most important to the elimination of payments imbalances – adjustment, liquidity and confidence. The process would take place over the course of four conferences as well as the intervening weeks, during which assumptions, beliefs and cognitions (including value judgements and political attitudes) are identified and associated with specific strategies, current or recommended. Advocates for each strategy are closely examined by their peers. Adjustment, liquidity and confidence are defined and prioritized in written drafts by each of the conference members – and revised from conference to conference through the fourth conference when the final drafts become part of the final conference report. The 'all hands on deck', intensive collaborative strategy approach, which would become very common to twenty-first century cross-functional strategy teams working for government agencies or Fortune 500 companies, was unique in its time to Machlup and the Bellagio Group conferences.

Establishing the Frame at the Bellagio Group Conferences

For Machlup, the critical problem was how to frame the problem so that each of these divergent solutions could be examined in terms of its ability to solve what was ailing the global economy. He saw three problems. His goal was to get the economists to see them, to define and prioritize them for themselves, and to set their sights on the end game, evaluating each policy change in terms of its ability to address the adjustment, liquidity and confidence problems. By adding to the discussion a consideration of the institutional and operational requirements of each policy option, Machlup was adding an opportunity cost dimension that was likewise an innovation.

With support from the Ford and Rockefeller foundations as well as Princeton University, four initial conferences were planned. The first conference was conceived as an experiment designed to isolate the assumptions underlying the major policy recommendations in order to determine where the policies diverged. As Machlup wrote to invitees in December 1963: '*I am writing to enlist your active participation in an experiment which may have significant results*'. Machlup called it a 'test' to find out whether this group could identify the differences in factual and normative assumptions that might explain the differences in prescriptions for solving the problems of the international monetary system. As Machlup argued, 'Presumably, we all use the same logic. Hence, if we arrive at different recommendation we evidently differ in the assumptions of facts or in the hierarchy of values. To identify and formulate these assumptions would, I believe be a major step towards a better understanding of the present conflicts of ideas'.[11]

Notes prepared by economist Burton Malkiel, a former student of Machlup who played a significant organizational role for the conferences, explained: 'In elaboration of these aims it was hoped that the reasons for disagreement could be isolated and classified according to a variety of separate categories. Nevertheless, the question of what the final result from such a conference would be was not to be prejudged. It was expected that this and future conferences would devote themselves to definition of the problem, examination of "ideal" solutions and an analysis of which negotiating compromises would be relatively harmless and which would detour us from a path towards an "ideal" solution'.[12] With only ten members and five observers, the first meeting was held at Princeton, 18–9 December 1963. The economists who attended were all but one from US institutions, many from Princeton, and included Arthur Bloomfield, University of Pennsylvania; Lester Chandler, Princeton; George Duncan, University of Dublin; William Fellner, Yale; Hourmouzis Georgiadis, Princeton; Gottfried Haberler, Harvard; George Halm, Fletcher School of Law and Diplomacy; Edward Kane, Princeton; W. Arthur Lewis, Princeton; Fritz Machlup, Princeton; Burton Malkiel, Princeton; Richard Musgrave, Princeton; Walter Salant, Brookings Institution; Tibor Scitovsky, University of California, Berkeley; and Robert Triffin, Yale.

Selection and Identity of the Bellagio Group Members

About the selection of a final group of thirty-two economists, Machlup wrote in *International Monetary Arrangements: The Problem of Choice* (1964) that group members should include several of the economists whose plans on international monetary reform had been widely discussed, especially those with notoriously divergent views. Keynesian, Austrian and Chicago school views and their variants were amply represented. Nevertheless, by neither recording nor transcribing participant discussions, Machlup hoped to encourage the exploration of alternative viewpoints. Machlup also specified that several economists should have achieved prominence in the field of international finance, especially those with an international reputation as writers or teachers. He wanted at least one economist, preferably in the field of international finance, from each of the eleven countries represented in the Group of Ten. No group members should be economists in full-time positions with national or international government departments or agencies. Less than half of the economists chosen should reside in the USA, or at least not so many members that fruitful discussion and effective composition of a report would be impossible. Finally, no economist would be chosen whose command of English was not adequate for oral discussion without translation services.[13] It would prove to be very important to the credibility of the group that nearly all of the economists who accepted the invitation to participate were former members of the Federal Reserve, the International Monetary Fund, the Bank for International Settlements, or had been or were still advisers to the heads of their national governments.

Although members of the Bellagio Group might have been born abroad and retained their native citizenship, Machlup considered the US contingent to be those currently working in US universities at the time of the Bellagio conferences. Nevertheless, there is sufficient arbitrariness in the selection. There were a number of senior economists in the group, so why not Paul Einzig? Perhaps his negative perspective on the French was perceived as a liability. Why not Friedrich Hayek? There is nothing in the Machlup archives to answer this question. Like Einzig, he does not appear on any list of potential invitees. We do know that the following economists were invited but could not attend the first four Bellagio Group conferences: James Meade, Milton Friedman, Richard Caves, James Tobin, Jan Tinbergen and Paul Samuelson. Meade, Friedman and Tobin would attend later conferences.

Arthur L. Bloomfield was a professor of economics at the University of Pennsylvania when he was invited to join the Bellagio Group. He had been a research economist with the Federal Reserve Bank in New York from 1941 to 1958, becoming chief economist of the Balance of Payments Division and later senior economist. According to Michele Alacevich and Pier Asso, Bloomfield was an expert in the financial and monetary systems of East Asian countries, heading missions to Korea and Indochina where he advised on central banking and financial policies, and reflecting a new multilateral role for the USA in foreign relations, one focused on internal stability and growth and on insulating national economies from international disruptions.[14]

Lester V. Chandler, a professor of economics at Princeton at the time he was invited to join the Bellagio Group, was associated with the rubber and chemical branches of the Office of Price Administration during World War II, first as price executive and then as economic adviser. After the war, Chandler conducted research for the Congressional Subcommittee on Monetary and Fiscal Policy of the Joint Economic Committee. In 1953 he became public director and deputy chair of the board of directors of the Federal Reserve Bank of Philadelphia. One of his major worries in the 1950s was the impact of low-interest easy money and increasing inflation on the government's mounting levels of debt. In 1949 he had written, 'It is common knowledge that money management in this country has been strongly influenced, if not dominated, by considerations related to the management of the Federal Debt'.[15]

Gottfried Haberler, a member of the board of governors of the Federal Reserve from 1943 to 1947, the director of the National Bureau of Economic Research (NBER), president of the American Economic Association and a professor of economics at Harvard when the Bellagio conferences began, was 'one of the first economists to make a rigorous case for the superior productivity and universal benefits of "free" or politically unrestricted international trade in terms of the modern subjective theory of value'.[16] Opposing both inflationary and protectionist policies, he advocated strict restraint in the growth of the money supply combined with free market-oriented microeconomic policies to reduce the monopoly power of labour unions and businesses, as well as the liberalization of international trade.

George N. Halm had been a professor of international economics at the Fletcher School of Law and Diplomacy since 1944. He was the doctoral mentor of C. Fred Bergsten, who became a member of the senior staff of the National Security Council under Richard Nixon. Halm was an advocate for what has become known as the 'band' proposal to extend exchange rate flexibility, a variant of a plan originally proposed by Robert Torrens in 1819 and similar to one suggested by Keynes in *The Treatise on Money* (1930) and *The Road to Prosperity* (1933).

Peter Kenen was a professor of economics at Columbia University when he was invited to join the Bellagio Group. He was a member of President Kennedy's Task Force on Foreign Economic Policy and the Review Committee on Balance of Payments Statistics.

Charles Kindleberger, a professor of economics at the Massachusetts Institute of Technology when he was invited to join the Bellagio Group, had been a research economist at the Federal Reserve Bank of New York from 1936 to 1939, a research economist for the Bank for International Settlements in Switzerland from 1939 to 1940, and a research economist for the Board of Governors of the Federal Reserve System from 1940 to 1942. In the period 1945–7 he served as chief of division, German and Austrian Economic Affairs for the US Department of State.

Robert Mundell was a professor of economics at McGill University in Canada when he joined the Bellagio Group. In the early 1960s he also worked in the research department of the IMF, where he began his macroeconomic analysis of exchange rates and their effect on monetary policies. In 1961 he put forward the theory that a single currency would be viable in an economic region, or optimum currency area, in which there was free movement of labour and trade.

Walter Salant had been a senior fellow at the Brookings Institution since 1954 when he was invited to join the Bellagio Group. He had served in the Treasury Department, the Securities and Exchange Commission and the Department of Commerce in the 1930s, and, in the 1940s, the Office of Price Administration and other agencies that designed the national strategy for wartime price controls. He was a senior staff member for international relations on the President's Council of Economic Advisers from 1946 to 1952. He later served as a consultant to NATO and in the Treasury Department in the Kennedy and Johnson Administrations. Salant argued that industrialized economies in depression were unlikely to recover on their own, but could use government spending and tax cuts to do so.

Among the internationals, perhaps the best known at the time of the Bellagio Group conferences was Sir Roy Harrod, a professor of economics at Oxford until his retirement in 1967. During World War II Harrod was invited to join the Statistical Department of the Admiralty (S-Branch), which Winston

Churchill had set up and moved to Downing Street when Churchill became Prime Minister in 1940. Harrod took an increasing interest in the international financial institutions – the International Monetary Fund and the World Bank – that would need to be set up after the war. He also became interested in national politics: he ran unsuccessfully for a Liberal seat in Parliament in the general election of 1945, and again in the 1950s with Churchill's support as a Conservative parliamentary candidate. He provided economic advice to Harold Macmillan, Conservative Prime Minister in the period 1957–63.

Before joining the Bellagio Group, Alberto Ferrari had been the first permanent Italian delegate of the Intra-European Payments Committee of the OEEC from 1948 to 1950, and Secretary General of the Bank for International Settlements from 1951 to 1961.

According to his biographer Jan-Otmar Hesse, Albert Hahn was never a regular university professor, but a private banker whose grandfather was the owner of a private bank in Frankfurt, the Bankhaus L. Albert Hahn, founded in 1821. During World War I Hahn wrote an article on inflation that was accepted as a PhD thesis at the University of Marburg, and in 1920 he wrote his *Economic Theory of Bank Credit*. Because of the numerous articles he wrote on the questions of inflation and monetary reform, he received an honorary (unpaid) professorship from the University of Frankfurt, which carried no teaching duties except for the occasional lecture. According to Hesse, 'Because of his experience as an international banker, his theoretical knowledge, and his knowledge of the German banking system, he was invited to participate in a meeting of international monetary experts in the Villa Serbelloni in Italy ... This conference, which led to the Bellagio Group, was the last appearance of the seventy-five-year-old Hahn among economists. Hahn died in Zurich in 1968.'[17]

Fred Hirsch was the financial editor at *The Economist* when he was invited to join the Bellagio Group. A graduate of the London School of Economics, he wrote *The Pound Sterling*, 'a major contribution to the then-heretical battle waged by many British economists in the mid-1960s to get the pound devalued', according to John Williamson.[18] In 1966 he took a job as senior adviser in the Research Department of the IMF, where he was regarded as an internationalist and a progressive, sympathetic towards greater exchange rate flexibility.

Dr Alexandre Lamfalussy was a professor of economics at the Université catholique de Louvain and at Yale and a banker with the Banque de Bruxelles at the time he became a member of the Bellagio Group.

Kioshi Kojima was a professor of economics at Hitotsubashi University in Japan. He is credited with the first Pacific Free Trade agreement proposal in 1966, leading to the establishment of both the Pacific Economic Cooperation Council (PECC) and the Asia-Pacific Economic Cooperation (APEC) forum.

Jurg Niehans had served in the Swiss Diplomatic Corps before becoming a professor of economics at the University of Zurich. He was an early critic of Robert Mundell's open economy targets and instruments approach to stabilization policy.[19]

Bertil Ohlin was professor of economics at Handelshögskolan in Sweden in 1963. He was also head of the Liberal Party in Sweden from 1944 to 1967 and a member of the Riksdag (parliament) from 1938 to 1970. He had been the minister of commerce (1944–5) in Sweden's wartime government.

Jacques Rueff, counsel for social and economic affairs, was economic adviser to French President Charles de Gaulle. Earlier, Rueff had been a major figure in the management of the French economy during the Great Depression. The 1958 Rueff Plan balanced the budget and secured the convertibility of the franc, which had been endangered by the strains of decolonization. In the 1960s, Rueff became a major proponent of a return to the gold standard, and was critical of the use of the dollar as a unit of reserve, which he warned would cause a worldwide inflation.

Dr Pierre Uri had been an aide to Jean Monnet, then in charge of the French Reconstruction Plan, part of the Schuman Plan that created the European Coal and Steel Community. At the time he was invited to join the Bellagio Group, he was counsellor for studies of the Atlantic Institute, an independent, non-governmental institute that promotes economic, political and cultural relations among NATO alliance members and the international community in general, based in Paris and founded in 1961.

A full listing of Bellagio Group members, their institutional affiliations and public policy experience appears below.

Table 5.1: Attending Bellagio Group Members, their Institutional Affiliations and Public Policy Experience

Member	Institution	Former Public Policy Role	Country of Citizenship (Birth)
Prof. Arthur L. Bloomfield	University of Pennsylvania	Federal Reserve	USA (Canada)
Prof. Lester Chandler	Princeton	Federal Reserve	USA
Prof. Alan C. L. Day	University of London	Member, Radcliffe Committee	UK
Prof. Pierre Dieterlen	National Center of Scientific Research	Author, with Charles Rist, of *The Monetary Problem of France* (1949)	France
Prof. Leon Dupriez	University of Louvain	National Bank of Belgium	Belgium
Prof. William J. Fellner	Yale University	Council of Economic Advisers	USA (Hungary)
Prof. Alberto Ferrari	University of Rome	Secretary General, Bank for International Settlements; Consorzio di Credito per le Opere Pubbliche	Italy
Prof. Gottfried Haberler	Harvard University	Federal Reserve; National Bureau of Economic Research	USA (Austria)
Prof. Albert Hahn	University of Frankfurt	Banker, Bankhaus L. Albert Hahn	Switzerland (Germany)
Prof. George Halm	Fletcher School of Law and Diplomacy	Doctoral mentor of C. Fred Bergsten, who became a member of the senior staff of the National Security Council under Richard Nixon	USA (Germany)
Sir Roy Harrod	University of Oxford	Economic adviser to Harold Macmillan, Conservative Prime Minister in 1957–63; Consultant, International Monetary Fund	UK
Prof. Michael Heilperin	Institut Universitaire de Hautes Études Internationales		USA (Poland)
Mr. Fred Hirsch	*The Economist*	Senior adviser in the Research Department of the IMF	UK (Austria)
Prof. Harry G. Johnson	University of Chicago		Canada
Prof. Fritz de Jong	University of Groningen	Labour Party of Groningen	Netherlands

Member	Institution	Former Public Policy Role	Country of Citizenship (Birth)
Prof. Peter B. Kenen	Columbia University	President Kennedy's Task Force on Foreign Economic Policy; Review Committee on Balance of Payments Statistics; Economic Advisory Committee of the Federal Reserve Bank of New York	USA
Prof. Charles Kindleberger	Massachusetts Institute of Technology	Federal Reserve; Bank for International Settlements	USA
Prof. Kioshi Kojima	Hitotsubashi University	Pacific Free Trade agreement proposal in 1966, leading to the establishment of both the Pacific Economic Cooperation Council (PECC) and Asia-Pacific Economic Cooperation (APEC)	Japan
Dr. Alexandre Lamfalussy	Banque de Bruxelles	Banker, Banque de Bruxelles; General Manager, Bank for International Settlements	Belgium (Hungary)
Prof. Friedrich Lutz	University of Zurich	International Monetary Fund	Germany
Prof. Fritz Machlup	Princeton University	Consultant, US Treasury	USA (Austria)
Prof. Burton Malkiel	Princeton University	Protégé of Machlup; Later, member of Council of Economic Advisers	USA
Prof. Hans Moller	University of Munich	Banker, Bank deuscher Länder; German Delgation, OEEC; Consultant, EED Brussels	Germany
Prof. Robert Mundell	McGill University	Adviser to the United Nations, the IMF, the World Bank, the European Commission, several governments in Latin America and Europe, the Federal Reserve Board, the US Treasury and the Government of Canada	Canada
Prof. Jurg Niehans	University of Zurich	Swiss Diplomatic Corps	Switzerland

Member	Institution	Former Public Policy Role	Country of Citizenship (Birth)
Prof. Bertil Ohlin	Handelshögskolan	Minister of commerce (1944–5) in Sweden's wartime government; Leader of the Liberal Party in Sweden from 1944 to 1967; Member of the Riksdag (parliament) from 1938 to 1970	Sweden
Prof Jacques Rueff	Consul for Economic and Social Affairs	Economic Adviser to French President Charles de Gaulle	France
Dr. Walter Salant	Brookings Institution	Treasury Department, Securities and Exchange Commission, Commerce Department in the 1930s; In the 1940s, the Office of Price Administration; Senior staff member for international relations on the President's Council of Economic Advisers from 1946 to 1952; Consultant to NATO and in the Treasury Department in the Kennedy and Johnson Administrations	USA
Prof. Tibor Scitovsky	University of California, Berkeley	OECD	USA (Hungary)
Prof. Egon Sohmen	University of the Saar	In late 1960s, with Herbert Giersch, wrote a defence of flexible exchange rates, submitted to the Saarbrucken government and drawing the support of one hundred economists in Germany when it went public	Austria
Prof. Robert Triffin	Yale University	Federal Reserve; IMF	USA (Belgium)
Dr. Pierre Uri	Atlantic Institute	Aide to Jean Monnet and the French Reconstruction Plan, which was part of the Schuman Plan that created the European Coal and Steel Community	France

Source: F. Machlup, *International Monetary Arrangements: The Problem of Choice* (1964a), and author's research into former public policy roles.

Use of the Frame in the Bellagio Group Conferences

In the morning of the first day, Robert Triffin provided a brief review of recent international monetary history. The first day's afternoon session and much of the second day's conference was devoted to a discussion of the objections to freely floating and fixed exchange rates. The purpose of the discussion was to identify and, if possible, to analyse the sources of agreement and disagreement. Some members of the conference felt that in addition it might be possible to evolve from the discussion of objectives, a set of objectives to be satisfied by proposals for reform of the present international monetary system. From the outset, Machlup posited four common sources of disagreement in the expressed opinions of reputable economists: logical fallacies, semantic confusion from ill-defined terms, different hunches 'about essential but unavailable information, [and] particularly the unpredictable responses of central bankers and other decision makers to future problems and developments'.[20] In accordance with the aims of the conference, a preliminary set of objections to freely fluctuating and fixed exchange rates was devised and an attempt made to indicate, where possible, how the arguments rest on specific factual assumptions or value judgements. In addition, the members attempted a partial reconciliation of opposing positions. Note that discussion of gold-based systems and centralized reserves was not part of the first conference (largely because of the absence of Europeans more closely associated with gold-based systems and centralized reserves).

A second conference was held from 17 to 23 January at the Villa Serbelloni in Bellagio, on Lake Como in Italy. Different value judgements and political attitudes were especially important to Machlup, who urged participants to state frankly what their recommendations would be if the constraints of 'political feasibility' were removed. At the second conference, advocates of each of the four alternative exchange rate regimes were asked to enumerate the positive assumptions associated with their plan and the reasons they preferred their plan to alternative systems. The inquiry took the form of hearings: one or two protagonists were asked to submit to cross-examination by the rest of the group. While no transcript of the Bellagio Group conference conversations exists, economist Robert Triffin acknowledged in a chapter for Jacob Dreyer's *Depth and Breadth in Economics* that 'Each of us had to defend his proposals against the criticisms of other participants and to explain why he could not agree with their proposals'.[21] On the basis of notes taken during these sessions, drafting committees worked every night on the formulation of statements of assumptions made in the advocacy of each major policy system which, if accepted as pertinent, correct and realistic, would justify the adoption or adaptation of a particular system and the rejection or modification of the others. Assumptions addressed the adjustment, liquidity and confidence problems (A), and covered three additional questions (B, C and D):

A. In what respects are the present-day system and the three other proposed systems inferior to the one under consideration? This question appears as 'Criticisms of the Present and Alternative Systems'.
B. What are the essential arrangements that characterize the system? This question was distilled as 'Institutional Arrangements under the Proposed System'.
C. What are some of the necessary conditions for the system to work in the intended fashion? This question appears as 'Operation and Implications of the Proposed System'.
D. What are the potential modifications to the system (suggestions made by economists to improve the exchange rate policy under discussion)?

The lists of assumptions concerning four systems (status quo, centralized reserves, multiple currencies, flexible rates) were uniformly organized under headings roughly corresponding to the questions posed above so that all the economists attending could compare them. Table 5.2 captures the differences between espoused plans. While the goal was not consensus around a single exchange rate policy, economists reached consensus around the 'desired changes' (that is to say, impact on adjustment, liquidity and confidence) they found most important to the strength and stability of the monetary system. This was the outcome Machlup had been looking for.

At the end of the second conference, following a survey format, members were asked to define, explain and prioritize three problems: 1) the problem of adjustment, i.e. of correcting imbalances in payments positions (a problem that would become known as the adjustment problem); 2) the problem of the aggregate amounts of international reserves, i.e. of providing such amounts as would avoid inflationary and deflationary swings in the world at large (a problem that would become known as the liquidity problem); and 3) the problem of consolidation of reserves, i.e. of avoiding sudden switches between reserve media (a problem that would become known perhaps not so intuitively as the confidence problem). The Robert Triffin papers preserve several of the responses. Canadian economist Robert Mundell would confirm that the problems of confidence, adjustment and liquidity were the three main problems under consideration. The confidence problem could be corrected easily by funding or guaranteeing exchange balances. As he saw it, confidence was both the most imminent threat to stability and the easiest problem to solve. Flexible exchange rates would speed adjustment, reduce liquidity and leave governments free to pursue full employment policies. Closely integrated countries may still opt for intra-currency area pegged rates.[22]

Table 5.2: Four Major Policy Proposals – Sources of Disagreement

Assumptions	Semi-Automatic Gold Standard	Centralized International Reserves	Multiple Currencies	Flexible Exchange Rates
	CRITIQUE OF PRESENT SYSTEM			
	Present gold exchange unsustainable, since it requires a progressive increase in the ratio of the liquid liabilities of reserve-currency countries to their gold holdings which threatens the value of the reserve holdings of other countries, undermining confidence in the stability of the system.	SAME	SAME	SAME
	Changes in domestic money supply are divorced from inflows/outflows of international reserves, permitting central banks to resist adjustment of imbalances in international payments: surplus countries can avoid domestic inflationary adjustments and deficit countries can postpone domestic deflationary adjustments. Meanwhile reserve-currency countries are able to finance deficits by increasing liabilities rather than losing reserve assets, hence they pursue inflationary domestic policies and leave adjustment measures to the surplus countries, biasing the system towards inflation.	The evolution of reserves to be expected from current gold production at current gold price and from deficits of the present reserve-currency countries is haphazard and does not ensure against excessive or deficient holdings.	SAME AS FOR CENTRALIZED INTERNATIONAL RESERVES	Presumed fixity of rates requires that adjustments be effected through changes in domestic price levels, domestic employment or restrictions on international transactions, which allows imbalances to be cushioned by the accumulation/decumulation of international reserves, leading to delayed adjustment, tariff/trade solutions or development tied to military aid. Furthermore, countries inflate/deflate in lock step, interfering with full employment and price stabilization.

Assumptions	Semi-Automatic Gold Standard	Centralized International Reserves	Multiple Currencies	Flexible Exchange Rates
	Deferment of adjustment measures leads to cumulative imbalances, which can only be corrected by large and disruptive changes in domestic prices and exchange rates.	Under existing and foreseeable circumstances, the adjustment mechanism will fail to work fast enough to enable countries to finance their deficits with available international reserves and borrowing facilities, with the result that satisfactory growth of world trade and capital movements cannot be reconciled with full employment and stable prices.	SAME AS CENTRALIZATION OF INTERNATIONAL RESERVES	Alternative systems that seek improvement by providing additional liquidity of a credit nature are unacceptable because they do not cope with the adjustment problem.
	Deficiencies will persist so long as national money supplies are determined by discretionary management dominated by political pressure to resist adjustment.	The use of national currencies as international reserves of national monetary authorities creates one of the main difficulties, interfering with parity adjustments by reserve-currency countries when needed.	The instability of the present currency-reserve system, largely due to its concentration on one or two reserve currencies, can be eliminated by a multiple reserve system that will also allow payments adjustments consistent with full employment and stable prices.	A semi-automatic gold standard would meet the adjustment problem, but would operate by deflation in deficit countries and inflation in surplus countries.

Assumptions	Semi-Automatic Gold Standard	Centralized International Reserves	Multiple Currencies	Flexible Exchange Rates
	INSTITUTIONAL ARRANGEMENTS UNDER PROPOSED SYSTEM			
	Each participating country fixes the gold value of its monetary unit and guarantees to maintain that gold value with the result that the exchange rate parities among the gold-standard countries are fixed.	Each country or each major reserve holder agrees to keep a fixed proportion of its gross international reserves in the form of gold-value-denominated sight deposits at the IMF or other international centre.	The monetary authorities of the major countries agree to diversify gradually their foreign exchange holdings so that the expansion of reserves will take the form of acquiring a mixture of currencies and gold, not merely gold, dollars and sterling.	Under this system, balance between international receipts and payments is achieved through the self-adjustment of the exchange rate to the existing supply and demand situation in free foreign exchange markets.
	OPERATION AND IMPLICATIONS OF PROPOSED SYSTEM			
	Changes in gold reserves and money stocks induced by imbalances in international payments will induce changes in interest rates.	The IMF will induce member countries to hold deposits by agreement, the payment of interest and the offer of guarantees against exchange rate changes and default. The IMF will increase/decrease the volume of world reserves by expanding or contracting the volume of its assets through open market operations, direct lending, modest overdraft or purchases of bonds.	The rate of increase of gross reserves needed to maintain full employment and price stability will be determined by major countries, ensuring that this increase in gross reserves will not erode the net reserve positions of the several reserve currency countries so rapidly as to jeopardize the system's stability within a few years.	Changes of a flexible exchange rate will provide an effective equilibrating mechanism by generating market forces, which tend to increase export revenues and decrease import expenditures of countries whose foreign receipts have been decreasing and/or payments increasing and inversely for countries whose receipts have been increasing and/or payments decreasing.
	MODIFICATIONS			
	NONE	Partial centralization of reserves, automatic credit line.	Composite currency reserve units.	Unlimited managed flexibility, limited unmanaged flexibility, limited managed flexibility.

For US economist Peter Kenen, the need for and size of reserves would depend on the size, frequency and duration of disturbances and on the speed with which countries are willing and able to offset or combat those disturbances. A monetary system that can bar governments from exercising discretion in their responses to payments disturbances must be avoided.[23]

German economist Egon Sohmen tied balance of payments adjustment to the price mechanism: Over the long run, only the domestic price mechanism in each country can be safely relied upon to ensure balance of payments adjustment. If it does not, the level of employment, the freedom of international payments or the long-run stability of exchange rates will have to yield. The abandonment of any one of these policy objectives would have most undesirable consequences for the operation of the world economy.[24]

Swiss economist Jurg Niehans would make the strongest defence of Machlup's frame: The various monetary projects put forward and debated in recent years do not all address themselves to the same problems. While from a purely academic point of view it might be interesting to analyse them *as if* each of them were meant to be a complete and self-contained solution to all our problems, from a practical point of view such an analysis would be in danger of being sterile. The various projects are, in fact, largely complements rather than substitutes. The real task, therefore, is to design a monetary strategy incorporating features of different plans at their appropriate place.[25]

By the third Bellagio Group conference (21–2 March 1964), conferees had further developed their position on the mechanisms necessary for payments adjustment. Planks included the continued addition to reserves in the hands of the international monetary authorities, and the importance of international reserve assets other than gold ('credit reserves') whose volume, composition and policies regarding balance of payments problems would be coordinated by the monetary authorities of large reserve-holding countries. Conferees also agreed that stability of the international monetary system would be improved by agreement among the major countries on the long-run rates of change in total reserves held by participating countries and on the 'normal' composition of these reserves; on the terms and criteria for extending special credit facilities to participating countries to cope with strains and crises resulting from international capital movements; and on the need to choose an international body to manage reserve use (e.g. International Monetary Fund, Group of Ten, etc.).

At the fourth conference (29 May to 6 June 6 1964), Machlup asked the Bellagio conferees to consider and rank in order their preferred adjustment, liquidity and confidence mechanisms. For adjustment, Bellagio Group conferees preferred managed flexibility of exchange rates (including adjustable pegs or wider margins); for liquidity, they preferred credit reserves; and for confidence, they preferred the consolidation of reserves into IMF deposits. At this conference all members, organized into several drafting committees, participated in the drafting and redrafting of the final report.

The outcome of the fourth conference was a report, *International Monetary Arrangements: The Problem of Choice; A Report on the Deliberations of an International Study Group of 32 Economists*, quite literally prepared by all members of the Bellagio Group. Even after all of the drafts prepared during the conferences and the weeks between conferences, handwritten notes in the Machlup archives depict the final report to be another collaborative decision-making exercise. Tibor Scitovsky and Fred de Jong, Friedrich Lutz and George Halm shared responsibility for the Objectives section. Assigned to discuss the adjustment, liquidity and confidence issues were Fred Hirsh, Harry Johnson and the team of Jurg Niehans and Peter Kenen, respectively. The team of Robert Mundell, Hans Moller and Gottfried Haberler was assigned the section on 'Relationships among the Three Problems – Objectives and Conflicts'. Even the final section, 'Towards a Consensus on Policy' (originally called 'Groping for a Consensus'), was drafted by Robert Triffin, Michael Heilperin and Alan Day.

What a Viable Solution Required

One might construe the Bellagio Group conferences as a series of scenario-planning exercises that allowed economists to investigate the relative impact on payments, liquidity and confidence of the four basic exchange regimes, given any one or combination of them might have been adopted. The experience also allowed economists to reach conclusions about the sine qua non of any acceptable exchange rate regime.[26]

1. Because balance of payments disturbances differ substantially in source and duration, the differences between them necessitate different responses.
2. Persistent adjustments of payments imbalances should be initiated promptly with the smallest loss of income and employment and, to this end, interim financing should be available.
3. The financing of reversible disturbances requires the use of official reserves and reserves should be expanded to meet needs.
4. The protection of the large outstanding foreign exchange component of the world reserve pool against sudden or massive conversion into gold should be a high priority.

All conferees agreed as well that an intelligent comparison of exchange rate regimes required a classification of payments disturbances into two types: temporary or reversible, and enduring. Temporary or reversible disturbance could be prevented by international financing and domestic offsetting operations. Adjustments to end enduring disturbances should be completed at the fastest rate consistent with high-level employment and continuing growth. There was broad consensus on the importance of exchange rate change as a method of adjustment.

Given the Bellagio Group's full-employment/stability concerns, one might say Keynes was at the table – as were Mises and Friedman –in spirit if not in fact. But theory was not under examination at the Bellagio conferences, which might seem surprising. It will be recalled that the methodologist Machlup's four-step adjustment model allowed the analyst/researcher to verify that a change which has occurred can traced back to specific assumptions without requiring a test of theory.[27] If empirics verified assumptions, then the theory underlying those assumptions was verified. At the conclusion of the four conferences, the focus had clearly shifted to payments adjustment and to market moderated exchange regimes (which included a number of policy alternatives – moving within a narrow or broad band, jumping or gliding parities, and fully flexible rates).

Finally, the series of iterations around fundamental assumptions – and the issue-raising exercise to differentiate institutions from policies – is reminiscent of contemporary strategic decision processes in which consensus is reached by weighting and ranking strategic factors and working through the process in stages to arrive at a collaborative view. In fact, the Bellagio conferences gave members the chance to formulate assumptions for major policy systems; revise and re-edit lists of assumptions and rank them in terms of their relevance to fundamental propositions, institutional recommendations and operating procedures; and in the end to examine and combine policy approaches to simulate alternative, possible exchange rate 'worlds', so that they would be ready to advise, consult or help their governments as necessary to implement policy, whatever the ultimate outcome for their own preferred theory or plan.

Conclusions

Machlup's use of framing in terms of adjustment, liquidity and confidence and his focus on the opportunity cost of policy decisions was both novel and strategic. While most Bellagio Group members would make common cause of a commitment to solve perceived problems, behind their espousal of one or another solution were underlying assumptions, values, even prejudices that muddied an attempt to focus on outcomes. Machlup's approach was to expose the assumptions, values and prejudices and rob them of their power.

He took another approach familiar to contemporary strategy consulting with its focus on cross-functional teams – engage every participant in every effort, so that all work belongs to every member of the group. While the notion of buy-in may be too simplistic, ownership of the whole discovery process is not. It was essential to the Bellagio Group's approach and, when depicted in the final conference report, very appealing to the international bodies – the Deputies of Group of

Ten and the IMF – that were pursuing official studies of the same issues and struggling with issues of group cohesion and focus on outcomes rather than blame.

For the Bellagio Group conferences, Machlup chose academic economists who were associated in print with a specific exchange rate policy, most of whom had prior public policy experience. All of the Bellagio Group participants were representatives of Group of Ten countries. This would prove enormously important to the group's credibility, as the power and influence of the Group of Ten continued to rise within the International Monetary Fund.

Fritz Machlup and the Bellagio Group would do much, through conferences and print media, to expose audiences of academics, bankers, business leaders and policymakers to exchange rate solutions to payments adjustment problems and, ultimately, to the logic of managed flexibility of exchange rates and credit reserves under the International Monetary Fund as a preferred, hybrid solution.

Meanwhile, discussion of the options available to solve the adjustment, liquidity and confidence problems identified by Machlup and the Bellagio Group continued. Chapter 6 will focus on the emerging popularity of a multiple reserve currency approach.

6 'ASSURING THE FREE WORLD'S LIQUIDITY' THROUGH MULTIPLE RESERVE CURRENCIES

Introduction

When Burton Malkiel (author of *A Random Walk down Wall Street* and a member of the Bellagio Group) wrote his analysis of the Triffin Plan in 1963, those working towards monetary reform were coming down strongly in favour of a multiple currency approach. The Triffin Plan, which had attracted so much initial attention after the publication of *Gold and the Dollar Crisis* (1960), had been rejected, but the arguments it raised against a world system dependent on the continuing deficits of a single key currency country continued to gain traction. These arguments had been raised before, first by Keynes and later by Harrod and Kaldor. Their origins lay in World War II, in the rise of multilateralism, in the fear that profligate partners threatened the system as a whole, and in the politics of European nations seeking a common voice and greater leverage as a community of states.

This chapter deals with plans for a system of multiple reserve currencies at a time when plan proponents believed in an international monetary system anchored in multilateralism. They sought to restore confidence by providing additional sources of liquidity through a basket of reserve currencies, significantly limiting dependence on the dollar and the pound sterling. Because this discussion is fundamentally about liquidity, it is separate from the discussion of special drawing rights in the Joint Meetings of Academics and Officials (the extended Bellagio Group), which were tasked with developing an implementation plan for SDRs; the focus had shifted to payments adjustment, correcting the profligacy of debtor countries and building safeguards into the SDRs to prevent the USA from misusing it. Special drawing rights and payments adjustment are discussed in Chapter 9.

Historical Context: Multilateralism – A Legacy of World War II

While World War II had caused a serious destruction of the factors of production, finished goods, and even land, by the end of the war the climate had warmed for international business activities. The mid-1940s saw the creation of several important institutions such as the IMF, the World Bank, GATT and the Bretton Woods system, focused on creating a favourable economic environment where currencies were stable and international trade and production were encouraged.

In 1945, the Articles of Agreement of the International Monetary Fund established as their main purpose 'to assist in the establishment of a multilateral system of payments in respect to current transactions between members and in the elimination of foreign exchange restrictions which hamper the growth of world trade'.[1] In 1947, there followed the General Agreement on Tariffs and Trade (GATT), based on the conviction that commercial and economic relations between the member countries should have as their aim, among other things, the raising of the standard of living, the achievement of full employment, the attainment of a high and continually rising level of real income and the full opening up of the world's resources. It is therefore the object of the General Agreement to bring about, for the common good, a considerable reduction of tariffs and other trade barriers and the abolition of discrimination in international trade. In 1948, the convention setting up the Organisation for European Economic Co-operation (OEEC) was signed, recognizing that its member economies were interwoven with each other and that the prosperity of each individual nation was dependent on the prosperity of them all. Its object was the early restoration of sound economic conditions that would enable the parties to achieve as quickly as possible a satisfactory state of economic activity without extraordinary external aid and, in particular, to remove the trade barriers between them and make the most effective possible use of available resources. In 1950, the European Payments Union (EPU) was set up within the OEEC to create a transparent system of payments for merchandise and other transactions and to promote the restoration of convertibility of currencies. In 1961, the OEEC was replaced by the Organisation for Economic Co-operation and Development (OECD), which extended the mainly European association to include the United States, Canada, Japan and Australia.

The International Monetary Fund and the Liability of Newness

It became apparent as early as 1947 that liquidity available from the IMF was inadequate. Throughout the 1950s, the IMF remained on the periphery of international monetary relations – so much so that outside observers prodded it to increase its activities. In 1950 the Economic and Social Council (ECOSOC), a founding charter body of the United Nations with economic social and environmental interests, commissioned a report entitled *Measures for International Economic Stability*. Published in July 1952, the report included the observation that 'our examination of existing resources has convinced us that they are not in general adequate'. The report ended with the recommendation that IMF resources be expanded.[2] The writers of the report included James Angell, Columbia University; G. D. A. MacDougall, Nuffield College, University of Oxford; Javier Marquez of the IMF; Hla Myint, University of Oxford; and Trevor Swan,

Australian National University. In a follow-on report published in the IMF Staff Papers, 'The Adequacy of Monetary Reserves', the IMF responded to the ECOSOC report, stressing three points: 1) Monetary reserves are meant to take care of swings between favourable and unfavourable but temporary payments positions. No amount of monetary reserves is sufficient to finance permanent payments imbalance; 2) The magnitude of monetary reserves of a given country tends to affect and be affected by that country's fiscal and monetary policies. Rigorous fiscal and monetary policies tend to increase monetary reserves. Countries should be on guard against relaxing their fiscal and monetary policies so far as to intensify domestic inflationary pressures; 3) A worldwide distribution of reserves in accordance with the apparent need for them is incompatible with the more fundamental consideration of the distribution of the real resources of each country in accordance with the highest priority for their use. Finally, 'The determination of adequacy in which any country falls, assuming that it means the fundamental condition of payments balance, is a matter of judgement'.[3]

The IMF again addressed the issue of liquidity in a report entitled 'International Reserves and Liquidity' in 1958. The IMF observed that 'Since the end of World War II, a large and growing supply of dollars, arising out of a steadily expanding volume of US import and payments for overseas services, capital export and aid, has been the dominant element in improving international liquidity. The European Payments Union (EPU) has provided additional liquidity by making it possible for intra-European payments to be settled partly in credits granted by the creditor members. The Fund made a substantial amount of resources available before the Marshall Plan went into effect. Subsequently, the countries that received Marshall Plan aid had no need to turn to the Fund'.[4] From 1947 to 1957, total international reserves had grown, reflecting a restriction of reserves as the reserves of the United States had fallen. The value of world trade had increased by 110 per cent and its volume by 90 per cent. The cost of goods traded internationally had increased 140 per cent between 1937 and 1957. The IMF acknowledged that a healthy and balanced growth of world trade depends on adequate and rising reserves and an efficient international credit system, both private and official. Nevertheless, a number of monetary crises have occurred in the post-war period as well as the multiple currency practices and exchange restrictions. The study concluded, 'It is doubtful whether, in the circumstances of the world today, with world trade greatly expanded in volume and value, the Fund's resources are sufficient to enable it fully to perform its duties under the Articles of Agreement'.[5]

Exorbitant Privilege

The French argument that the United States enjoyed an 'exorbitant privilege' as a reserve currency that made the world dependent on dollars for trade and investment, even as the United States continued to run up huge deficits, was shared by many European allies as well. The French and the Dutch had disagreed with the United States and Britain on the terms of the proposed General Arrangements to Borrow, which ultimately added $6 billion in commitments by member nations to be used by the Fund for emergencies, including the defence of the dollar against speculative attacks. They feared that the scheme would thus water down the 'discipline' imposed on national financial policies by the existing system. At the annual IMF meeting in 1961, the French Minister of Finance Wilfrid Baumgartner defended his opposition to the British-American scheme, recommending that care should be taken to avoid having currency convertibility jeopardized by insufficiently precise procedures. After a meeting of the Finance Ministers of the Group of Ten in Paris, Baumgartner announced that the additional credits would be submitted to examination and subordinated to guarantees to be discussed by meetings of Finance Ministers of member countries of the Group of Ten.[6]

Meanwhile, the United States had replaced the United Kingdom as the most important source country of foreign direct investment (FDI). By 1960, the United States accounted for around 60 per cent of the developed economies' outward stock of FDI.[7] A process had also started where developing economies became less important as host countries for FDI. Whereas in 1938 close to two-thirds of FDI flowed to the developing economies, in 1960 two-thirds of global FDI flowed to the developed economies.[8] The volume of FDI flows as well as trade flows increased strongly after the end of World War II. During the high-growth period of the 1960s, flows of FDI grew twice as quickly as global GNP and 40 per cent faster than world exports.[9] The primary sector became less important as a destination for international investment, and the decreasing importance of the developing economies as host countries for FDI continued. Instead, FDI increasingly tended to flow between the developed economies.

A Call for Multiple Reserve Currencies

Arguments on behalf of multiple reserve currencies emerged from many quarters, specifically from the largest Marshall Fund recipient countries – France, Germany, Italy, UK and the Netherlands. Long after the dollar was delinked from gold, the arguments were no less trenchant. We have seen as recently as 2008 the effect of an erosion of confidence on the world monetary system. Fear that even a system based on multiple currency reserves might be gamed to the advantage of deficit countries, particularly the United States, has stymied attempts to make extensive use of such a system even after it was created in 1969. The special drawing right (originally special reserve asset) is such a system. Its origins are in multiple reserve currency proposals of Xenophon Zolotas of the Bank of Greence, Friedrich Lutz of Switzerland and a professor at the University of Zurich, Robert Roosa, former assistant director of the US Treasury, and Edward Bernstein, former director of research at the IMF and now at the

Brookings Institution, among many others working with Fritz Machlup and the Bellagio Group in the 1960s. In this section, we review these plans, beginning with the early plans advanced by Keynes but later abandoned.

Keynes International Clearing Union

As early as September 1941, the first draft of Keynes' plan for a Clearing Union was circulated within the British Treasury. The final draft was issued by the British Government in April 1943 as a white paper.[10] In his *Proposals for an International Currency (or Clearing) Union*, Keynes envisioned a post-war international economic system with the least possible interference with internal, national policies. He envisioned the plan would operate to general and to the individual advantage of participants, requiring no special economic or financial sacrifice from any country. He added:

> It must be emphasized that it is not for the Clearing Union to assume the burden of long-term lending which is the proper task of some other institution. It is also necessary for it to have means of restraining improvident borrowers. But the Clearing Union must also seek to discourage creditor countries from leaving unused large liquid balances which ought to be devoted to some positive purpose. For excessive credit balances necessarily create excessive debit balances for some other party.[11]

In recognizing the mutual responsibilities of creditor and debtor for imbalance, the Clearing Union would be breaking important ground.

Keynes expressed the objectives of the plan in a series of 'We need' statements. The object of the plan was to provide an instrument of international currency having general acceptability between nations to be used in international transactions by treasuries and central banks. Private individuals, businesses and banks other than central banks would continue to use their own national currency. There would be an orderly and agreed method of determining the relative exchange values of national currency units, so that unilateral action and competitive exchange depreciations are prevented. We need a quantum of international currency, which is neither determined in an unpredictable and irrelevant manner as, for example, by the technical progress of the gold industry nor subject to large variations depending on the gold reserve policies of individual countries. We need a system possessed of an internal stabilizing mechanism by which pressure is exercised on any country whose balance of payments with the rest of the world is departing from equilibrium in either direction, so as to prevent imbalance among its neighbours. We need an agreed plan for starting off every country after the war with a stock of reserves appropriate to its importance in world commerce. We need a central institution of a purely technical, non-political character. We need a means of reassurance to a troubled world by which any country conducting its affairs prudently is relieved of anxiety for causes not of its own making concerning its ability to meet its international liabilities.[12]

Keynes's plan called for all members of the United Nations to become original members of the International Clearing Union. The governing board of the Clearing Union would be appointed by the governments of the several member states. Routine business with the Union would be carried out through the central banks or other appropriate authorities of the member states.

Member states would agree between themselves the initial values of their own currencies in terms of an international bank money or 'bancor'. Having established its value, a member state could not subsequently alter the value of its currency in terms of bancor without the permission of the governing board except under certain conditions. Nevertheless, during the first five years the governing board would consider appeals for an adjustment.

Both deficit and surplus countries had responsibilities in Keynes's system. He did not contemplate that the debit or credit balance of an individual country should exceed a certain minimum, its quota. In the case of debit balances this maximum would be a rigid one, and countermeasures would be called for long before the maximum was reached. In the case of credit balances no rigid maximum had been proposed. Keynes thought the appropriate provision might be to require a cancellation or compulsory investment of persistent bancor credit balances accumulating in excess of a member's quota.

It was Keynes's intention to promote an expansionist pressure on world trade. By allowing each member state overdraft facilities of a defined amount and the obligation to repay within a certain interval of time, the Clearing House would operate like a national bank. Gold would have a role in Keynes's plan, although the purpose of the Clearing Union was to supplant gold as a governing factor, not eliminate it. Bancor would be defined in terms of a weight of gold. No member state would be entitled to demand gold from the Clearing Union against its balance of bancor. Bancor would be available only to transfer to another clearing account.

EPU (EMA) Unit of Account

With the institution of the European Payments Union (EPU) in 1950, a unit of account was established – the European unit of account – to be used in various international loans. Its purpose was twofold – to discourage bilateralism and to facilitate clearing operations between European central banks and the convertibility of European currencies.[13] The EPU unit of account was expressed in terms of 0.888 grammes of fine gold, the equivalent at that time to one US dollar.[14] Changes in the value of the EPU unit could be made only by unanimous action by member states.[15] A similar provision was included in the European Monetary Agreement, signed in 1955, which came into force after the dissolution of the EPU in 1958. A definition for the unit of account was created after the dissolution of the EPU in terms of present value and the gold values of the reference currencies of the seventeen members of the EPU.[16] The treaties signed in Rome in 1957 establishing the European Economic Community and the European Atomic Energy Community also provided for a unit of account, which was identical to that of the EPU. The statutes of the European Investment Bank stipulated that the capital of the bank should amount to 1 billion units of account.[17] Emmanuel van der Mensbrugghe wrote of bond issues in European units of account, issued between 1961 and 1964, sponsored by Belgian banks and offered to European capital markets with a limited exchange guarantee. 'All were subscribed without hesitation by the general public', although there was some opposition to the sale of bonds denominated in units of account.

The Zolotas Plan

A plan for broadening the gold exchange standard was made by Xenophon Zolotas, governor of the Bank of Greece, who recommended that the current 'reserve countries should build up sufficient balances of major, convertible currencies to be used as "masse de manoeuvre" in the foreign exchange market and to serve as the first line of defence of the key currencies'. Zolotas called the new system 'the multi-currency international standard'.[18] To make it more attractive for central banks to hold their reserves in foreign exchange rather than gold, the Zolotas Plan would have offered a 'gold guarantee', that is, protection for foreign monetary authorities against losses from devaluation. Another feature of the plan was preferential treatment regarding interest rates and taxation for official foreign depositors of short-term balances.

The Lutz Plan

Friedrich Lutz endorsed the 'multiple currency standard'. This was his second choice, after flexible exchange rates, for the reform of the international monetary system. Lutz distinguished this 'multiple currency standard' – where 'every country is prepared to hold its international reserves in other foreign currencies besides dollars' and 'America too is ready to hold foreign exchange balances' – from a 'multiple currency standard with gold' – and contrasts both with 'two key currencies with gold'.[19] He believed that the distribution of reserves among several currencies would make the system less sensitive to crises of confidence.[20]

The Lutz Plan says nothing about gold guarantees or gold clauses, but 'it does require that all of the reserve currency countries should be ready ... to surrender gold to the monetary authorities of other countries on request'.[21]

The Roosa Plan

Robert Roosa, US Treasury undersecretary during the early 1960s, had early on advocated an increased role for currency swap arrangements. By 1962, in 'The Beginning of a New Policy', Roosa announced that the USA had already begun to hold foreign currencies in its reserves and would, in the event of surplus in its overall balance of payments, acquire foreign currencies. Hence, whether the USA was in deficit or in surplus, the net effect would be an increase in world reserves. In the event of deficits, the USA could use foreign exchange to meet its obligations, avoiding further liabilities or an outflow of gold. The Roosa Plan for multiple currency reserves did not include any gold guarantee or compensation for losses in the event of devaluation.[22] In addition to a plan that still put the United States in the decision maker's seat, Roosa held that confidence in the dollar as a reserve currency must be above suspicion, not bolstered by gold guarantees. In the future, he anticipated that 'the new arrangements also are capable of providing for a steady growth in the monetary reserves needed to service the trade requirements of an expanding world'.[23]

The Posthuma Plan

S. Posthuma, director of the Netherlands Bank, introduced a plan in 1962 that was discussed in the Monetary Committee of the European Economic Community and among the central bankers at the Basle Club, but not published.[24] Another version of the Posthuma Plan appeared in the *Banca Nazionale del Lavoro Quarterly Review* in 1963. Here the emphasis was on fixed proportions in which countries have to meet deficits in their payments balance to other countries. The member countries of the Organisation for Economic Co-operation and Development should by agreement fix these proportions for several years to come: for example, any deficit would have to be paid three parts in gold, two parts in foreign exchange, and two parts in the paying country's own currency. Less than 43 per cent would be paid in gold. The number of currencies accepted as official reserve currencies would be equal to the number of parties to the agreement, each giving an exchange value guarantee for its currency in the official holdings of the other countries. The difference between this system and a system of two or three key currencies would be, according to Posthuma, that 'all countries would be treated the same way'.[25] Every country would be able to cover a portion of its deficit with its own liabilities. The addition to these liabilities to the gross reserves of the monetary surplus countries would provide more or less regular increases to the monetary reserves of the free world. These two features make the Posthuma Plan similar to the Roosa Plan. One additional feature unites the Zolotas, Lutz, Roosa and Posthuma plans: confidence in the credit and fiscal policies of the reserve currency countries is essential.[26] The Trustee in the Posthuma Plan was the IMF, as in other multiple reserve currency plans, but also the Bank for International Settlements.[27]

The Bernstein Plan

In 1963 Edward Bernstein proposed an agreement among the Group of Ten countries to standardize the composition of their holdings of gold and foreign exchange and their use in international settlements with each other. The best way to accomplish this, according to Bernstein, was to establish a composite reserve unit (CRU) equivalent to a gold dollar, consisting of a stated portion of each of the eleven currencies. Thus, a reserve unit might consist of about 50 cents in US currency and lesser amounts in sterling, French francs, Italian lire, Canadian dollars, Japanese yen, Dutch guilders, etc. The proportion of each currency should be agreed on the basis of its present role as a reserve currency and its importance in international trade and investment.[28]

Each country would hold reserve units amounting to at least one-half of its gold reserves. The plan would be put into effect in stages to avoid an excessive upsurge in monetary reserves.[29]

Group of Ten participating countries would effectively create reserve units by depositing their own currencies with the International Monetary Fund, in return for which each would be given a credit on the books of the IMF as Trustee denominated in reserve units, 'Thus, the trustee would hold $3.5 billion in the currencies of the eleven Group of Ten countries and they, in turn, would hold $3.5 billion in reserve units.'[30] All currencies held by the IMF would be guaranteed against exchange depreciation – a feature the Bernstein Plan had in common with the Zolotas Plan.

Alone among multiple currency reserve systems, the Bernstein Plan required participating countries to hold the foreign currencies not directly in their own portfolio, but indirectly in the form of reserve unit credit balances in a central reserve pool. Further, to safeguard the system against hot money movements, the reserve currency mix would be standardized and not subject to changes at the discretion of the separate monetary authorities.

The Jacobsson Plan

Similar to the strategy employed in the General Arrangements to Borrow, Jacobsson's plan called for Group of Ten countries in payments surplus to make loans to the IMF, enabling it to place funds at the disposal of other Group of Ten countries suffering from outflows of short-term capital. Lending central banks would have to approve the IMF's use of funds in each case. In the Zolotas, Bernstein and Jacobsson plans, the IMF's role was that of a guarantor not a banker. Again, in the Zolotas, Bernstein and Jacobsson plans, the emphasis was on hot money movements, not on balance of payments problems.[31]

The D'Estaing Plan

A plan introduced by French Finance Minister Giscard D'Estaing at the IMF Annual Meeting in October 1963 called for a collective reserve unit (also known as a CRU), linked to an increase in the price of gold and composed of the currencies of Group of Ten countries. The gold price increase ensured that additional reserves would not be required. The detailed proposal focused on tight controls to avoid the importation of US inflation on what was anticipated to be conditional liquidity. Hence, the plan required a 'much more powerful role for the IMF'.[32]

Plan Commonalities

Common to all of these plans was their concern with international liquidity and confidence, and not with adjustment. Common to all was the concern that additional unconditional reserves would eliminate the conditionality and surveillance measures that attended a country's request to draw more than their gold tranche from the Fund, or if they were to borrow under the General Arrangements to Borrow. According to Harold James, they seemed an easy way to defend national policy autonomy in the international monetary debate.[33] Common to all was the obligation of countries in balance of payments surplus to make loans to the IMF, enabling it to place the acquired funds at the disposal of the authorities of important industrial countries suffering from outflows of short-term capital. All of the plans were designed to reinforce the gold-exchange standard of the time against hot money movements. In each plan, the IMF would operate as an intermediary or a guarantor, not that of a bank of issue or a commercial bank engaged in the creation of credit. The IMF would borrow liquid international means of payment in the form of demand liabilities of central banks in strong positions and pass them on to the central banks experiencing hot money movements.

These 'arrangements to borrow' reflect a change in thinking from the early Bretton Woods era, when international loans were designed to help countries in balance of payments difficulties that were not caused by capital or hot money movements. The main idea then was that central banks assisted by international loans might be spared painful adjustments through 'deflationary' methods. Under the 'arrangements to borrow', international loans are specifically designed to help countries in difficulties arising from short-term capital outflows. And the main idea was to keep an eye on countries to see that they do not pursue unsound policies, e.g. policies of undue monetary expansion.

The danger that a central bank in trouble will use international assistance for an extension of its credit will be much smaller if only hot money movements are the cause of its difficulties.

Plan Differences – Role of Gold, Credit or Asset, Ad Hoc or Permanent, Plan Only or Actual Use in Practice

The plans discussed above differed in their provision of a role for gold, their perception of the instrument as credit or reserve asset, and their desire to create an ad hoc, as required solution rather than a permanent one. Only one of these plans has been put into practice, the 1950 EPU unit of account that became the 1959 EMA unit of account and later the ECU, although a variation of the D'Estaing CRU became the special reserve asset, renamed special drawing right.

Table 6.1: Multiple Reserve Currency Plans, 1943–63

Plan Proponent	Role Of Gold	Credit Or Asset	Ad Hoc Or Permanent	
Keynes 1943	Gold link	Asset	Permanent	Central Bank
EPU, later the European Monetary Agreement unit of account 1950	Gold link	Credit	Permanent	Central Banks
Zolotas 1961	Gold link (protection against devaluation losses)	Asset	Permanent	Central Bank
Lutz 1962	Gold link	Asset	Permanent	Central Bank
Roosa Plan 1962	None	Asset	Permanent (originally stand-by, and at that time credit not asset)	Central Bank
Posthuma 1962 (unpublished); 1963	Gold link	Asset	Permanent	Central Bank
Bernstein 1963	Gold link	Credit	Stand-by	Central Bank
Jacobsson 1963	Gold link	Credit	Ad hoc or stand-by	Central Bank
D'Estaing 1963	Gold link with gold price increase	Credit	Permanent in fixed proportions of G10 currencies	Central Bank

Source: Author's own research. 'Asset' encompasses foreign exchange holdings or a substitute for foreign exchange (e.g. currency swaps, bancor, some variations on Composite Reserve Unit). 'Credit' includes reciprocal credit obligations or drawing facilities.

Implications of the European Unit of Account for Today

The history and problems surrounding the European unit of account provided lessons to central bankers, bankers and investors in the 1950s. One might otherwise wonder why the EUA was not an acknowledged model for the development of a global unit of account or an Atlantic unit of account (a nod to the terminology Triffin had used when contemplating alternative uses for the Triffin Plan).

History

The European Payments Union owes its life to a US initiative, the Economic Cooperation Administration (ECA) proposal, which stressed two points: complete transferability to OEEC-area currencies used for current transactions and the elimination of all quantitative restrictions on imports. It also called for the ultimate restoration of multilateralism. Each member country was given a line of credit, a definite amount of credit it would receive from, or be obligated to grant to, the Payments Union. All transactions of the member countries were to be carried out using a common unit of account, and countries whose OEEC-area imports exceeded their exports to that area could finance the difference (the imbalance) with credit granted by the Union and through partial gold payments to the Union. Countries whose exports exceeded their imports in the OEEC area would receive their surplus in part by gold payments from the Union and in part by extending credit to the Union. In case the Union's payments of gold exceeded its receipts, a fund of dollars contributed by the USA was to finance the difference.

Transferability of currencies and the abolition of quantitative restrictions on impacts called for some kind of coordination among the European countries, hence the ECA provided for a supervisory board (including ECA representation) to maintain a kind of surveillance over the internal financial policies of member countries. This idea was eventually abandoned by the ECA because most European countries were reluctant to grant strong discretionary powers to such a body, especially if the USA were to share in it. The history of problems and compromises in the formation of the EPU and the role of the ECA is told by Kurt Flexner with acknowledged assistance from the notes of Robert Triffin, who represented the ECA during the negotiations.[34]

With the dissolution of the EPU in 1955, the European Monetary Agreement that replaced it continued to offer increased international liquidity by making additional credit available in the system; increased flexibility of exchange rates within the system (up to 12 per cent between two currencies, moving from one set of two opposite extremes to the other); increased flexibility of monetary and fiscal policies within OEEC countries – a consequence of threats of retaliation and acts of compromise; and the maintenance of multilateralism of payments and trade within the OEEC area.[35]

The EUA and Multiple Currency and Gold Value Clauses

The holder of the European unit of account had a right to demand payment of principal or reimbursement in any one of the seventeen reference currencies (the seventeen currencies of the OEEC members). In a typical multiple currency clause, the creditor has a right to demand reimbursement of principal or payment of interest in one of several currencies at the rate of exchange existing on the issue date of the obligation. Should the creditor choose, as is likely, repayment in a currency revalued upward, the debtor would find the amount of his debt increased in proportion to the amount of revaluation. If the debt is expressed in EUA, the revaluation of a single currency (or less than two-thirds of all currencies) will not affect the value of his debt obligation in EUA.

The required weight of the EUA in terms of grammes of fine gold does not constitute a gold clause. Because the EUA derived its gold weight only from the gold weight of the seventeen reference currencies, it was an index. In other circumstances, it could have been indexed to GDP or purchasing power or hamburgers. Hence, the EUA was not fixed to the official price of gold. The EUA was an artificial currency.

Conclusions

The purpose of all of these multiple reserve currency plans, with the exception of the European unit of account, was to avoid the problems associated with a single key currency as well as to address liquidity problems that might arise and threaten world trade. All fundamentally were still-born, except the European unit of account. D'Estaing's CRU was a stage in the evolution of Special Drawing Rights. The discussion of special drawing rights is reserved for Chapter 9. Adoption of special drawing rights would require discussion and resolution of payments adjustment issues, specifically the responsibilities of deficit and surplus countries and safeguards against the anticipated abuse of new liquidity by deficit countries, particularly the USA. The adoption would require that European nations within the Group of Ten industrial countries set ground rules for the special type of instrument (asset or credit; the final name – special drawing right – reflects the decision to make this an instrument of credit), as well as the allocation of special drawings rights by country and distribution as a whole (industrialized countries versus the whole world).

The growing importance of the Group of Ten (because of their commitment to bail out countries in chronic deficit through the General Arrangements to Borrow) is discussed in Chapter 8. The General Arrangements to Borrow created the burning platform necessary to bond European policymakers and to seek a European voice in the IMF. Fritz Machlup and the Bellagio Group would play a critical role in the development of that voice in the resolution of payments adjustment issues and in the adoption of special drawing rights through a series of conferences from 1964 to 1977. Discussion of those conferences, the Joint Meetings of Officials and Academics, begins in Chapter 8 and continues through Chapter 9.

Chapter 7 adds another element important to the story of payments adjustment and special drawing rights – the increasing exposure and acceptability of flexible exchange rates.

7 MILTON FRIEDMAN AND THE ARGUMENTS FOR FLEXIBLE VERSUS FIXED EXCHANGE RATES

Introduction

Many of the economists drawn into the flexible versus fixed debate had been writing on adjustment and liquidity issues since shortly after the Great Depression and through World War II. Others were young scholars eager to make their mark in the innovative and interdependent areas of international economics and economic policy, tied to theories of comparative advantage, factor-price equalization, trade and welfare, exchange devaluation and forward exchange. Paul Einzig, no enthusiast for flexible exchange rates, considered the focus on flexibility a consequence of the drive for growth at all costs.[1] As previously noted, employment and growth were major issues, as was stability, leading to many different versions for flexible or fixed rate plans.

Chapter 7 examines some of the major arguments for variations in flexible and fixed exchange rate policy options as well as contributions to a theory of payments balance made by the Bellagio Group economists and by their contemporaries. The chapter begins with a brief history of exchange rate choice, moves to a general consideration of floating rates, then considers managed flexibility (slides, glides, crawls, etc.) and a theory of payments balance. The second half of the chapter considers the arguments of economists committed to fixed exchange rates and to an increase or decrease in the price of gold.

History behind the Theory

Economists writing about exchange rate solutions to adjustment or liquidity problems had significant experience with both fixed and flexible rates. To an extent, their preference for one or the other is the result of experience with a regime, belief in the underlying principle or moral suasion rationale or trust in national institutions. The litmus test of exchange regimes is response to financial crises, although there may be significant lag. Michael Bordo (2003) surveyed the history of exchange rate choice by fourteen industrialized countries, demonstrating that as countries become more financially mature, they tend towards floating and away from pegging.[2] The countries are Belgium, Canada, Denmark, Finland, France, Germany, Italy, Japan, Netherlands, Norway, Sweden, Switzerland, United Kingdom and United States.

Bordo's research finds that during the gold standard period (1880–1914) most countries adhered to fixed rates; in the interwar period and World War II (1914–45), with the exception of the gold-exchange standard (1926–31), most countries had some kind of floating; under Bretton Woods (1946–71), with the exception of Canada (1951–61) which floated, most countries had adjustable pegs; and since 1971 most countries were managed floaters, with the exception of the European Monetary Eurozone.[3] In terms of stability, the gold standard and convertible (after 1958) Bretton Woods periods were extremely stable, World War I, World War II, interwar and early Bretton Woods the most unstable. Inflation was lowest in the gold standard and early Bretton Woods periods and highest during the wars. Inflation was low in the late 1950s through the 1960s, the convertible Bretton Woods period.[4] Economic growth was highest during the Bretton Woods period (and higher, 4.1 per cent versus 3.6 per cent during convertible Bretton Woods) versus the gold standard period (1.6 per cent), and lowest during the wars.

Barry Eichengreen and Ricardo Hausmann (1999) examined three views of the relationship between exchange rate regime choice and financial fragility: the moral hazard hypothesis, according to which pegged exchange rates offer implicit insurance against exchange risk and encourage reckless borrowing and lending; the original sin hypothesis, where incompleteness in financial markets prevents the domestic currency from being used to borrow abroad or domestically long term (in which case a country literally uses another country's currency in parallel to or as a substitute for its national currency as its unit of account and medium of exchange); and the commitment hypothesis, which sees financial crises resulting from the weakness of institutions (failure to commit includes fear of bailouts and refusing to be the lender of last resort).[5] Each of these hypotheses expresses a connection between the exchange rate and financial fragility. To shed light on this connection, Eichengreen and Hausmann examine three cases: Argentina under the gold standard; Panama, a fully dollarized economy in the 1990s; and Australia, whose flexible exchange rate regime, after its struggles in the 1980s, successfully weathered the Asian financial crisis. Australia's success with floating required adopting securities-market regulations to discourage opportunism and make market participation attractive to investors; reforming monetary and fiscal institutions to improve transparency; and establishing a track record of sound and stable policies that improved the credibility of policymakers. For Australia, it meant privatizing social security systems to generate broad participation by domestic investors.

As Jeffrey Frankel (1999) wrote about currencies, so too about exchange rates: 'no single currency regime is best for all countries and that even for a given country it may be that no single currency regime is best for all time'.[6]

The Case for Flexible Rates

Milton Friedman (1953) is associated with the modern case for floating. According to Friedman, floating has the advantage of monetary independence, insulation from real shocks, and a less disruptive adjustment mechanism in the face of nominal rigidities than is the case with pegged exchange rates. But Friedman was not the first theorist arguing on behalf of floating rates. There were others before him, like Benjamin Graham and David Whittlesey (1934); Graham (1949); Whittlesey (1937); Haberler (1937, 1954); James Meade (1948, 1955, 1961); Lloyd Mints (1950); and Roger Dehem (1952); and many who wrote contemporaneously: John Burr Williams (1954); Lutz (1954); Sohmen (1961, 1963); Halm (1962, 1963); Caves (1963); and Johnson (1962, 1963). A number of these were members of the Bellagio Group, specifically Haberler, Lutz, Hahn, Sohmen, Hahn, Halm and Johnson, as well as Machlup and Fellner as previously discussed. The major point to be made here is that significant groundwork for flexible exchange rates had been laid and continued to be laid by scholars working within academe and within government in the USA, Germany and the UK. This section explores their thought in detail.

Anthony Endres (2008) argued that Frank Graham was the first twentieth-century economist to make a coherent case for flexible exchange rates, a forerunner of the post-war Chicago school advocacy of flexible rates that culminated in Milton Friedman (1953).[7] Graham (1949) argued that 'Uncoordinated national monetary policies, non-discriminatory multilateral trade on the basis of free enterprise, and exchange rates fixed, cannot be made to mix. We must choose between them'.[8] Graham and Whittlesey (1934) argued, 'If we are to have a dollar of stable purchasing power we must, in the absence of effective international action to stabilize all national price levels, espouse fluctuating exchange rates'.[9]

In *Prosperity and Depression* (1937), Haberler made a strong intellectual case for floating exchange rates as a mechanism to insulate countries from the transmission of booms and depressions.[10] His view was a clear predecessor to the open economy Fleming-Mundell model. Bordo and James (2001) argued that Haberler's approach was not taken seriously until the 1950s. Their main conclusion was that Haberler himself failed to offer a sufficiently clear blueprint for his approach at the time.[11] Haberler would appear to be sending mixed messages. This is evident from Haberler (1945):

If it were possible to prevent speculative capital movements, one of the most serious disadvantages of frequently changing exchange rates would be removed. But there remain other objections. There are speculative anticipations of changes in the exchange rate, which are not in the nature of capital movement ... [which] would tend to bring about the expected depreciation of the currency and to intensify exchange fluctuations. They could be eliminated only by a more severe type of control which went far beyond the prevention of capital movements. Moreover, frequent changes in the exchange rate are very disturbing to international investment.[12]

Two decades after *The Theory of International Trade* and *Prosperity and Depression*, Haberler came out as a strong advocate for floating exchange rates, and he reversed a number of the positions he had taken in the 1930s and 1940s. In *Currency Convertibility* (1954), Haberler made the case that European countries should remove their exchange controls and restore current account convertibility, but not to the adjustable peg of the Bretton Woods Articles.[13] Instead, they should adopt floating rates as had been done by Canada in 1950. Bordo and James (2001) found Haberler very close to Friedman on adjustable pegs and the need for well-functioning forward markets in foreign exchange to reduce the inconvenience of fluctuating rates.[14]

Considering the trade-off necessary in exchange rates versus import controls, Meade, another early proponent of flexible rates, argued that 'the method of exchange rate adjustment is to be greatly preferred to that of direct trade controls'.[15] Flexible rates allowed countries to pursue independent monetary practices while also preserving open trade. Also embracing this view was Mints (1950), who wrote about the 'irreconcilable conflict between the requirements for international equilibrium and for domestic stability' that came with fixed exchange rates.[16] In his review of Meade's *Theory of International Economic Policy: The Balance of Payments*, Canadian economist Roger Dehem (1952) commented on Meade's distinction between the 'adjustable peg' (Bretton Woods system) and 'freely fluctuating rates', drawing on Canada's positive experience with the latter: 'The author favours freely moving rates because under them speculation would be more stabilizing, and because direct control of capital movements, involving necessarily the supervision of current transactions, is inevitable under the system of adjustable pegs'.[17] Under adjustable pegs the amount of speculation is not regulated by automatic price adjustments: speculators may periodically obtain a 'free ride' on the currency without risk of loss – Canada's experience prior to the switch to flexible rates in the 1950s.

Lloyd Mints defended flexible rates against those (like Ragnar Nurkse 1944) who would argue that exchange rate flexibility leads to monetary instability. Mints saw no direct relation between monetary instability and fixed or flexible rates, even if under the latter, payments by an importer or receipts of an exporter, in his own currency, may differ from the amount that would have been paid or received had the exchanges been fixed. In that case, the risk will be priced into the final cost of commodities. Nevertheless, if there is a well-organized market for forward exchange, traders themselves can avoid the exchange risk at a negligible cost.[18]

John Burr Williams (1954) also defended floating exchange rates in a series of questions: 'Inasmuch as no gold is needed to keep the equilibrium, because the equilibrium is automatic and self-maintaining, why mine gold? And inasmuch as any arbitrary rate is sure to be more or less wide of the mark, why set an arbitrary rate? And finally, since changes in the rate only reflect changes in the underlying conditions of supply and demand, why seek to stabilize the exchange rate, and why set up an International Monetary Fund?'[19]

Like many economists, Friedrich Lutz had more than one exchange rate plan in his back pocket. While his thoughts about a multiple currency reserve system are discussed in Chapter 6, here we consider the 'Case for Flexible Exchange Rates' (1954). Taking on the well-known arguments against flexible rates, Lutz argued that 'Under flexible rates a deficit does not force a country into a contraction of its money supply with unemployment as a result, nor does a surplus force it into an expansion of its money supply with rising prices as the consequence.'[20] Citing the success of flexible rates in Britain in the 1930s and Canada in the 1950s, Lutz recommended a system that allows exchange rates to fluctuate only between well-defined limits, which would need to be wider than those permitted under the Bretton Woods system.[21]

Egon Sohmen (1963) supported flexible rates because of their role in reinforcing national monetary policy:

> If ... on the other hand, the movement of exchange rates is not hemmed in by rigid limits and the authorities refrain from direct intervention in the foreign-exchange markets, the response of international trade and capital movements in a regime of convertibility will act as a powerful factor *reinforcing* monetary policy. It would undoubtedly prove to be the most important channel through which monetary policy can act as a countercyclical tool ... [This] property of a system of freely fluctuating rates ought to be the principal reason for endorsing it.[22]

Richard Caves (1963) argued that a country has the strongest case for flexible exchange rates when disturbances to its balance of payments typically come from outside its borders. 'Ruling out induced changes in capital movements, a fluctuating exchange rate averts changes in the trade balance and blocks transmission of the business cycle by that route.'[23]

The Case for Greater Flexibility: Bands, Slides, Glides and Crawls

As the 1960s advanced, most economists became convinced of the desirability of greater exchange rate flexibility, but were also aware of the political difficulties of realizing freely floating exchange rates in practice. In his article 'Recent Trends in International Economics', Arthur Bloomfield noted that interest had begun to shift from the issue of 'fixed' versus 'flexible' rates to the pros and cons of more limited forms of exchange flexibility. 'The main proposals recently advanced, along with numerous variants thereof, are the "band" scheme for a wider spread around parities within which exchange rates would be allowed to fluctuate; the "sliding parity" (or "crawling peg") under which parities would be continuously changed by small amounts in the face of continuing payments disequilibria; and some combination of both.'[24]

Even economists who might have favoured freely floating rates were apt to support managed floating alternatives as a transition from fixed rates, as acceptance of greater exchange rate flexibility grew. Among these economists was George Halm (1965): 'A system of freely fluctuating exchange rates has no chance whatever of being accepted in the foreseeable future in spite of the strong support which it enjoys among economists.'[25] Instead, the band proposal was a compromise 'between the principles of fixed and flexible exchange rates, between internal and external equilibrium, and between theory and practice'. The band would permit greater exchange rate variations (within predetermined limits) around a fixed parity after the abolition of the fixed peg system. 'The inescapable need for harmonizing national policies will strengthen the central banks of the member countries in their difficult stand against the inflationary consequences on monopolistic wage and price policies ... promoting monetary discipline.'[26]

A Theory of Payments Balance

In *The Balance of Payments* (1952), Meade stated that to achieve internal balance (defined as full employment without inflation) and external balance (defined mainly in terms of current-account transactions), a country needed two instruments or policy variables: an expenditures (aggregate demand) policy and exchange rate variation (or wage price flexibility). If only one instrument is available, as when exchange rates are fixed, it is possible for conflicts of objectives to arise. Mundell (1962) introduced capital movements into the model and showed that fiscal policy and monetary policy (the two components of expenditures policy) have differential effects on the capital account of the balance of payments. He demonstrated that an appropriate mix of fiscal and monetary policies, whatever the exchange rate system, could simultaneously attain the two goals of internal and external balance. Essential to balance was the 'assignment' of each policy variable to that goal on which it exerted the relatively greater effect; under fixed exchange rates, this meant that monetary policy should be directed to maintaining external balance and fiscal policy to internal balance. The opposite pairing of instruments and targets, he argued, would lead to dynamic instability. Given balance can be achieved whatever the exchange rate regime, flexible rates might not be best for every country. For many centuries, the gold standard and other commodity-based systems provided a monetary anchor, as well as a standard for financing international transactions. Nevertheless, the modern case for fixed rates need not have a commodity basis. Countries may anchor to a currency with a credible central bank, a useful strategy if their own financial institutions are less well developed.[27]

While a single currency implies a single central bank (with note-issuing powers), a currency area with more than one currency requires the cooperation of an equal number of central banks. There will be a major difference between adjustment within a currency area with a single currency and a currency area involving more than one currency, even though exchange rates in the latter are fixed. Analysing Mundell's implications, Eichengreen stated: 'In Mundell's paradigm, policymakers balance the saving in transactions costs from the creation of single money against the consequences of diminished policy autonomy'. Eichengreen argued that the loss of national monetary authority will be more costly when macroeconomic shocks are more region- or country-specific, when monetary policy is a more powerful instrument for 'offsetting them and when other adjustment mechanisms are less effective'.[28]

The Mundell model attracted much attention in the literature and a torrent of followers with modifications and extensions to his theory. In 'Equilibrium Under Fixed Exchanges', Harry G. Johnson (1963) used an argument similar to Mundell's to argue the disadvantages of fixed rates. He treated fixed exchange rates as a device for achieving on a world scale the advantages of a unified currency secured at the national level by a national currency, with the same inherent problems.[29] The advantages of a unified currency are those of a measure of value, a standard for deferred payments, an acceptable medium of exchange and a store of value subject only to price fluctuations. These advantages are interrelated with and dependent on freedom of competition in goods and factor markets in the economy, which tends to equalize the purchasing power of money throughout the economy. This raises unavoidable risks for the national economy when it is adversely affected by real or monetary disturbances from outside. A system of fixed exchange rates is intended to secure the advantages of a unified currency on a world scale; but fixed exchange rates differ from a unified national currency in respects that limit both advantages and disadvantages as well as create new problems. Fixed exchange rates do not carry with them the freedom of competition necessary to realize the full benefits, or the taxing power that compensates a nation for the disadvantages of participating in the national currency area. Fixed exchange rates do not provide the same technical convenience of a unified currency, and the fixed rate system of 1963 was not really fixed: countries were allowed to vary rates by 1 per cent of par value, which introduced some risk into the system as well as hedging costs. Johnson found that perhaps the most important difference between fixed exchange rates and a unified national currency concerns the use of monetary reserves. In a national system, any individual bank must maintain one-to-one convertibility between liabilities and reserves, whereas in the international system, any nation has the ultimate right and power to alter the exchange ratio between its national money and the international reserve money. The role of gold is another important difference between the national and unified banking systems. The national system creates its own reserves and is focused on monetary stability and economic growth; the international system depends on gold, the supply of which depends on production and the degree of hoarding.

Johnson (1969) would put the case for flexible rates more directly: 'The fundamental argument for flexible exchange rates is that they would allow countries autonomy with respect to their use of monetary, fiscal and other policy instruments, consistent with the maintenance of whatever degree of freedom in international transactions they chose to allow their citizens, by automatically ensuring the preservation of external equilibrium'.[30]

In 'Macroeconomic Policy Adjustment in Interdependent Economies', Richard Cooper (1969) explored the effects of coordination between policymakers in two countries adjusting to disturbances, given different degrees of interdependence between them. He found that as interdependence increases, effectiveness of decentralized policymaking decreases and policy coordination needs increase, requiring the alignment of policy instruments to all targets.[31] Against the idea of fixed targets (and the Meade, Mundell and other models based on them), Jurg Niehans (1968) in 'Monetary and Fiscal Policies in Open Economies' made the case for optimizing the results of monetary or fiscal policy instruments against a 'target frontier' to get the best policy combination for each nation in a system of nations where there is some level of policy coordination.[32]

The Case for Status Quo, Improvements or Changes in the Price of Gold

The gold-exchange standard under the Bretton Woods system was a system of exchange rates with some variability within a predetermined limit, dependent on gold, dollars and the convertibility of dollars into gold on demand. After acknowledging problems that the current system could not fix – balance of payments deficits, inadequacy of reserves, the role of gold, generalized fear of collapse leading to speculative movements – a number of Bellagio Group economists and their peers argued for the status quo, for improvements in the current system, or for a return to gold. Improvements included increases in dollar and sterling reserves as well as increases and decreases in the price of gold.

The case for automatic adjustment mechanisms continued to be made in the work of Tibor Scitovsky. In 'The Theory of Balance of Payments Adjustment' (1967), Scitovsky argued that international asset immobility makes balance of payments adjustment painful (and interregional adjustment painless); nevertheless, for the international movement of transferable assets to perform a payments-equilibrating function, they must only move in response to price changes and to changes in the individual economic position of individual issuers of assets and never in response to political and economic changes, or the results will be disequilibrating.[33]

Paul Einzig argued that the Bretton Woods system of the 1960s had given rise 'to an overdose of international financial cooperation'. He saw the willingness of monetary authorities and private holders of dollars to finance US trade deficits and US investment abroad as the proximate cause of US reluctance to take the steps necessary to stop the country's decline in financial strength, and he urged an increase in the US price of gold leading to a substantial general alignment of parities.[34]

In 'Imbalance of International Payments', Roy Harrod argued for an increase in reserve position because monetary authorities would be more inclined to expand credit to pursue full employment and growth policies. Given reserve shortage and left to their own devices, 'each nation ... bethinks itself of an alternative remedy, and finds it in direct import restriction'.[35] Urging the USA to continue investing its way out of recession, Harrod (1958) also argued for raising the price of gold: 'If they raised the dollar price of gold somewhere in proportion to the decline in the goods value of the dollar, the rest of the world would soon have reserves comparable to those before the war ... That involves money ten times as great as anything you can possibly imagine they could do in the way of adding liquid resources to one or other of the international institutions'.[36] Harrod did not propose to abolish the gold-exchange standard. Rueff and Heilperin did.

Also supporting a rise in the price of gold, Jacques Rueff (1961) indicted American monetary policy. In 'The West is Risking a Credit Collapse', Rueff declared that the 'United States was not really required to settle its debts abroad'. That is, 'the country with [the reserve] currency is in the deceptively euphoric position of never having to pay off its international debts. The money it pays to foreign creditors comes back home, like a boomerang'.[37] In *The Monetary Sin of the West* (1972), Rueff identified the gold-exchange standard as the monetary sin. While economists blamed the gold standard for its role in transmitting the Great Depression internationally, Rueff argued that the real culprit was the gold-exchange standard, with its dependence on reserves. The gold standard would have been stable; the gold-exchange standard was not. When questions of confidence in reserve media are raised, gold alone historically has inspired confidence as money.[38]

Like Rueff, Michael Heilperin's convictions about gold go back before World War II. In *International Monetary Economics*, Heilperin said, 'the only successful experience of monetary internationalism (apart from monetary unions) has been under the gold standard'.[39] He discussed the mechanisms behind its operation and the means by which it facilitates the restoration of equilibrium in a disturbed balance of payments. He showed that maintenance of the gold standard depends upon the coordination of national monetary policies and adherence to 'the rules of the game'.[40] The advantages of monetary internationalism are durable stability of exchange rates and long-run equilibrium of international payments. In an interesting twist, Heilperin can conceive of these advantages being realized in the absence of a gold (or other common monetary) standard, that is to say, when a system of free paper currencies exists, but only providing that similar mechanisms are allowed to operate as under the gold standard and that a long-run stability of the exchanges is maintained, with fluctuations limited to mere oscillations around the long-run equilibrium position.[41] With a shared standard, it is likely that claims of national 'autonomy' will triumph over those of international stability.[42]

Arguments in favour of a decrease in the price of gold were made by L. Albert Hahn (1963), Arthur Dahlberg (1962), Paul Wonnacutt (1963) and Fritz Machlup (1961). In 'Anachronism of the Gold Price Controversy', Hahn (1963) recommended reducing the price central banks pay for gold. Among his proposals was that central banks sell gold only to other central banks, taking speculators and hoarders out of the picture. Additionally, Hahn proposed that private ownership of gold be forbidden in all countries.[43]

Arthur Dahlberg called for a reduction of 2 per cent per year in the US Treasury's purchase price of gold and a 2 per cent tax on bank deposits and currency. The title of his book *Reduce the Price of Gold and Make Money Move* expresses the book's purpose – to discourage the holding of inactive cash balances and increase the velocity of circulation.[44] The notion that inactive money is dangerous to the health of the economy grew out of the analysis of government policy during the Great Depression. The point was made by Salant (1941): 'The existence of excess reserves establishes the existence and importance of the speculative motive for liquidity on the part of banks, with whom it is easily observable ... The vulnerable position of the government bond market in 1936 and 1937 may be traceable to our neglect of the important question of why excess reserves exist, which in turn reflects our failure to analyse adequately the nature of the demand for money'.[45]

Seeing loss of confidence and speculation as the cause of the liquidity problem, Machlup proposed that the dollar price of gold be reduced in two, three or more instalments. This would reverse historical experience, and those who persist in holding gold would lose money.[46]

Laffer (1969) argued that 'Any problem that we actually face would be more accurately associated with the role of gold in the international monetary system and not with the existence of US deficits. The measures to "cure" the US payments deficits, although they have not cured the US balance of payments, have contributed significantly to the misallocation of world resources'.[47]

The IFI Hypothesis

Salant picked up the 'idle money' thread again in 'Financial Intermediation as an Explanation of Enduring "Deficits" in the Balance of Payments' (1972). Salant, as well as co-authors and Bellagio Group members Emile Depres and Charles Kindleberger, would move to a consideration of the liquidity issue in terms of who needs liquidity, from whom and why, to support their hypothesis that the enduring deficits of the USA were attributable to its historic role as a financial intermediary.[48] To make their case, the authors draw on the John Gurley and E. S. Shaw study of debt and money in the USA in the period 1800–1950. Beginning in 1950, the USA had persistent 'liquidity deficits' accompanied for some years by great strength of the dollar in the foreign exchange market. This strength reflected a demand for dollar assets by both private foreigners and foreign monetary authorities, who, on balance, preferred dollars to gold for at least most of the 1950s. Even after 1957, when liquidity deficits grew to a size that caused alarm, private holders continued to accumulate liquid dollar assets. In the ten years beginning in 1960, when the data first permit separating increases in holdings of liquid dollar assets by monetary authorities from increases in holdings by other foreigners, the recorded holdings of others have risen in every year; in six of these ten years they rose by more than $1 billion a year. At the same time, outflows of American private capital, mainly long term, increased. Thus, the United States was increasing its foreign financial assets and its liquid financial liabilities to foreigners at the same time. The simultaneous strength of the dollar and the accumulation of dollar assets by foreign monetary authorities during the 1950s showed that the increase in the liquid liabilities of the United States was a response to an increasing total 'stock demand'. It appeared, therefore, that the United States was performing the role of a financial intermediary.[49] Commenting on the International Financial Intermediation (IFI) hypothesis, Franco Modigliani warned,

> The analogy with financial intermediaries and the implication that one need not be concerned with the rate of increase in liabilities has some validity as long as the increased liabilities are willingly held by private foreign holders, i.e. as long as there is no deficit on the official-settlements basis ... But the conclusion that in employing an analogy with conventional financial intermediation, one need not be concerned with the rate of growth of liabilities or the size of the deficit, loses much of its validity when it comes to the official settlements deficit ... [B]eyond some point, a deficit on an official-settlements basis will become excessive, a conclusion with which Salant would presumably not disagree ... Unfortunately, it also is clear from these remarks that the IFI hypothesis, however interpreted, cannot be of much help in identifying just where that border line lies.[50]

Conclusion

Both fixed and flexible rates had their advocates before and throughout the period covered in this book, many as early as the 1930s. By *not* focusing on the originator of the case for flexible or fixed or hybrid solutions, what emerges is a large group of thinkers driven to understand what policy instruments are necessary to maintain full employment while balancing international payments, as well as to develop their own plans to solve the problems in an increasingly interdependent world. Some trusted an automatic mechanism; others sought to use interdependence to advantage. It is clear they were also reading each other's work, cherry-picking innovative policy and theory, and modifying or extending it. In economic policy and theory, there was significant appeal in coming up with 'the next new thing', an exciting proposition for technology innovators and quantum physicists today. It was that cool to be an economist in the 1960s.

In many respects, this study of the Bellagio Group is a study of individual voices addressing needs for collective action. That Machlup, Triffin and Fellner were able to orchestrate the group to ask the right questions and make sense of many potential answers was demonstrated by the Bellagio Group conferences. Policymakers heard about the collaborative exploration of alternatives through the publication of *International Monetary Arrangements: A Problem of Choice* (1964). The approach would be invaluable to the representatives of the Group of Ten countries, who had laid their economic fortunes on the line with the signing of the General Arrangements to Borrow. The increasing importance of the Group of Ten and their relationship with the Bellagio Group are discussed in Chapter 8.

8 COLLABORATION WITH THE GROUP OF TEN

Introduction

IMF and Group of Ten studies were announced by US Treasury Secretary Douglas Dillon at the IMF Annual Meeting in September 1963 (the same time a commitment to pursue a similar study was made by Machlup, Triffin and Fellner, who were attending the same meeting). The Group of Ten study was undertaken in the period 1963–4 by the deputies of the Group of Ten. Machlup had scheduled the publication of the Bellagio Group's final report for June 1964, preceding by two months the official publication of the IMF staff and Group of Ten reports. The Bellagio Group's report, *International Monetary Arrangements: The Problem of Choice* (1964), was shared with the IMF and deputies of the Group of Ten and attracted significant attention, especially from the chairman of the deputies of the Group of Ten, Otmar Emminger, and the chairman of the OECD's Working Party 3, Emile van Lennep. Their interest in the Bellagio Group coincides with the rising importance of the Group of Ten countries and the assignment of major IMF projects to the deputies of the Group of Ten. Chapter 8 first explores the historical context of the rising importance of the Group of Ten. This chapter then discusses the reports published by the Group of Ten and IMF, and the difference between them and the Bellagio Group's final report; Machlup's decision to explore the origins of these differences at the first joint meeting of Group of Ten members and academics; the private thoughts of Group of Ten members about the Bellagio Group's approach and advantages as a non-governmental, independent think tank; and Otmar Emminger's assignment to the Bellagio Group, which led to a thirteen-year collaboration.

Historical Context

The creation in 1962 of the General Arrangements to Borrow (GAB) caused a virtual split in the IMF between GAB member nations and the rest of the IMF, the latter of which were convinced that cooperation between industrial countries had replaced 'the universalist aspirations of Bretton Woods'.[1] The ten industrial nations that agreed to participate in the GAB (Belgium, Canada, France, Italy, Japan, the Netherlands, the United Kingdom, the United States, and the central banks of Germany and Sweden, followed by Switzerland in 1964) effectively put their own banks on the line for $6 billion to cover IMF loans to member (and sometimes non-member) nations with the consent of GAB members and the IMF's Executive Board. As Harold James explained, 'The creation of additional resources through the GAB produced a new sort of conditionality, intended to calm continental European fears about the possible use of the GAB by the major reserve centres of the time, the US and UK'.[2] The GAB continues to the present. In March 2011, the New Arrangements to Borrow (NAB) added $330 billion in new borrowing capability. Cooperation between the G10 members became institutionalized through study meetings of deputies. The group committed itself to 'undertake a thorough examination of the outlook for the functioning of the international monetary system and of its probable future needs for liquidity'.[3] It defined its task as 'multilateral surveillance' (the first use of the term in discussions about the international economy), which it interpreted as an appraisal of 'the various means of financing surpluses and deficits' in order to develop 'a common approach to international monetary matters'.[4]

Increasingly, the Group of Ten would meet separately from the IMF as a whole and would undertake independent efforts – like the Group of Ten report on the international monetary system, timed to coincide with the IMF staff report. A second 'split' occurred when the six countries that were part of the European Economic Community also met separately to discuss a common position in the reform discussions so as to safeguard their legitimate interests.[5] Note that the Joint Meetings of Officials and Academics would begin to focus on the European role in meetings beginning in 1969 and running through 1977.

Table 8.1: GAB Participants and Credit Amounts

Participant	Original GAB (1962–83) Amount (SDR million[1])	Enlarged GAB (1983–2008) Amount (SDR million)
Belgium	143	595
Canada	165	893
Deutsche Bundesbank	1,476	2,380
France	395	1,700
Italy	235	1,105
Japan[2]	1,161	2,125
Netherlands	244	850
Sveriges Riksbank	79	383
Swiss National Bank[3]		1,020
United Kingdom	565	1,700
United States	1,883	4,250

Participant	Original GAB (1962–83) Amount (SDR million[1])	Enlarged GAB (1983–2008) Amount (SDR million)
Total	6,344	17,000
Saudi Arabia (associated credit arrangement)		1,500

[1] SDR equivalent as of 30 October 1982.
[2] 250,000 million yen entered into effect on 23 November 1976.
[3] Switzerland was not an original member of the G10 and signator of the General Arrangements to Borrow, but signed in 1964 and renewed in 1967.
Note: Total may not equal sum of components due to rounding.

Source: International Monetary Fund. Updated 31 December 2010.

Even the formation in 1961 of the OECD's study group called Working Party 3, whose task was to analyse the effect on international payments of monetary, fiscal and other policy measures and to consult on future policy measures, replicated the composition of the Group of Ten. In this way, the industrial countries, with a heavy over-representation of Europeans, appeared to be on their way to establishing their own international financial system. Their actions challenged the IMF's vision of a more global, inclusive international economy.

Liquidity versus Adjustment

As the debate over liquidity requirements and payments adjustment became more heated, the speeches of the central bank governors of the Group of Ten showed a divergence of views between those who favoured expansion of the world's supply of liquidity and those who emphasized elimination of balance of payments deficits. Those who urged attention to payments adjustment argued that liquidity would encourage deficits and over-expansive financial policies in countries running persistent balance of payments deficits, especially in the UK and USA. Valery Giscard d'Estaing (France) argued that the fundamental difficulties confronting the international monetary system were structural weaknesses, not liquidity. These were: the advance of mechanisms to correct payments deficits; the asymmetry between reserve currency countries and the rest of the world; and the unevenness between countries of the risks of holding reserves – with those holding gold having the least risk.[6] Douglas Dillon (USA) argued that improvements in supplying liquidity did not absolve the United States from reducing its own payment deficit. The critical question was how the adjustments were to be made. Balance had too often in the past been forced by measures that endangered domestic stability or the prospects for growing international trade.[7] Reginald Maudling (UK) argued that the primary purpose of international liquidity is to give time for individual countries to make adjustments in their balance of payments without sharp changes to the volume of imports or domestic demand growth. While the availability of additional liquidity should not be such as to promote unsound domestic or international positions in the guide of temporary fluctuations, the availability of prompt liquidity in times of trouble is necessary. [8]

On 15 and 16 June 1964, the deputies presented to their ministers and governors the report that they had prepared in response to the request of the previous September. The report was largely the work of Emminger, de Lattre, Roosa and van Lennep. The report was attached as an Annex to the Group of Ten's Ministerial Statement. By design, it was released to the public on the same day, 10 August 1964, as the IMF's Annual Report.

We know from 'The Final Report of International Monetary Arrangements Undertaken by a Group of Nongovernmental Economists from 11 Countries; Sponsored by Princeton University with the Support of Grants from the Ford Foundation and the Rockefeller Foundation' that the IMF, Group of Ten and Bellagio Group reports were discussed and compared at a two-day session of the American Bankers Association conference prior to the Fund's Tokyo meeting in September 1964.

There was further discussion of the three reports at the Annual Meeting of the American Economic Association in December 1964. The papers presented at the meeting were published in the 'Papers and Proceedings' issue of the *American Economic Review*, May 1965.[9] There was also extensive media coverage of the Bellagio Group conferences in the *New York Times,* the *Economist* and the *Financial Times.* As a result of this attention and the network of contacts Robert Triffin had with the EEC, Fritz Machlup was able successfully to join Bellagio Group academics with IMF officials whose mandate was reform of the world monetary system, particularly the deputies of the Group of Ten countries. Marius Holtrop (Netherlands) found in the three reports evidence of general agreement on the pursuit of national policies aimed at the avoidance or early correction of major and persistent imbalances; the use of reserves and international liquidity to cushion temporary imbalances but not to finance more fundamental imbalances; a limited increase in liquidity to avoid inflation or deflation at the extremes; a limit to liquidity generated by continued US payments deficits; as well as new techniques for generating reserves independent of the supply of gold.[10]

Nevertheless, there was also serious disagreement among Group of Ten countries on the relative importance of national payments adjustment policies versus increased liquidity. A second area of disagreement was the role of the IMF or other agency in managing an increase in liquidity. A third area of disagreement was whether liquidity should be available to all countries or to a limited group of countries.[11]

The debate over adjustment policies and the creation, allocation and distribution of special reserve assets would consume the deputies of the Group of Ten. Joseph Gold considered all of the basic reforms incorporated into IMF amendments at this time to have been the work of EEC members.[12] Among these amendments was the need for a special majority of 85 per cent of voting strength required to allocate or cancel special drawing rights or to increase quotas. A second group of amendments now requiring an 85 per cent voting majority was related to the repurchase and calculation of monetary reserves, earlier seen to favour reserve currency countries. Finally, a Committee on the Interpretation of the Board of Governors was created to hear members who dispute a finding of the IMF and appeal to the Board of Governors of the Fund. The Committee ruling holds sway unless overridden by an 85 per cent voting majority of the Board of Governors.[13] The story that unfolds here is one of the obligations Group of Ten nations felt as a result of the GAB, their need for control over liquidity and its use, their increasing demand for 'adequate safeguards', 'conditionality' in the provision of Fund resources to members, and 'surveillance'. This is a story that European Union members of 2012 dealing with sovereign debt crises know only too well.

A Comparison of the Bellagio Group's Final Report and the Group of Ten and IMF Reports

The first difference between the Bellagio Groups report and the reports of the Group of Ten and of the IMF lies in the affiliations of the authors. The Group of Ten is a group of governments; their statement and the Annex, the report of the deputies, were written by representatives of national governments. The IMF is an international organization of national governments; its report was written by staff members and officers representing international government. The Bellagio Group was an international study group of thirty-two economists not affiliated with national or international government, at least not directly and full time. The official inquiries reflected a consensus view, whereas the private character of the economists' study permitted the consideration and discussion of proposals that were 'out of bounds' in an official inquiry (such as proposals for changes in the price of gold or in foreign exchange rates). Furthermore, economists speaking only for themselves, in an atmosphere like that of a university seminar, can more easily examine all sides of an issue than can experts speaking for their governments and instructed to defend more or less fixed positions.

Another difference deserves emphasis: the difference in purpose. The two official studies were designed to seek agreement on courses of action; the private study was designed to interpret disagreement and identify the sources of disagreement.

In the Bellagio Group's final report, Machlup explained, 'Among the valuable results of a study undertaken by experts known for their diametrically opposite recommendations may be the specification of the particular judgements of facts and objectives which are responsible for the conflicting conclusions. Perhaps some of the differences in judgements of fact can be resolved by further study, and some of the differences in judgements of value may be reduced by a non-emotive analysis of their places in a common hierarchy of higher goals'. [14]

The Bellagio Group conferences (and the final report) took a novel approach by identifying adjustment, liquidity and confidence as the three overriding social objectives against which to compare alternative potential solutions. The Group of Ten and IMF reports fundamentally took liquidity as their objective and preservation of the existing fixed-rate, gold-based system as given.

The Group of Ten report drew six conclusions and recommendations. The current system with fixed exchange rates and present price of gold was adaptable and flexible enough to serve present and near-term needs. International liquidity, including the entire range of resources available for financing payments imbalances, was also fully adequate for current and near-term needs, especially since a moderate increase in IMF quotas was being recommended at the same time. To strengthen international cooperation, a process of 'multilateral surveillance of bilateral financing and liquidity creation' was recommended. Studies of the adjustment process and the need for an additional source of owned reserves would be undertaken'. [15]

Group of Ten recommended that Working Party 3 of the OECD undertake a study of the adjustment process. The Group of Ten also set up a Study Group for Creation of Reserve Assets, centred on two types of proposals: 1) the establishment of a collective reserve unit (CRU) among a limited group of countries, presumably the Group of Ten; and 2) the acceptance and development of gold tranche or similar claims on the IMF as an international reserve asset. By late fall 1965, the Bellagio Group had already been engaged by the chairman of the deputies of the Group of Ten, to assist in the study of special reserve assets and adjustment processes.

In 'The Report of the International Monetary Fund', Jacques Polak acknowledged that the IMF staff report was published as chapters 3 and 4 in the IMF's Annual Report. Chapter 3 dealt with general issues of international liquidity, while chapter 4 analysed the Fund as a source of liquidity and the further contributions the Fund could make to liquidity, including an immediate increase in Fund quotas. Polak noted a difference between the two reports – the Group of Ten report was a document written by high officials of ten governments; the report of the Fund was a staff report for an organization with 102 country members, discussed and amended and then released by the Fund's nineteen executive directors. He acknowledged one area of commonality: the Group of Ten and

IMF reports represented first steps towards understanding the problem of international liquidity.[16] However, the problems involved more than liquidity, but also the notion of payments balance and the roles of surplus and debtor countries. Before any member of the Group of Ten would authorize more liquidity, responsibility for payments balance had to be ironed out and even then liquidity had to be handled judiciously to avoid encouraging further imbalance and spreading inflation.

Criticism and Defence of Machlup's Approach

At the American Economic Association Conference in 1965, J. Herbert Furth of the Federal Reserve, Milton Friedman of the University of Chicago and Milton Gilbert of the Bank for International Settlements would critique Machlup's approach because it offered no preferred solution to the current crisis. As Machlup would argue in his 'Report of the Nongovernmental Economists Study Group', presented to the American Economic Association and published by the *American Economic Review* in 1965, 'I am quite ready to admit that most policy recommendations consist of ready-made prescriptions, prejudged solutions without full awareness of the major and minor premises on which they supposedly rest. Only when challenged by critics or confronted with conflicting recommendations will most advocates begin to rationalize their proposals by exposing the underlying suppositions. But precisely this is needed, since the validity of the solutions can be judged only by evaluating the validity (or comparative probability) of the relevant factual assumptions and the acceptance (or comparative weight) of the relevant value judgements'.[17] For example, Machlup argued, advocacy or rejection of flexible exchange rates rested to a large extent on assumptions regarding future attitudes of central bankers and private traders and investors. Concerning central bankers, the question is whether their resistance to inflationary pressures will or will not be reduced if the fear of dwindling international reserves is removed. Advocates of exchange rate flexibility assume that central bankers will fear drastic exchange depreciation under flexible rates no less than they fear reserve depreciation under fixed rates. Opponents of flexible rates assume that a loss of reserves always impresses central bankers more forcefully than would a drop in the exchange rate.

Advocates of the semi-automatic gold standard want to remove the central banks' power to meet a payments deficit by anything other than a sale of gold and to extend domestic credit to offset the deflationary effects of gold outflow. Advocates of flexible rates want to remove the central banks' power to intervene in the foreign exchange market by official sales and purchases or to interfere by restrictions on private transactions.

Machlup repeated for his critics the statement made in the final conference report that 'The consensus that mattered most to some of the members of the Study Group was not on the questions of what to do now and what to recommend for the future – an objective they considered inconsistent with the recognition of divergent value judgements and divergent assumptions about unknown facts – but rather a consensus on what were some of the things on which the consequences of particular measures or arrangements would depend. This consensus permits those who know what they want and who believe they know the most probable answers to the open questions of fact to make rational decisions on alternative courses of action. A consensus of this kind was achieved without reservations'.[18] In other words, the Bellagio Group report left to policy-makers explicit choices among the most plausible assumptions of fact and the most worthwhile social objectives.

Problems within the Group of Ten and between the Ten and the IMF – What the Bellagio Group Had to Offer

In a letter of 5 October 1964 to Machlup, Triffin wrote about the IMF Annual Meeting in Tokyo: 'In brief, I anticipate continued and fierce squabbling between the French and the Anglo-Saxons over the next six months or so ... We and the British should, I think, concede the correctness of Giscard D'Estaing's basic diagnosis of instability rather than under-liquidity, but should also press him to accept its full implications by recognizing that the inflationary impact of US deficits is not the only danger that should be guarded against in light of such a diagnosis itself'.[19] D'Estaing also wanted multilateral surveillance to prevent destabilizing policies and an end to financing of long-term deficits with short-term assets.

Triffin touched on the conflict between the Group of Ten and the IMF as a whole: 'As to the institutional conflict between the Fund and the Group of Ten as a framework for future action, I am confident that the power problem involved will be considerably eased by the development of the EEC monetary system itself, and the contribution of such a development to the decentralization of the IMF'.[20] Chapter 9 of this volume deals with this conflict and the emergence of a European voice at the IMF.

We learn from Triffin's notes that Group of Ten members saw the usefulness of the Bellagio Group as a non-governmental, independent think tank. Emminger found the Bellagio Group conferences invaluable to policy deliberations. Rinaldo Ossola, chair of the Ossola Committee on Creation of Reserve Assets (Special Drawing Rights) of the Group of Ten, liked the Bellagio Group's connection between liquidity and payments adjustment, and Robert Roosa, deputy secretary of the US Treasury and member of the Ossola Group, found the Bellagio Group's contribution important to the 'evolution' of emerging public policy. Emminger, Ossola, Roosa and van Lennep, chair of Working Party 3 of the OECD, would become exceptionally close working partners with the academic economists of the Bellagio Group, joining them for seminars under the 'Bellagio Group' name some eighteen times through 1977.[21] The impetus for collaboration was created by Machlup. In a letter to Robert Triffin on 30 October 1964, Machlup wrote:

> The discussions of the three reports – Group of Ten, the IMF and Group of 32 – have made it clear that certain disagreements must be further discussed. The Ossola Committee and Working Party 3 of OECD are at work, and several of their problems have not been discussed by the Group of 32. It is desirable that we make an effort to clarify some of the issues that need to be resolved in the near future.
>
> Among the questions to which we ought to give attention are certain technical problems connected with the composite reserve unit; certain differences between the Bernstein Plan and the French plan; the significant differences between solutions stressing owned reserves, borrowed reserves and borrowable reserves; and the creation of a new reserve asset.
>
> I propose that a small sub-group of the 32 meet in the period between December 17 and 22 – perhaps not more than ten of us ... Robert Roosa, Otmar Emminger and Rinaldo Ossola have indicated an interest in participating in our discussion in an entirely informal capacity. I am inviting several other government economists and it is quite likely they will agree to join our conference for two or more days, coming immediately from a Paris meeting of Working Party 3. Their participation in our discussions should, of course, not be publicized. The idea is that they will talk much more freely and discuss the issues much more effectively if they come as economists interested in the same problems and not as representatives of a government.[22]

First Joint Meeting of Officials and Academics:
An Assignment from Dr Emminger

A first meeting was planned at the Villa Serbelloni on Lake Como for December 1964. A second meeting was also anticipated as 'suggestions emerging from it need to be talked over again at a later date'. In a letter of 19 October 1965, Fellner discussed funding with the Ford Foundation's Shepard Stone, intimating that he planned to approach Emminger: 'The Machlup conferences were undoubtedly very successful, so much so that (as you know) Emminger, who is very influential among the decision makers of the Central Banks, suggested repeatedly that a further conference of central bank officials with part of the Bellagio group of non-official economists would be distinctly useful. The conference would be concerned primarily with the balance of payments adjustment problem. Emminger did not say that the conference would be useful at this time *because* important decisions are in the offing – and he probably would not like to put it that way – but it is quite generally believed that important decisions are in fact in the offing'.[23]

In December 1964, the first Joint Meeting of Officials and Academics took place in Bellagio, Italy. In his very few notes for this conference, Machlup wrote, 'Idea for this conference – wearing hats, wearing masks ... Not mutual criticism – except perhaps as a starting point. Problems that are now occupying us, problems that perhaps were not treated in the reports'.[24] Topics of discussion included the impact of the growing Eurodollar market on US deficits (a topic proposed by Roy Harrod and Peter Kenen); too much liquidity or too little (Dennis Rickett, Treasury, UK); liquidity – quantitative or qualitative (J. Martens de Wilmars, Ministry of Finance, Belgium); stability versus growth, securing flexibility (Marcus Fleming, IMF); and any chance that the present system will improve? How to make it workable? Important for monetary order (Jacques Rueff). The meeting generated a final list of questions and suggestions for further work:

1. Why not G10 consolidation?
2. Inadequate or unstable provision of liquidity.
3. No automatic lending to deficit countries. No automatic distribution by formula. Effort to accelerate adjustment mechanism.
4. Adjustment mechanisms and policies:
5. The Six and the Ten and the 102: Monetary integration of the Six – implications for liquidity arrangement for the Ten and for IMF.
6. Developing nations and the Ten.

Among members of the deputies of the Group of Ten who attended the first meeting were de Lattre, Emminger and van Lennep as well as Dennis Rickett (UK) and J. Martens de Wilmars (Belgium). In August 1965, the report of the Ossola Committee was published. Various techniques for deliberate reserve creation were examined, but no preference was expressed. Differences of view persisted on such questions as the link, if any, between reserve assets and gold, the role of the IMF, and the rules by which decisions to create liquidity would be made.

In September 1965 the Ministers and Governors of the Group of Ten gave instructions to their deputies to resume discussions leading to agreement on arrangements for the future creation of reserve assets, as and when needed, to permit adequate provision of the reserve needs of the world economy. The deputies report was due in the spring of 1966.[25]

In preparation for that report, Emminger requested that the Bellagio Group put some focus on devising adjustment policies for countries in payments imbalance and the creation of new reserve assets. In fact, in his letter of 2 November 1965, Emminger outlined exactly what he wanted the Bellagio Group to work on in devising adjustment policies for countries in payments imbalance and the creation of new reserve assets. He suggested the group focus on three themes: the possible creation of a set of standards against which members could justify their adjustment policies; objective criteria for the respective responsibilities

of surplus and deficit countries; and improvements in international consultation and cooperation on balance of payments policies of member countries.
Emminger thought the first two problems would be well suited for analysis and
recommendations by a 'Bellagio-type' study group; the third problem would, of
necessity, have to be dealt with entirely by Working Group 3 itself, which can
draw on eight years of practical experience (with a number of successes but also
of failures). Emminger requested that the study group base their work on the
assumption that exchange rates remain fixed per the IMF's Articles of Agreement and general policies.

The Zurich Conference on Payments Adjustment

It was with this in mind that Emminger suggested in the autumn of 1965 that a
number of academic economists should be invited to join some of the officials
who constitute Working Party 3 for informal discussions. William Fellner was
charged with developing a draft agenda for the second Joint Meeting of Officials
and Academics, planned for Zurich in January 1966. In addition to Emminger
and van Lennep, attendees at the Zurich conference included Frederick Deming, undersecretary for monetary affairs of the US Treasury; JCR Dow, assistant
secretary general of the OECD; Rolf Gocht, ministerial director, Bonn; Marcus
Fleming, deputy director, IMF; RW Lawson, deputy governor, Bank of Canada;
Robert Neild, economic adviser, Her Majesty's Treasury, UK; Rinaldo Ossola,
Banca d'Italia and chair of the Ossola Committee; M. Brossolette, Treasury,
Paris; Dennis Rickett, economic adviser, Her Majesty's Treasury, UK; T. de
Vries, director of economic and financial affairs, CEE, Brussels; Milton Gilbert,
Bank for International Settlements. Fourteen academics, mostly drawn from the
original Bellagio Group, also attended.

In remarks preceding his draft, Fellner noted, 'It seems to me that a set of
standards for the adjustment policies of individual countries at fixed exchange
rates can be formulated only in a very general way and that the operational
content of such standards must inevitably become a matter of interpretation
in specific situations. Personal judgement of a legitimately controversial kind
must be expected to enter into these interpretations'.[26] The notion of procedures
raised the question of whether only the committees of international bodies
should be involved – or independent experts should also be consulted. Fellner
was inclined towards the latter. Would the interpretation of procedures be bind-
ing? Or merely carry the force of international public opinion? As concerned
Emminger's second question, it seemed to Fellner that general standards were
apt to be neutral with respect to surplus and deficit countries – and the question
of just how the two should behave was apt to become a matter of ad hoc interpretation, lacking operational content. Fellner's agenda for the conference was

based on contributions from Emminger and J. C. R. Dow. It focused on these areas: alternative sources of disturbances (monetary and non-monetary, shifts in demand, productivity changes) and the diagnostic indicators that permit a first alert; remedies and the criteria for using them (including surplus versus deficit country adjustments and financing); multilateral compatibility of forecasts, remedies and diagnostics; and the relationship of adjustment to liquidity.

Very rarely were notes taken during any of the conferences (because Machlup preferred participants to speak candidly and to feel free to change their minds, if they chose). In the case of the Zurich conference, the Machlup Papers preserve some notes so that we have a flavour of the conversations – not presentations or read statements, but informal conversations among policymakers and academics. While the planned agenda was broad, the issue of the relative responsibility of deficit and surplus countries for adjustment appeared to engulf the agenda, generating deep disagreement. The Zurich meeting was also a testing ground for Working Party 3's report on adjustment policies and for some of the papers (written by Fellner, Triffin and Machlup) to be included in a book to be called *Maintaining and Restoring Balance in International Payments*. Some fourteen academic economists who attended the Zurich conference would also contribute papers to the book.

The Link between Adjustment and Liquidity

We know that Fritz Machlup began the conversation on the link between adjustment and liquidity. Machlup said the liquidity problem would not be solved if the adjustment process were not improved, because nations wanting deficit countries put under pressure will not agree to a liquidity increase otherwise. The officials objected that a general scarcity of liquidity is not an adequate way of enforcing adjustment since, even then, some countries will have large reserves and may go on a spending spree, inflating others. Without an agreed-upon code of behaviour, there is no way of disciplining surplus countries. It is better to have adequate reserves plus an adjustment code, even though good adjustment permits getting along with lower reserves. An annual addition of $1 billion to world reserves created by US deficit is much more inflationary than one created by increment of reserves, since deficits raise demand and liquidity. The academics suggested that an attempt to reduce demand by limiting growth and raising unemployment is merely palliative, in addition to being immoral.

A second, follow-up conference on adjustment was held in Princeton on 23–4 April 1966. At Emminger's suggestion, the following were invited: Dennis Rickett (UK), Emile van Lennep (Netherlands), G. A. Kessler (Netherlands), R. W. Lawson (Canada), Rolf Gocht (Germany), Rinaldo Ossola (Italy), Frederick Deming (USA), Milton Gilbert (BIS) and Maurice Perrouse (France). These officials would also be meeting in Washington with the executives of the IMF from 18 to 22 April. Machlup added with Emminger's permission the following: J. J. Polak (IMF), Marcus Fleming (IMF), Richard N. Cooper (USA), J. Dewey Daane (USA) and Maurice Parsons (UK). Along with the revised papers previously submitted to participants of the Zurich conference, some eleven additional papers on balance of payments adjustment issues were disseminated for comment.

Maintaining and Restoring Balance in International Payments

The primary purpose of the papers submitted to the Zurich and Princeton conferences was to be of help to the officials of the governments in their inquiry into the balance of payments problems, so essential in their negotiations on the necessary improvements of the international monetary system. The participants concluded that the papers should be made available through publication in the form of a book. Fellner, Triffin and Machlup reviewed and edited the submissions. Machlup provided a rough draft of the foreword to Emile van Lennep for his signature. The text notes that government officials and academics tended to view the adjustment process from rather different angles. 'We concentrate very closely on the policy adjustments that seem immediately practicable, sometimes perhaps at the expense of what would be nearer to the ideal. Academic thought tends to approach the subject from the other end. There is therefore good reason to believe that a discussion between officials and the academic profession can provide a useful process of cross-fertilization, with mutual benefit to both parties'.[27]

Published by Princeton University Press, the book is divided into two parts – Part I consists of three comprehensive papers, written by Fellner (the article, 'Rules of the Game', is discussed here in Chapter 3); Machlup ('In Search of Guides for Policy'); and Triffin ('The Balance of Payments See-saw'). Part II consists of fourteen papers on specific issues by Fellner, Gottfried Haberler, Sir Roy Harrod, Harry Johnson, Peter Kenen, Alexandre Lamfalussy, Friedrich Lutz, Fritz Machlup, Jurg Niehans, Walter Salant, Tibor Scitovsky, James Tobin, Robert Triffin and Robert West. The concluding section, 'Notes on Terminology', is a glossary prepared by Fritz Machlup.

The comprehensive papers were intended to be useful to government officials in their attempts to formulate general principles and policies. In their joint introduction, Fellner, Machlup and Triffin explain that the three comprehensive papers were written without an attempt to homogenize their viewpoints. There are some similar characteristics: each author stressed the desirability of prompt action to prevent major imbalances of aggregate demand. All proposed prompter consideration of exchange rate adjustments as a solution to fundamental disequilibria. The authors hoped that their separate papers reflected the candour and directness they sought to preserve.

The style of the comprehensive papers and special issue papers reflected what has become the essence of the Bellagio Group approach: independent perspectives on a myriad of issues raised by a chosen topic area, together creating a hologram on the topic – in this case, payments balance.

Fritz Machlup's comprehensive paper, 'In Search of Guides for Policy', was intended to give policymakers a set of rules telling them exactly who should do what to assure payments adjustment, what, how much, when and how quickly. The paper appeared to meet Emminger's requirements for a Bellagio-style approach to a set of standards. A close reading of the paper might suggest that the long list of criteria and adjustment options is not an exercise in comprehensiveness, but a demonstration of how many and how problematic are the choices available under a system of fixed rates. For a system of flexible exchange rates, there were only two criteria to consider: criteria of recognizing the emergence of imbalance not yet manifest, a kind of early warning system, and criteria for ascertaining the source of disturbance leading to imbalance, its geographic location, nature and probable duration. The paper ends with the recommendation that recognizing impending imbalances and taking preventive measures is the way to go. Where exchange rate adjustment is deferred, remedial measures in situations of fundamental disequilibrium are, from an economic viewpoint, more appropriately the business of surplus countries; preventive measures are the obligation of prospective deficit countries. If proposals for greater flexibility of exchange rates remain unacceptable, the only solution may be the creation of a system of continuous intervention, surveillance and consultation aimed at harmonizing national monetary policies.[28]

Robert Triffin's paper, 'The Balance of Payments Seesaw', made the point that imbalance requires mutual adjustment by surplus as well as deficit countries. The primary aim of international consultation on adjustment policies should be to maximize the compatibility and effectiveness of measures and policies adopted – and avoid 'beggar thy neighbour' policies. Again, his paper dealt squarely with Emminger's desire for improvements in consultation and cooperation (the surveillance problem).[29]

Several of the special issue papers stood out. In 'Adjustment Responsibilities of Surplus and Deficit Countries', James Tobin classified the adjustment responsibilities of surplus and deficit countries, and the impact of action on employment and inflation.[30] In 'Capital Markets and the Balance of Payments of a Financial Center', Walter Salant focused on the balance of payments problems of a reserve currency country.[31] In 'Limitations of Monetary and Fiscal Policy', Alexandre Lamfalussy identified the institutional and political constraints facing governments in their monetary-fiscal policy choices. [32]

Within the first few months of publication, more than 1,400 copies of *Maintaining and Restoring Balance in International Payments* had been sold. The book was also reviewed in the mainstream economics media, including the *Southern Economic Journal, The American Economic Review, Economica, The Journal of Finance, International Affairs* and *Weltwirtschaftliches Archiv.*

Conclusions

Fritz Machlup's plan to build the reputation and visibility of the Bellagio Group was aided by the emergence of the importance of the Group of Ten within the IMF. It was aided as well by fears the European members of the Group of Ten felt after the creation of the General Arrangements to Borrow, when the weight of the Group's responsibility for the payments imbalances of member states, particularly the USA and UK, was clearly on their heads. Machlup's emphasis on prevention by deficit countries lest surplus countries pick up the slack had a strong appeal. Certainly, van Lennep and Emminger were impressed with the success of the Zurich and Princeton conferences, and the sales of *Maintaining and Restoring Balance in International Payments.* Thus began a correspondence between Machlup, van Lennep and Emminger around a series of conferences that ran through 1977 (and a continuation of the conferences under a different guise into the present, discussed in Chapter 11). Chapter 9 continues the story of the Joint Conferences, this time focusing on a second phenomenon: the Europeanization of the Group of Ten and the emergence of the Bellagio Group/Joint Conferences as a social interest NGO.

9 ADJUSTMENT POLICIES AND SPECIAL DRAWING RIGHTS: JOINT MEETINGS OF OFFICIALS AND ACADEMICS

Introduction

The creation of special drawing rights (SDRs) was designed to solve the liquidity shortage that might delay balance of payments adjustment or provoke financial crises. How SDRs were distributed – to whom, how much and how often – was influenced by the ministers and bank governors of the Group of Ten, a group of mostly European officials from countries that had signed the General Arrangements to Borrow, and their deputies. The deputies of the Group of Ten met separately from the IMF in a series of eighteen conferences called the Joint Meetings of Officials and Academics (1964–77), organized by economists Fritz Machlup, Robert Triffin and William Fellner as an early social interest non-governmental organization (NGO). The conference organizers sought to provide a framework within which to manage issues where international management had become inadequate, and, increasingly, to provide a voice and identity for the European nations who were part of the Group of Ten.

While the Fritz Machlup and Robert Triffin Papers confirm the Bellagio Group's recommendation of a special reserve asset as early as 1964, the group's real work on adjustment and special drawing rights (as it came to be called) was done at the Joint Conferences of Officials and Academics from 1964 to 1977.

As discussed in Chapter 8, the Group of Ten countries had emerged as a powerful sub-group, often pursuing their own versions of projects that the IMF as a whole had in progress. Increasingly important were the finance and treasury officials who supported the ministers and central bank governors of the Group of Ten. These were the deputies of the Group of Ten, the officials who attended the Joint Conferences of Officials and Academics. Here they could talk not as country representatives or political appointees as at the IMF meetings, but as individuals whose identities were closely guarded. This chapter explores the meetings that followed from the publication of *Maintaining and Restoring Balance in International Payments*, and begins with a discussion of the Bellagio

Group Joint Meetings as a social interest NGO, then discusses the Joint Meetings themselves. The timetables of IMF, Group of Ten and Bellagio Group/Joint Meetings of Officials and Academics are also compared. The chapter concludes with a discussion of the impact of the Joint Meetings in setting adjustment policies and establishing the ground rules for the initial distribution of special drawing rights (SDRs), as the special reserve assets came to be called, and of the increasing Europeanization of the Joint Meetings.

The Bellagio Group Joint Meetings as a Social Interest NGO

Machlup made the point often in his private correspondence and his publications that this was a non-governmental group. As the United Nations first used the term non-governmental organization in 1950, the intention was to distinguish governments from private, non-profit organizations that were independent of governments.[1] Hildy Teegen, Jonathan Doh and Sushil Vachani defined NGOs as 'private, not-for-profit organizations that aim to serve particular societal interests by focusing advocacy or operational efforts on social, political and economic goals, including equity, education, health, environmental protection and human rights'.[2] Classifying NGOs in terms of the benefits they provide, Teegan et al. distinguished between membership NGOs and social purpose NGOs. The Joint Conferences fall into the latter because the group promoted a broader social interest. The Joint Conferences are a hybrid of advocacy and operational NGO, providing to the deputies of the Group of Ten an opportunity to think critically and candidly without fear of political repercussions. The expertise and reputation of the academics facilitating the Joint Conferences put them in a trusted position vis-à-vis the Group of Ten, the greater IMF and the world of corporate executives and private sector bankers to whom the conference model would later be extended.

Social NGOs are created to fulfil unmet needs, even to fix what is broken in existing management systems.[3] Membership in the deputies of the Group of Ten was by appointment and political: the governors and their deputies belonged to the leading political party in the country they represented. Nevertheless, the deputies were functional experts who were increasingly tasked with major projects and expected to work together – sharing ideas, compromising and otherwise behaving like members of a cohesive team – even as their respective governments took divergent positions on the same issues. As Teegen et al. acknowledged: 'Unlike democratically elected governments, which are accountable to their citizens, and firms, which are accountable to their owners and shareholders, NGOs serve diverse principals … and operate in environments that provide them with relative "immunity from transparency"'.[4] The Joint Conferences permitted participants to 'wear many masks, try on many hats', as Fritz Machlup would say in his introduction to the group at the first Joint Conference in 1964. Machlup would strive to keep the names of officials participating in these conferences out of print. Research into the conference files among the Fritz Machlup papers in the Hoover Institution allowed the production of a spreadsheet of the officials and academics who attended each of the eighteen conferences held between 1964 and 1977, the country represented and the institution of employment. See Appendix: Table 9.1 Joint Meetings of Officials and Academics, 1964–77. Machlup would write:

> I have avoided saying that the national and international monetary authorities were 'represented' by the officials participating in our conferences. The officials represented only themselves and spoke in the capacity of specialists, not as spokesmen for their governments or agencies. This, indeed, was the great advantage of our conferences over the intergovernmental meetings, in which some of the most important issues were 'out of bounds' or 'off limits'. The officials were not supposed to discuss certain questions 'officially', but they could discuss them as members of a 'seminar' chaired by an academic economist responsible to no one.[5]

In contrast, the IMF fits Michael Barnett and Martha Finnemore's bureaucratic universalism pattern: 'Bureaucrats necessarily flatten diversity because they are supposed to general universal rules and categories that are, by design, inattentive to contextual and particularistic concerns. Part of the justification of this ... is the bureaucratic view that technical knowledge is transferable across circumstances ... [when] particular circumstances are not appropriate to the generalized knowledge being applied, the results can be disastrous'.[6]

Bureaucracies 'establish rules to provide a predictable response ... in ways that safeguard against decisions that might lead to accidents and faulty decisions. Over time, small, calculated deviations from established rules may become the norm'.[7] According to Ngaire Woods (2000), 'In the IMF there were originally very few categories of decision for which special majorities applied. But, decisions taken in 1969 and in 1978 increased the number of categories from nine to 64'.[8] Normalized deviation explains the IMF's increasing use of voting majorities, like the 85 per cent voting majority that effectively gave the United States (or the European delegation, depending on one's perspective) a veto over the adjustment of quotas, establishment of councils and (important to this discussion) the allocation of SDRs. In 1977, this majority was extended to include political decisions as well.[9] The deputies of the Group of Ten were, however, largely drawn from the EEC countries. Of the 125 Joint Conference participants listed in Appendix Table 9.1, 56 per cent were from Europe, a handful from countries other than the Group of Ten. While the individual countries of the EEC were engaged in economic cooperation and problem solving, an early legitimating strategy Erik Eriksen and John Fossum characterized as 'the problem solving regime',[10] the deputies of the Group of Ten, by virtue of their collective tasks and need to compromise, sought and achieved a 'deeper sense of unity and community' based on shared values.[11] By the mid-1960s, the USA was seen to have too much influence in the IMF, as was clear from Emminger's objections as head of the European Monetary Committee to the Triffin Plan, which would have invested more power in the IMF as a lender of last resort.[12] Throughout 1964–9, when they were tasked with exploring solutions to the adjustment problem and the need for special reserve assets, the Joint Conferences would devote a significant part of the agenda and discussion (where notes taken by Walter Salant allow us a feel for the flow of conversation) on assigning responsibility for deficit, focusing on what the USA and UK needed to do to reform. By the time of the second Basle conference in 1977, sponsored by the BIS, Machlup reported that the European officials had asked him for 'new faces from the academic community ... fewer Americans and more Europeans.'[13]

The Joint Conferences of Academics and Officials

In the period 1964–9, Joint Meetings of Officials and Academics would focus on balance of payments adjustment and later special reserve assets to achieve payments adjustment. From 1970 to 1977, discussions would focus on the increasing liberalization of the international capital market and the wisdom of special drawing rights for developing countries. The archived notes on conversations would suggest that for this group of predominately European officials and academics, the most important issues were identifying who was responsible for payments imbalance, the roles of surplus as well as deficit countries, and the rules and regulations necessary to keep payments balanced – far more so than additions to liquidity. The Joint Meetings tended to precede meetings of the Fund as well as, increasingly, planned discussions between the executive directors of the Fund and the deputies of the Group of Ten. While distribution of special reserve assets to all IMF members was recommended in the July 1966 deputies report to the Ministers and Governors of the Group of Ten, the discussion of extending the distribution of special reserve assets beyond Group of Ten countries was added to the Joint Meetings of Officials and Academics agenda only in 1970. It appears that the inclusion of the executive directors of the Fund at the deputies meetings forced issues that the European deputies were uncomfortable with or thought marginal to their real concerns.

After the publication of *Maintaining and Restoring International Payments Balance*, a third joint meeting of the IMF's executive directors and the deputies of the Group of Ten was held in Washington, DC on 24–6 April 1967. Two illustrative schemes were considered: reserve policy inside the existing system and an entirely new reserve policy. Following the meeting, agreed answers still had to be found for: 1) the decision-making process; 2) rules for the use, transfer and acceptability of the new reserve; 3) the nature of the resources backing the new reserves, and whether such reserves would be merged with or separated from other reserves of the Fund; and 4) whether there would be any reconstitution or repurchase provisions linked with the prolonged or extensive use of the new reserve assets. In May 1967, Otmar Emminger prepared an 'Outline of a Reserve Drawing Rights Scheme' for consideration by the deputies. In May–June, during a meeting of the deputies, the US delegation, in an effort to pull together the results agreed on so far, submitted two papers on reserve creation. The Fund staff prepared new drafts and shared them with Emminger. Consensus appeared to be building on some of the features a final outline should have.[14]

A fourth joint meeting of executive directors and the deputies of the Group of Ten was held in Paris in June 1967. It had become clear that some EEC countries preferred drawing rights (which implied credit obligations), rather than reserve units (which might be considered new money and a substitute for gold). Some agreement was reached on the relationship between the reserve and gold (the reserve would have a gold-value guarantee) and interest (the reserve would earn interest). How participants would use reserves was agreed: use was to be for balance of payments needs only. It was agreed that two subjects be referred to the ministers and governors of the Group of Ten: the provisions for reconstitution, i.e. payback of used reserves, and for the voting majorities that would be necessary to create liquidity.[15]

Later in the same month, a Joint Meeting of Officials and Academics was held at Bellagio to discuss: 1) the payments imbalance between the United States and Europe; 2) capital movements between the United States and Europe, and the implications of the role of the USA as a world banker for the reforms now under negotiation; and 3) the influence that deliberate creation of new forms of reserves would exercise upon the balance of payments policies of the reserve currency countries and of the European countries. Gottfried Haberler urged the group to consider the problem of gold guarantees to secure the continued overhang of dollars. Milton Gilbert pointed out a conundrum: doesn't the shortage of new gold contribute to US payments deficits? Given the European six demand that the USA get into equilibrium before any reform of the system takes place, is this impossible given the shortage of new gold? Van Lennep added that he thought it urgent that the USA and Europe resume talks about their respective responsibilities in the case of payments imbalance. Another point raised by Fellner and some others was the consequences to be foreseen in the event of total or partial failure to reach agreement in time, and the measures that might still be envisaged to avoid the worst and to enhance chances for a later resumption of cooperative efforts to reach agreement.[16] At the conference itself, each participant was given no more than five minutes to identify what policies were needed to 'Reduce or Remove the Deficit in the US Payments Balance'.

From Reserve Assets to Special Drawing Rights: Link to Gold

The Ministers and Governors of the Group of Ten met in London twice and the deputies met several times between July and August 1967 to discuss voting procedures and reconstitution obligations under what were now being called 'special drawing rights', given the desire articulated by Giscard d'Estaing that the potential for increased liquidity be expressed in terms of credit, not owned reserves. After considerable discussion, the ministers and governors agreed that decisions on the basic period for, timing of, and allocation rate for special drawing rights should be taken by the Board of Governors of the IMF by a majority of 85 per cent of the total voting power.[17] Given that Europe's share of the voting power within the IMF at the time was 17.5 per cent, this effectively allowed the European members to own the decision. The ministers and governors agreed as well that the process for allocating special drawing rights would be complicated, involving the managing director, executive board, consultation with countries and the board of governors, and that participants would incur reconstitution obligations according to rules that would be specified in the Rules and Regulations of the Fund rather than put into the amended articles.

In September, the IMF Annual Report of 1967 devoted a whole chapter to developments in world reserves. At the Fund's Annual Meeting in Rio de Janeiro in the same month, the board of governors adopted a resolution, to which was attached the 'Outline of a Facility Based on Special Drawing Rights in the Fund', requesting the executive directors to submit no later than 31 March 1968 a report proposing amendments to the Articles of Agreement and By-Laws.[18] A Joint Meeting of Officials and Academics was also held in Rio in September 1967. Only the names of the attendees remain.

In December, the Fund's executive board considered a draft amendment to the Articles of Agreement and a related report to the board of governors.[19] The ministers and governors of the Group of Ten met in Stockholm in the early spring of 1968 to resolve their differences on ten points still at issue. They approved a draft amendment to the Articles of Agreement.[20] In April the Executive Board adopted the report 'Establishment of a Facility Based on Special Drawing Rights in the International Monetary Fund and Modifications in the Rules and Practices of the Fund', and recommended the board of governors adopt a resolution approving the amendment. The board of governors did so without meeting, effective 31 May 1968.[21]

Following closely on the March gold crisis, the next Joint Meeting of Officials and Academics occurred in May 1968 in Bologna to discuss: 1) the current and prospective problems arising from the devaluation of the pound, the gold rush, the US and UK programmes, etc.; (2) the short-term and medium-term proposals relating to the Rio agreement and other possible national and international agreements regarding the co-existence of the various forms in which reserve assets are or could be held (gold, reserve claims in the Fund, 'traditional' and other types of foreign exchange holdings, etc.); and 3) a longer-run view of alternative reserve systems and adjustment mechanisms.[22] We know from Machlup's few notes on this conference that he introduced to the group his proposed techniques for bringing about adjustment without demand deflation in the USA or demand inflation in the surplus countries – that is, via the introduction of a 5 per cent band of exchange rate flexibility and universal reserve pooling, at least by the major countries, depositing both their gold reserves and their currency reserves, apart from working balances in stipulated amounts, with an international agency such as a settlements account of the IMF. As a result, the participating nations would hold neither gold nor dollars in their monetary reserves, but only IMF certificates (or IMF deposits) and SDRs and DRs in the General Account of the Fund. Afterwards it would be easy to arrange for periodic adjustments or continual flexibility of exchange rates: a) by stipulated rules; b) by negotiations; or c) by market mechanism. He also introduced the idea of cutting the official link between the dollar and gold by terminating both sales of gold to official holders of dollars and purchases of gold from official holders of gold. Machlup noted that this would be tantamount to a suspension of the US obligation under the Fund agreement, since the USA could not replace its gold-price peg with exchange-rate pegs. The measure would also leave the decision about the dollar exchange rate to other countries; they would have to decide whether a) to accumulate inconvertible dollars at the present fixed rate; b) to buy and sell inconvertible dollars at a reduced price – say 5 or 10 per cent less than at present; c) to leave the exchange rate to the free foreign exchange market, either without any interventions or with official sales and purchases only a limit prices, or d) to establish a two-price system for the dollar with strict exchange controls, fixing the present exchange rate for current account dollars and lower rates for capital account dollars. (Note that alternatives a, b and c would all be agreeable to the USA. Only alternative d would be deplorable, for the USA as well as for all other countries, including those introducing the controls.)

The Link between SDRs and Development Finance: Floating Rates and the Role of Gold

At a meeting in Torremolinos in March 1970, the topic of the international capital market was narrowed to a discussion of the Eurodollar market which had seen explosive growth in the 1960s, EEC monetary integration, the link between SDRs and development finance, capital movements and other non-monetary disturbances. Again the discussion of the link between SDRs and development finance was the focus of the Joint Conference in Taormina in January 1971. US participants Frederick Deming and Dewey Daane, as well as van Lennep and G. A. Kessler of the Netherlands, had been in favour of SDRs for all countries. Kessler's paper, 'Should Development Aid Be Linked to SDR Creation', was presented. Kessler argued for the link; Professor Nino Andreatta of the University of Bologna argued against it.

By the Vienna meeting of 1973, after Germany had floated and the USA had gone off gold, the agenda had four major areas. Questions of exchange rates and the role of gold reflected the fact that things had changed, but no one knew whether the changes were permanent.

The Basle meeting of 1977 reflected a changed world. As Machlup would write, 'The agenda for the meeting [is] almost dictated by the present international monetary situation: the two main themes for discussion will be "Managed Floating" and "International Liquidity". It has been proposed however that we start with a general discussion of current imbalances in world payments, of the issue of adjustment versus financing, and of the advisability of expansionary policies in the countries with the strongest balances of payments'.

Emminger, van Lennep and Rene Larre requested that the meeting immediately follow the governors' meeting at the Bank for International Settlements, and in preparation for the interim committee report due March or April, for 'it would surely be wrong to hold the Bellagio meeting after they have made up their minds. If we can make a contribution it would be by having several members – or their deputies – of the interim committee in our discussions'.[23] It was at this meeting that for the first time the officials sought to limit the US academic group and increase the number of European academics invited. Machlup was uncomfortable with the request, but suggested that the invitations be issued by the funder, for the first time not the Ford Foundation but the Bank for International Settlements.

The Basle meeting of 1977 was the last meeting of the Joint Meetings of Officials and Academics. By 1978 a new group had been assembled with funding from the Rockefeller Foundation, under the leadership of Geoffrey Bell, formerly an adviser to the Banque of Venezuela and head of his own consulting firm. In October 1978 Machlup wrote to Emminger, Rene Larre and van Lennep to discuss their thoughts about the meaning of the new venture for the Bellagio Group:

> The purpose of this letter is to ask for your opinion as to whether the new group should be considered a kind of successor to the Bellagio Group, the Joint Conference of Officials and Academics on International Monetary Reform, and whether the Bellagio Group should therefore be considered dead; or whether I can inform my colleagues of the Bellagio Group that we are still alive and may become active again whenever you or other officials think that another meeting should be planned.

It can be argued ... that the new group does not supersede the Bellagio Group: 1) Its scope is wider in that it is concerned also with other than monetary questions, for example, trade policies and development policies. 2) Its membership is different in that it includes commercial bankers and other practitioners (like our old Bürgenstock Group and does not include the 'Deputies' except Dr Emminger). 3) Its method of operation is different in that the meetings will be supported by commissioned papers rather than by informal on-the-spot and off-the-cuff presentations. On the other side it can be said that there may be no need for two groups with overlapping membership and overlapping interests.[24]

In the end it came down to a new funding opportunity, secured because of the promise of a group with a stronger representation of developing and emerging market countries. Machlup and other members of the Joint Meetings of Officials and Academics would be among the original members.

The Impact of the Joint Meetings of Officials and Academics

The Joint Meetings of Officials and Academics played an important role in the history of adjustment policy recommendations, and in the case of special reserve assets (or SDRs as they came to be called) a limiting role, given the fear that SDRs would be used by deficit countries like the USA to delay adjustment and support a profligate lifestyle. The limited distribution of SDRs from the outset reflected those fears. While SDRs were originally envisioned as a means of alleviating a shortage of international reserves, or maintaining confidence in the convertibility of US dollar-denominated foreign exchange assets into gold, the suspension of gold convertibility, elimination of par values and development of international credit markets during the 1970s eliminated the role of SDRs in helping to maintain gold convertibility. Nevertheless, other aspects of SDRs became more salient, including reserve supplementation, reserve refinancing, and an alternative to international financial markets when the creditworthiness of individual countries or confidence in the system as a whole is in crisis. While distributions had been limited until 2009 (when SDR holdings/allocations rose from 21 billion to 204 billion), SDRs remain a potential source of cost-less, lower-risk, owned (rather than borrowed) reserves[25] – an existing system that might still be further modified to create the kind of 'supernational' currency envisioned by China's central banker Zhou Xiaochuan.[26]

Figure 9.1 depicts the timeline of conferences and deliverables from the first Bellagio conference to the first allocation of SDRs in 1970.

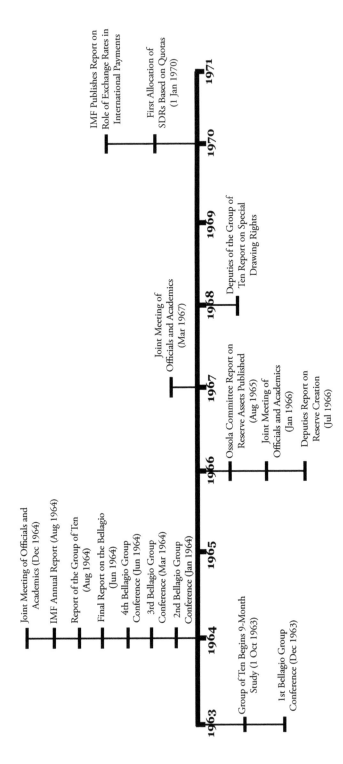

Figure 9.1: Bellagio Group and Joint Meetings of Official and Academics in International Monetary History, from First Bellagio Group Conference to First Allocation of Special Drawing Rights (SDRs). Source: Author's own research.

Conclusions

The Joint Meetings of Officials and Academics reflected the decision of the deputies of the Group of Ten both to separate themselves from the IMF as a whole, and to meet separately from the executive directors of the Fund to formulate their own platform on issues of balance of payments adjustment, SDRs and the inclusion of developing countries in the allocation of SDRs. We have argued here that the Joint Conferences of Officials and Academics preceded the required submission of major reports promised by the deputies to the ministers and governors of the Group of Ten. Further, the Joint Meetings of Officials and Academics also tended to precede meetings of the deputies and executives of the IMF. Harold James and others have argued that the move to separate meetings reflected the increasing Europeanization of the deputies of the Group of Ten. The research presented here supports that argument and demonstrates where these separate meetings took place, who organized them, what was on the agenda, and – for the first time – who attended these meetings. The data suggests as well that the deputies were often far from ready to reach the agreement on issues necessary to satisfy the IMF executive directors. Meeting together, the executive directors doubtless sought to reach faster closure on key issues and to identify next steps. At the Joint Meetings of Officials and Academics, there was far more open-ended discussion and seldom a neatly packaged set of recommendations and conclusions. In that respect, the Bürgenstock conferences (an extension of the Bellagio Group model to include bankers and corporate executives) would be closer in format to the original Bellagio Group conferences. The Bürgenstock conferences are discussed in Chapter 10.

Appendix

Table 9.1: Joint Meetings of Officials and Academics, 1964–77

Official/Academic	Country	INSTITUTION	12–64 Bel	1–66 Zur	4–66 Prin	3–67 Bel	6–67 Bel	9–67 Rio	5–68 Bol	9–68 Prin	3–69 Lug	9–69 Prin	3–70 Torr	1–71 Taor	9–71 DC	3–72 Cas	1–73 Vien	2–74 Vers	1–75 Basle	3–77 Basle
Adler, John H.	USA	IBRD																		
Andreatta, N.	Italy	University of Bologna																		•
Claassen, E.	France	Université Paris-Dauphine													•					
Barilla, Umberto	Italy	Banca d'Italia																	•	
Barre, Pierre	Belgium	CEE, Brussels								•										
Bennett, Jack	USA	Asst. Treas. Sec. Intl. Mon. Af.												•						
Bergsten, Fred	USA	Economist, IMF													•					
Bourginat, M.	France	Université de Bourdeaux																		•
Brossolette, M.	France	Treasury, Paris		•												•				
Bryant, Ralph	USA	Federal Reserve																		
Carli, Guido	Italy	Banca d'Italia					•	•	•											
Conti, Suzanne	UK	London School of Economics					•			•										
Cooper, Richard	USA	Yale			•		•			•	•	•	•		•	•	•	•	•	•
Daane, Dewey	USA	Federal Reserve			•					•	•	•	•			•	•	•	•	
Dale, William	USA	IMF	•							•	•	•	•			•	•		•	
De La Giroday, Boyer	France	CEE, Brussels									•						•	•		•
De Larosiere, J.	France	Banque de France																	•	
De Lattre, Andre	France	Finance Minister, FR	•																	
De Strycker, C.	Belgium	Nat. Bank of Belgium									•									
De Wilmars, Mertens	Belgium	Nat. Bank of Belgium	•						•							•		•		
Deguen, Daniel	France	Banque de France															•			
Deif, Nazih	Egypt	IMF Exec. Director															•			

Official/Academic	Country	INSTITUTION	12-64 Bel	1-66 Zur	4-66 Prin	3-67 Bel	6-67 Bel	9-67 Rio	5-68 Bol	9-68 Prin	3-69 Lug	9-69 Prin	3-70 Torr	1-71 Taor	9-71 DC	3-72 Cas	1-73 Vien	2-74 Vers	1-75 Basle	3-77 Basle
Dell, Sidney	UK	UN, Tariffs and Trade													●					
Delectenhove, Albert Kervyn	Belgium	University of Louvain									●									●
Deming, F.	USA	US Treasury	●	●	●	●	●	●	●	●										
Devries, Thomas	Belgium	CEE, Brussels	●	●	●	●	●	●												
Dornbusch, Rudiger	Germany	MIT																		●
Dow, J. C. R.	UK	OECD	●	●												●	●			
Elliott, George P.	USA	University of Syracuse	●			●	●													
Emminger, Oscar	Germany	Deutsche Bundesbank	●	●	●	●	●		●	●	●	●	●	●		●	●	●	●	●
Fellner, William	USA	Yale	●	●	●	●				●	●	●	●	●		●	●	●	●	●
Figgures, F.	UK	Treasury, London		●							●									
Fleming, J. Marcus	UK	IMF	●	●	●	●	●		●	●	●	●	●	●		●	●	●	●	
Frenkel, Jacob	Israel	U. of Chicago																		●
Fried, E.	USA	White House Staff; later Brookings													●					
Friedman, Milton	USA	U. of Chicago							●	●	●					●				
Giersch, Herbert	Germany	U. of Saar		●	●	●	●				●								●	●
Gilbert, Milton	USA	BIS		●	●	●	●	●	●	●	●	●	●	●	●	●	●	●	●	●
Gocht, Rolf	Germany	Ministerial Dir, Bonn																		
Gutowski, Armin	Germany	Kreditanstalt fur Wiederaufbau																		
Haberler, Gottfried	USA	Harvard	●	●	●	●	●		●	●	●	●	●	●	●	●	●			
Harrod, Sir Roy	UK	Oxford	●	●	●	●	●		●											
Hiss, Dieter	Germany	Fed. Ministry for Economy and Finance																		
Hood, William C.	Canada	Asst. Dep. Minister Finance								●										
Horie, Shigeo	Japan	Bank of Japan					●												●	

Official/Academic	Country	INSTITUTION	12–64 Bel	1–66 Zur	4–66 Prin	3–67 Bel	6–67 Bel	9–67 Rio	5–68 Bol	9–68 Prin	3–69 Lug	9–69 Prin	3–70 Torr	1–71 Taor	9–71 DC	3–72 Cas	1–73 Vien	2–74 Vers	1–75 Basle	3–77 Basle
Houthakker, H.	USA	Harvard													•					
Hovey, Mrs Arthur	USA	Yale University			•								•		•	•	•		•	
Inamura, Koichi	Japan	Ministry Finance, Tokyo					•										•		•	
James, Emile	France	University of Paris				•											•			
Jayawardena, Lal	Sri Lanka	Ministry Planning and Employment, Sri Lanka																		
Joge, Sven	Sweden	Sveriges Riksbank	•																•	•
Johnson, Harry	USA	U. of Chicago				•		•	•	•	•	•		•	•	•	•	•	•	•
Kafka, Alexandre	Brazil	IMF											•			•	•	•	•	•
Kashiwagi, Y.	Japan	Finance V. Min., Toyko						•		•	•		•			•	•		•	•
Keller, Pierre	France	Lombard Odier & Cie.																		
Kenen, Peter	USA	Columbia U.	•			•		•	•	•	•	•		•	•	•	•	•	•	•
Kessler, G. A.	Netherlands	De Nederlandsche Bank															•	•	•	•
Kindleberger, Charles	US	MIT				•	•													
Lamfalussy, Alexandre	Belgium	Banque de Bruxelles		•																
Larre, Rene	France	IMF, BIS					•		•						•					
Lawson, R.W.	Canada	Bank of Canada			•															
Luening, Otto	USA	Columbia U.					•													
Leutwiler, F.	Switzerland	Swiss National Bank															•		•	
Lundberg, Erik	Sweden	Stockholm S. of Economics															•		•	•
Lutz, Friedrich	Switzerland	U. of Zurich	•	•		•				•	•	•		•	•	•	•	•	•	•
Machlup, Fritz	USA	Princeton	•	•		•		•	•	•	•	•	•	•	•	•	•	•	•	•

Official/Academic	Country	INSTITUTION	12-64 Bel	1-66 Zur	4-66 Prin	3-67 Bel	6-67 Bel	9-67 Rio	5-68 Bol	9-68 Prin	3-69 Lug	9-69 Prin	3-70 Torr	1-71 Taor	9-71 DC	3-72 Cas	1-73 Vien	2-74 Vers	1-75 Basle	3-77 Basle
Magnifico, Giovanni	Italy	Banca d'Italia																	•	•
Mangone, Gerard	USA	University of Syracuse					•													
Marris, Stephen	UK	OECD																•		•
Maude, Evan W.	UK	IMF							•											
Mayakawa, Hauro	Japan	Bank of Japan											•						•	
Mcmahon, Christopher	UK	Bank of London									•	•					•			
Meade, James	UK	Cambridge U.				•		•												
Mikesell, Raymond	USA	University of Virginia																		
Mitchell, Derek	UK	IMF								•	•	•	•		•		•		•	
Morse, Jeremy	UK	IMF, Committee of 20																		
Mosca, U.	Belgium	CEE												•						
Mundell, Robert	Canada	McGill U.															•			
Neild, Robert	UK	Adviser, Treasury, Britain																		
Neufeld, E.R.	Canada	Bank of Canada				•	•	•	•	•	•	•	•	•					•	
Niehans, Jurg	Switzerland	U. of Zurich		•																
Oort, C.J.	Netherlands	Treasurer-Gen, Holland		•																
Ossola, Rinaldo	Italy	Banca d'Italia	•	•		•	•	•	•	•	•		•	•		•	•			
Palamenghi-Crispi, Francesco	Italy	IMF			•											•	•			
Parsons, Maurice	UK	Bank of England			•															
Patel, I. G.	India	Indian Ministry of Finance																		
Perez-Guerrero, Manuel	Venezuela	UN, Tariffs and Trade; Sec'y Gen., UNCTAD																		•

Official/Academic	Country	INSTITUTION	12–64 Bel	1–66 Zur	4–66 Prin	3–67 Bel	6–67 Bel	9–67 Rio	5–68 Bol	9–68 Prin	3–69 Lug	9–69 Prin	3–70 Torr	1–71 Taor	9–71 DC	3–72 Cas	1–73 Vien	2–74 Vers	1–75 Basle	3–77 Basle
Perouse, M.	France	Treasury, Paris		•															•	
Pohl, Karl Otto	Germany	Deutsche Bundesbank		•	•															
Polak, Jacques	Netherlands	IMF			•			•					•	•						
Rawlinson, Anthony	UK	Her Majesty's Treasury													•					
Reuss, Henry	UK	US House of Rep.		•			•			•	•		•	•		•	•			
Rickett, Sir Dennis	UK	Treasury, London	•	•	•					•	•		•	•		•	•			
Roosa, Robert	USA	Brown Brothers Harriman																•		
Rota, Giorgio	Italy	IBRD	•																	
Rueff, Jacques	France	Conseil Economique												•						
Salant, Walter	USA	Brookings Institute		•					•	•	•	•	•	•	•	•	•		•	
Salin, Pascal	France	Université de Paris-Dauphin									•	•	•	•		•	•			
Schleiminger, G.	Germany	Deutsche Bundesbank																		
Schmitz, Wolfgang	Austria	Austrian Nat. Bank		•															•	
Scitovsky, Tibor	USA	U. of California														•	•			
Segre, C.	Belgium	CEE, Brussels; Lazard Freres					•		•	•	•	•								
Sohmen, Egon	Germany	Alfred Weber Institute											•	•	•	•	•		•	
Solomon, Robert	USA	Federal Reserve																		
Stein, Herbert	USA	Council of Economic Advisers																		•
Stone, John	Australia	IMF Exec. Director																		
Stutzel, Wolfgang	Germany	U. of Saarbrucken					•													
Swoboda, A.	Switzerland	Grad. Institute of International Studies										•								
Szefzel, Marc	USA	U. of Washington	•																	
Tobin, James	USA	Yale		•						•										

Official/Academic	Country	INSTITUTION	12-64 Bel	1-66 Zur	4-66 Prin	3-67 Bel	6-67 Bel	9-67 Rio	5-68 Bol	9-68 Prin	3-69 Lug	9-69 Prin	3-70 Torr	1-71 Taor	9-71 DC	3-72 Cas	1-73 Vien	2-74 Vers	1-75 Basle	3-77 Basle
Travers, Harry	France	OECD		•	•	•	•	•	•	•	•	•	•	•	•	•	•	•	•	•
Triffin, Robert	Belgium	Yale		•															•	
Thygesen, Niels Christopher	Denmark	University of Copenhagen			•	•								•					•	•
Van Lennep, Emile	Netherlands	Treasurer-Gen, Holland	•	•	•	•	•		•		•		•	•		•	•	•		
Van Ypersele, J.	Belgium	Pres, Monetary Com'tee								•		•								•
Volcker, Paul	USA	Treasury, DC									•									
Wallich, Henry	USA	Yale											•	•		•	•	•	•	•
Weber, Hans Herbert	Germany	IMF											•	•		•	•			
West, Robert L.	USA	Rockefeller Foundation		•																
White, Howard	USA	New School					•													
Whitman, Marina	USA	Council of Economic Advisers															•			
Willett, Thomas	USA	Harvard													•					
Williamson, John	USA	IMF													•	•	•	•		
Willis, G.	USA	Treasury Dept, DC	•													•	•		•	
Zijlstra, J.	Netherlands	Bank of Netherlands						•												

Legend: Bel – Bellagio; Zur – Zurich; Prin – Princeton; Lug – Lugano; Torr – Torremolinos; Taor – Taormina; Cas – Cascais; Vien – Vienna; Vers – Versailles.

Source: Author's own research based on Fritz Machlup Papers, copyright Stanford University.

10 FROM THE BELLAGIO GROUP TO THE BÜRGENSTOCK CONFERENCES

Introduction

Through 1967, the IMF and the Group of Ten continued publicly to insist that the prevailing system of fixed parities had worked well, and they showed no desire to consider greater exchange rate flexibility as a means to improve the international monetary system, having recently created special drawing rights (SDRs) on the IMF to address the liquidity problem. No success had yet been achieved in integrating the domestic monetary and fiscal policies of the members of the international monetary system, although currency convertibility at fixed exchange rates was expected. Nevertheless, behind the scenes and in academic circles, greater exchange rate flexibility had begun to gain traction.

Chapter 10 deals with the extension of the Bellagio Group model to a new audience. The focus of these meetings was the choice of exchange rate regime, particularly floating in a variety of guises. Like the first four Bellagio Group meetings, the Bürgenstock meetings were orchestrated by Machlup, using his tools for defining terms and sniffing out value judgements; the meetings also introduced the group to Machlup's variations on scenario analysis. Unlike the Joint Meetings of Officials and Academics, the agenda was firmly in his control. Like the first Joint Meetings around payments adjustment, the outcome of the Bürgenstock conferences was the publication of a book. This time, whether corporate, official or academic, every attendee submitted and actively revised his paper per Machlup's edits for publication in the Princeton University Press volume *Approaches to Greater Exchange Rate Flexibility* (1970). Chapter 10 begins with a discussion of scenario analysis and its fit with Machlup's Austrian economics background.

Scenario Analysis in the Literature

Scenario analysis attempts to capture the nonlinearity, complexity and unpredictability of turbulent environments, macroeconomic and corporate, by incorporating techniques for eliciting and aggregating group judgements. If this sounds very much like the nature of strategic planning itself, that is because the exploration of alternative futures has become important to strategic planning in governments as well as corporations. Linked to methods like Delphi (a non-quantitative forecasting method based on aggregated responses to a series of questions administered to a group of panellists who are experts in their respective fields), scenario analysis was used in 1944 for a US Defence Department project undertaken by the RAND Corporation. It was also used for cross-impact analysis, first pioneered at General Electric by Ian Wilson in the 1950s: a complex technique sometimes performed by hand, sometimes by computer, that plots future changes across the column headings left to right, specific corporate activities down the rows of the first column, and inserts into each row – across what is essentially a grid or matrix – an entry for anticipated impact of decision making. Herman Kahn and Anthony Wiener (1967) constructed similar matrices to compare hypothetical sequences of events, in order to focus attention on causal processes and decision-points, and designed to answer two kinds of questions: 1) how might some hypothetical situation come about, step by step; and 2) what alternatives exist, for each actor, at each step, for preventing, diverting or facilitating the process, facilitating preparedness and flexibility in the face of high-velocity environments.[1]

Machlup may have learned scenario analysis from contemporary planning literature. Certainly, the corporate banker and executive audience he sought to attract would have been familiar with the approach. There is, however, an established relationship between scenario analysis and strategic planning, and Austrian economists from Bohm-Bawerk and Menger to Mises and Hayek. The connection has received attention from Robert Jacobson (1990, 1992), Brian Loasby (2002), Joseph Salerno (2006), Nicolai Foss (2007) and Peter Klein (2008).[2] Paul Aligica (2007) found the roots of scenario analysis in the methodological individualism and uncertainty of Menger, Mises and Hayek.[3] John Proops and Paul Safonov (2005) tracked the use of alternative futures to Bohm-Bawerk at the turn of the century, arguing that the Austrian approach was significantly different from the dominant neo-classical approach in that the former is empirically oriented, so the prime aim is to represent activities observed rather than preconceptions about human behaviour and human motivation.[4] Fritz Machlup's model was designed not to put the assumptions of economic theory to empirical test, but only the predicted results that are deduced from them, empirically verifying the results by observed data.

Purpose of the Bürgenstock Conferences

In 1968, Machlup again applied for funding from the Ford Foundation for two and possibly more conferences to explore a number of enhanced flexibility options – including a wider band of permissible fluctuations of exchange rates around established parities, and those for permissible small and frequent changes in parities, limited to 2 or 3 per cent per year, described under the name of gliding or crawling pegs. In a letter to the Ford Foundation, Machlup argued that a growing body of opinion on both sides of the Atlantic looked to a greater use of exchange rates to help smooth international payments imbalances. The alternatives – excessive deflation or inflation of national economies and controls over international transactions – are often undesirable because of their costs in terms of other national and international objectives. Large discreet changes permitted under the present rules of the game were seldom used because they generated big disturbances, while smaller, more frequent adjustments seemed to be a more reasonable route. There remained reluctance among practitioners to place the entire adjustment on exchange rates by allowing them to fluctuate freely, but there was serious interest in exploring the possibility of letting rates play a significantly greater role. Economists, on the other hand, had come to the view that limited flexibility was the best way to resolve the issue. Machlup emphasized that recent monetary crises made it clear that the continued evolution of the international monetary system was necessary for both economic and political reasons.

This time, Machlup proposed to combine academic economists (most of whom had been attendees of the Bellagio Group conferences) and officials (some of whom had attended the Joint Meetings) with a group of practitioners drawn from international corporations, including many international banks, active in foreign exchange dealings.

The first conference was planned to discover the extent to which support for the principles of the 'band' existed, and to aim at identifying the problems that needed to be resolved. Specific topics would be assigned to individual participants. The second conference would be devoted to intensive discussion of the resulting papers (and previously distributed papers), some of the conclusions regarding the desirability of official adoption of the 'band', and how the various problems which might arise could be resolved.

A compendium of the papers, possibly together with some of the dialogue at the conference itself, could then be published. Machlup suggested that the first chapter of such a publication would be of great use to government officials dealing with the problem. The first chapter might be an overall statement of the desirability of official adoption of the 'band' – if indeed such a conclusion was ultimately reached – perhaps signed by as many of the conference participants and other leading authorities in the field as would wish to be associated with it.

In a letter of invitation to the first Bürgenstock conference, Machlup wrote, 'We understand that the staff of the IMF is about to embark on a study of these same problems and that parallel studies by non-governmental specialists will be considered very helpful. We may in fact wish to invite a few observers from the IMF and some member governments.'[5] The signatories of the letter (and the editors of the final volume) were Fred Bergsten, a visiting fellow at the Council on Foreign Relations; George Halm and Fritz Machlup, members of the original Bellagio Group; and Robert Roosa, now a partner at Brown Brothers Harriman. Each would also play an active role in facilitating conference discussions.

Preparation for the First Bürgenstock Conference

In preparation for the first conference, Machlup commissioned a poll of industrial, banking and government-services firm leaders by Emil Kuster, senior vice president of J. Henry Schroeder Banking Corporation, and George H. Chittenden, senior vice president of Morgan Guaranty Trust. Five questions were asked:

1. In your international financial operations, have you experienced problems or difficulties that can be ascribed primarily to the system of fixed change rates?
2. Do you feel that a different system allowing for wider fluctuations or for periodic and systematic increases or decreases in parities would facilitate your operations?
3. Would you prefer a system allowing wider trading ranges?
4. Would you prefer a system in which demonstrably overhauled currencies would be devalued fractionally over a period of time, and demonstrably undervalued currencies would be revalued fractionally over a period of time (the 'crawling peg' concept)?
5. Would you prefer a system with no fixed parities, based on floating rates?

The initial response to all five questions was an overwhelming 'no'. But this status could change dramatically as a result of rigorous conference discussion. The comments of survey participants supported the conclusion that most had only begun to think about these questions. Pollsters Kuster and Chittenden drew several major conclusions from the survey results:

1. The mentality of the business community is worth appraising by academic and market operators alike. That mentality would seem to be sophisticated, deeply concerned, susceptible to persuasion that changes are necessary, but highly suspicious of fairy-tale formulae, the application of which to their practical problems is difficult for them to see.
2. Any scheme for reform should be based on a profound understanding not only of the existing system, how it works and why it falters, but also of the mass mentality of those involved in international commercial and financial affairs who use, and perhaps abuse, the system. One cannot wisely design a new race track for Sammy to run on until one understands what makes Sammy himself run.

3. Businessmen are far more suggestible as to rational changes in the monetary system, and more freely disposed towards open-minded discussion of change, than:
   a. academics probably give them credit for; and
   b. central bankers and finance ministries have until very recently shown themselves to be.
4. These thoughts suggest that a conference group composed of equal parts bran (academics), oats (market operators) and hay (corporate financial officials) might be highly productive.

The first conference, held at Oyster Bay, Long Island on 29–31 January 1969, sought to identify reasons for differences of opinion, to clear up misunderstandings and to develop a convergence of views among the fifteen practitioners and twenty academics attending. The second meeting was held at Bürgenstock, Switzerland on 22–8 June 1969, this time with twenty practitioners and eighteen academics from ten different countries. Table 10.2 (Appendix) presents the list of attendees at all five Bürgenstock conferences.

Importantly, Machlup's intention was not only that academics and practitioners should present their views at the conferences, but also that their papers should be published by the Princeton Finance Section. They were published in 1970 under the title *Approaches to Greater Flexibility of Exchange Rates: The Bürgenstock Papers*, arranged by C. Fred Bergsten, George Halm, Fritz Machlup and Robert Roosa, and edited by George Halm. Understanding the potential impact they had on public policy, most of the practitioner conferees sought also to publish versions of their work in professional journals.

Setting the Ground Rules for Scenario Discussion

Machlup opened the first conference with a talk on the definition of terms, later published as *On Terms, Concepts, Theories and Strategies in the Discussion of Greater Flexibility of Exchange Rates* (1970). 'Since a great deal is said in the current discussions about pegs and parities, we ought to decide whether we understand these words to mean the same thing or different things'.[6] Again, speaking about alternative exchange rate systems, he argued:

> It will be helpful to have terminological consistency in talking about alternative exchange systems ... To be sure there can be systems that prescribe, by unchangeable legal requirements, fixed ratios between the supply of money and the official gold holdings (with an unchangeable price of gold). Such orthodox gold-standard systems would be comparable with unchangeable exchange rates, but could endure only if the people in the countries concerned were willing to forget about stable rates of employment, economic growth, and several other national objectives. It is a waste of time to discuss this theoretical possibility. Whether we like it or not it is not in the cards. This reduces the choices to three: jumping, gliding or no parities.[7]

About flexibility, Machlup wrote: 'Flexibility is often confused with instability. This is understandable since, if flexibility is the opposite of inflexibility or rigidity, it means that it permits variations, and wide variations represent instability ... History tells us little about the relationship between flexibility and instability of exchange rates. Of course, many countries had very unstable rates in periods when they had flexible rates, but in these periods flexible rates would not have worked at all. History provides examples of very stable flexible rates, and many examples of very unstable rates fixed and refixed over time ... Confusion between flexibility and instability must not be tolerated.'[8]

John H. Watts, a banking executive with Brown Brothers Harriman, took notes on the discussion of each alternative. In all of the conferences Machlup convened, notes were kept on only two occasions: during the Zurich conference of 1966 and during the first Bürgenstock conference of 1969. The notes give us a feeling for the conversation – how animated it was, who contributed – that is missing unless there was a memoirist, like Robert Triffin, who wrote about the first four Bellagio Group conferences in 1978. A bit of the conversation appears here.

Scoping the Problem

Machlup opened the first conference with a talk on the definition of terms and the need for clarity. He then put up a 2 × 2 matrix for the discussion of nine scenarios for exchange rate flexibility, including unmanaged and managed rates with unlimited and limited variability and with varying degrees of discretionary action by national authorities, international agreement or fixed formula.

Table 10.1: Variations on the 'Band' Proposal

	Unlimited Variability	Limited Variability	
		Around Parity	At Parity
Unmanaged	Freely flexible (floating)	Intervention at edges only	n/a
Managed	a. by discretion of national authorities b. by international agreement c. by discretion of interest authority	Intervention within band also	a. by discretion of national authorities b. by international cooperation c. by fixed formula

Source: Machlup's notes from first Bürgenstock conference, January 1969; author's own figure.

At the outset, the group began with several questions about classification. Professor Erik Lundberg asked if 'passive' intervention could be judged simply from the size and direction of reserve changes. Several European conference members noted that the close relationship between central banks and government made this kind of intervention more difficult to track. Swiss banker Max Ikle observed that as long as the dollar is exchangeable into gold, it cannot be considered to be 'managed'. George Chittenden of Morgan Guaranty Trust then asked if the intention of the group was to assume a continuation of the dollar-gold relationship. Professor Harry Johnson responded that there were two systems to consider: one in which gold is the numeraire and other currencies move, perhaps in terms of a key currency, but finally with respect to gold; and two, without gold or any non-currency numeraire. Stephen Marris of OECD and Robert Roosa of Brown Brothers Harriman then suggested the group assume first that the discussion be based on a continuation of the fixed gold-dollar relationship; later, the group could consider the implications of relaxing the assumption.

Machlup intervened to limit the scope of the problem: our task is to try to find an international currency technology that could improve the present degree of rate stability. Machlup then suggested that the group begin a series of individual opening comments, beginning with the bankers and businessmen, in alphabetical order. George Chittenden argued that he would vote for maintaining the system as is, having served world trade and investment well thus far. The only missing ingredient, in his view, was the lack of sufficient pressure on governments to accept the discipline of the system when its signals were contrary to domestic political desire. Disagreeing with Chittenden's claim that the current system was working well, IBM's Chief Economist David Grove said that the present resistance by officials to change had led to interventions, political stresses between countries and controls with more frequent and more disruptive crises, followed by illiberal controls. Seconding dissatisfaction with the present system, Marius Holtrop of Nederlandsche Bank noted that pressures to make appropriate internal corrections or to change the currency rate seemed to be stronger and more effective during times of crisis than during times of surplus, hence the system is asymmetrical.

Wider Bands, Limited Variability

Wider bands had limited appeal for the corporate participants. W. F. J. Batt of Westminster Bank argued that if currency bands were wider and important currencies could fluctuate by several per cent, bank customers would desire a much greater amount of forward cover, without which rates could skyrocket. More importantly, banks would be in the position of finding and matching buyers and sellers, difficult given their limited capacity for two-way forward exchange. Ake Lundgren of Scandinaviska Bank said there were two major discrepancies in the current system: first, that creditor countries do not hew to the rules, and wider bands might encourage deficit countries to react less quickly to inflation and impose an inflationary bias on the system; second, that wider bands would change the liquidity picture, with currency rate fluctuations tending to enlarge customs or border hurdles for trade, reducing the level of trade and contradicting the goals of the General Agreement on Tariffs and Trade. Donald Marsh of the Royal Bank of Canada agreed that forward markets might well be weak under wider bands, but in his experience with Canada's floating rate period of the 1950s, forward cover was not a problem, and many large firms did not have currency exposures. On the other hand, in the first quarter of 1968, under fixed rates, a real difficulty in providing forward cover occurred. Marsh suggested turning the emphasis around: instead of fixed rates with fluctuating reserves, the authorities would keep reserves at a fixed level and let rates float freely, the precise opposite of the Bretton Woods system, with International Monetary Fund oversight.

Bank of America's Van Vlierden said he was worried about widening the bands because trade was not the primary motivator in international transactions, but instead direct and portfolio investment were more dynamic. In his view, widening bands would create disproportionate demands for forward contracts and the present commercial banking system could not meet it. George Chittenden then commented that there was no pure speculation in the world's foreign exchange markets; instead, what appears to government officials and economists as 'speculation' is commercial banks running scared. David Grove countered that it should not be concluded from the problems in the present banking structure that wider bands would not work, but only that institutional changes might have to be made. Emil Kuster argued that there was also the possibility that the volume of foreign exchange transactions might shrink with wider bands if underlying trade shrank from greater uncertainty about exchange rates. Conference Co-Chairman Robert Roosa then summarized the discussion and invited the academics in the group to comment.

Floating Rates, Unlimited Variability

Focusing the group now on flexible exchange rates with unlimited variability, Machlup raised the question for discussion: if totally fixed currency rates are impossible, as they obviously are, how often should changes occur in different situations – on a ten-year frequency or daily? Where in this spectrum is the optimum for any country? Machlup asked the group to consider a second question: how would one go about effecting a transition from fixed rates to a system of 'gliding adjustments' or a wider band? And finally, he posed a third question: should peg adjustment be discretionary or based on a formula? Stephen Marris of Brookings asked whether more flexibility would be useful for the 'dilemma' case where the adjustment indicated for external equilibria is dysfunctional to internal economic needs: how would greater flexibility affect adjustment? Professor Mundell pointed out that part of the world moved with the economic centre of gravity, e.g. the USA, Japan and Latin America. Others like the UK and Germany do not or cannot so move and so their policies do not match. The problem is how to adjust for this mismatch. Central banks could conceivably run the entire monetary system, taking the uncertainty away, but the tendency in monetary management today is towards decentralization, so institutional change may be necessary and the problem would be how to get it. Professor Francis Bator commented that had it not been for the USA's unwillingness to correct its balance of payments, the country would have more controls on trade and funds and no foreign aid.

Managed Flexibility – Public Policy Impact

When Donald Marsh asked whether the foreign exchange rate was in fact a policy target, Professor Johnson put the question to the group: did they believe the exchange rate to be a relevant instrument for affecting the composition of the balance of payments, or was it to be used for hoodwinking the public into accepting other economic objectives? Dr Holtrup said that automatic peg ideas only invite intervention via other financial routes by authorities who are frustrated by automaticity. Robert Roosa agreed that asking governments to submit themselves to automatic exchange rate regimes was similar to asking them to subject themselves to a fixed gold standard: they would need to express their policy aims through other parallel means. Pushing forward, Machlup noted that economists had for years taken as given its imminence of collapse and, therefore, now accepted as undeniable the need for major reform in the present structure.

After some discussion about the politics of arguing effectively for modification of the present system, Fred Bergsten introduced a detailed summary of the headings that the group had discussed to date. The method of assigning papers to be presented at the next conference was then discussed. Conference attendees made their choice of topic, committing themselves to the research and preparation necessary.

The Second Conference: Reaching Consensus

The conference papers prepared by Bürgenstock members were presented and discussed at a follow-up conference in Bürgenstock, Switzerland. By the time the conference ended, the conferees had arrived at an unexpected consensus on smaller and more frequent exchange rate changes, by widening the range within which exchange rates respond to market forces and permitting a more continuous and gradual adjustment of parities.

The consensus statement appeared in the *New York Times* on Monday, 30 June 1969, in an article entitled 'Wild Flexibility in Rates Favored; Businessmen and Bankers from 10 Countries Back Elasticity in Exchange', under Edwin Dale's by-line. Dale had been a long-time media supporter of the Bellagio Group. Throughout the Bürgenstock conferences, media had been handled by

Fred Bergsten. The consensus statement also appears in the Foreword to the Bürgenstock volume. It read:

> There was a consensus that such changes when appropriate should take place sooner, and thus generally be smaller and more frequent, than during the past two decades.
>
> Following their analysis of all of the current proposals for change, some participants pointed toward a need for greater readiness by countries to adjust the established parities of their currencies within the existing framework.
>
> A majority favored widening the range (or 'band') within which exchange rates may respond to market forces may respond to market forces, and permitting a more continuous and gradual adjustment of parities ...
>
> Throughout the participants had in mind the need for improvements which would facilitate balance of payments adjustment in ways consistent with the domestic objectives of Governments and the elimination of many restrictions on trade, current payments and capital movements.[9]

The statement also clarifies that Bürgenstock participants were neither government officials nor central bankers and that they participated as individuals, not as representatives of their school, organization or firm. This was standard operating procedure for the Bellagio Group model: allowing individuals to feel free to try on 'new hats, new masks' was crucial to the examination of problems and the consideration of solutions.

During the second half of 1969, the papers prepared for the conference, or as a result of it, were assembled for editorial work with a view to publication. In preparation, a brief meeting of some of the conferees was held in October 1969 at the Brookings Institution in Washington in connection with the annual meeting of the IMF.

Publication of *Approaches to Greater Flexibility of Exchange Rates: The Bürgenstock Papers*

The volume of collected papers was published by Princeton University Press in 1970 as *Approaches to Greater Flexibility of Exchange Rates: The Bürgenstock Papers*, edited by George Halm and 'arranged by' Bergsten, Halm, Machlup and Roosa. The papers made the case for and against variations of exchange rate flexibility, and dealt with the practicalities and problems of implementation, the effect of greater flexibility on the forward market and the experience with flexible rates of Canada, Germany, Switzerland and Sweden. A final section dealt with taxation and a critique of Roosa's paper, which had likened government loss of control when confronted with flexible rates with a corporation making a foreign investment decision.

The book opened with a set of papers by the editors that made the overall case for change. Also included in that group was Stephen Marris of Brookings.

Among the contributions, George Halm's essay 'Toward Limited Flexibility of Exchange Rates' identified the rationale behind flexible and fixed rate prejudices and explored the range the flexible solutions. The most insightful part of his essay is the set of questions he raised that make the case for change: If the present system were working adequately, why the repeated monetary crises? Why should it be justifiable to violate the principles of market economy in the area of foreign exchange? Why must it be taken for granted that international monetary cooperation will cease with flexible rates? Could a wider band combine the discipline of fixed rates with sufficient flexibility within the band?[10]

Robert Roosa's paper 'Currency Parities in the Second Decade of Convertibility' decried full and free flexibility. 'Such an approach implies an unworldly detachment on the part of governments and monetary authorities, from forces they are most reluctant to leave out of control.'[11] Even if 'managed money' had its pitfall, Roosa argued, 'they were found to be fewer than the hazards of relying upon the market to perform for the economy as a totality the kind of role that a market may quite rightly be expected to fulfill for the individual parts of the economy'.[12] Roosa accepted limited flexibility within 'a politically tolerable framework' as the solution 'that involves the least abrasive adaptation of present central banking practices and arrangements, including the IMF provisions themselves'.[13]

C. Fred Bergsten's essay 'The United States and Greater Flexibility of Exchange Rates' discussed the effects of more limited flexibility on the United States as a key currency country. Not only are there no overriding reasons why the United States should oppose greater flexibility of exchange rates, but 'greater flexibility of exchange rates would "bottle up" inflation or deflation to a greater extent within its country of origin, reducing the possibility that Europe would have to "import inflation" from the United States or that the United States could "export unemployment" to the rest of the world'.[14]

Stephen Marris's paper 'Decision-making on Exchange Rates' makes the case for limited flexibility. Marris looks at recent history (the devaluation of the pound and franc, the revaluation of the mark) to argue that large-scale changes in exchange rates have major impact on demand-management policies and on the level and distribution of income in the country concerned. Hence, governments are loath to act. Under a system of limited flexibility with small parity changes, there would be little risk of a chain reaction. 'It should become normal for a country's exchange rate policy to be examined regularly in the same way as its fiscal, monetary and other policies are already scrutinized in such international organizations as the IMF, OECD, the BIS and the institutions of the EEC'.[15] In the same year, Marris also published an in-depth review of the case for limited flexibility for Princeton Essays in International Finance.[16]

The case for greater exchange rate flexibility was made in part two by Harry Johnson, Gottfried Haberler, George Halm, Marius Holtrop, Herbert Giersch,

David Grove of IBM and John H. Watts of Brown Brothers Harriman. The papers of the two corporate representatives are particularly interesting. Grove explored the impact of a wider band on foreign direct investment through a series of cases or scenarios. Using a methodological approach similar to Machlup's partial equilibrium adjustment model, he concluded, 'By starting with an equilibrium situation under the present international monetary system, and then introducing departures from the initial position, and by doing the same for the proposed wider band, we conclude that, on balance, the greater flexibility in rates permitted by the wider band (or floating exchange rates without a band) would create considerably more favourable conditions for sound international investment. By "sound" we mean investment that moves mainly in response to the workings of a competitive price mechanism, under conditions that minimize uncertainties'.[17] IBM (like Shell and other companies dependent on massive amounts on R&D) had adopted a variety of methodologies, including scenarios and competitive options, to investigate alternative strategies, their benefits and risks. Within a wider band, Grove argued, 'speculators would be set against speculators, instead of all speculators ganging up against the central bank'.[18]

In 'The Business View of Proposals for International Monetary Reform', John H. Watts explored the impact of exchange rate fluctuations on types of firms, their geographic location and strength of national currency, as well as the type of transaction and the nature of markets for traded goods and degree of firm diversification. The approach provided some insight into the perceived and actual risk involved for business operations as well as trends. Watts concluded, 'The more serious risk to business ... is quite often not that of somewhat greater fluctuations in currency prices, but the risk of controls, higher tariffs, blocker currencies, and the possibility of monetary disintegration and international economic conflict. More and more businessmen consider the devaluations and fluctuations experienced from 1967 to 1969, bad as they were, to be less of a threat to profits than the trade and investment controls ... erected during the same period'.[19]

Peter Oppenheimer, Max Ikle, Antonio Mosconi, Giuliano Pelli, Emil Kuster and Richard Cooper make the case against exchange rate flexibility. Among these, Fiat's Mosconi, not otherwise listed as an attendee, defended his perspective that exchange rate flexibility is incompatible with the goals of the European Economic Community. In his 'Notes for the Bürgenstock Conference', Mosconi wrote, 'In the post-war period it has been possible to achieve a far wider ... international cooperation with more viable schemes for economic integration for specific multinational areas, such as the one set in motion in 1958 by the Treaty of Rome for the European Common Market – a process I should like to call irreversible. Fixed exchange rates (or exchange rates varying within the smallest possible limits, if need be) between the EEC currencies constitute the first step towards a common monetary policy'.[20] A system of greater exchange rate flexibility would 'jeopardize progress made towards a common monetary policy, a common administration of reserves and, ultimately, a common currency for the Six'.[21]

Mosconi continued to write on cooperation, a new Bretton Woods and the crisis of the international role of the dollar (2008) as well as on the need for a global currency (2010).[22] Importantly, most of the Bürgenstock conference participants had a paper published in this volume, including the corporate executives, who were also encouraged to publish their papers in journals important to their functional area. For example, David Grove, formerly with the IMF, had a substantial record of publication in finance on topics from Chilean inflation to monetary policy, plans for international liquidity, the dollar overhang and devaluation of the pound. Paolo Rogers of Olivetti wrote a paper on the impact of US foreign direct investment on the growth of European corporations.[23]

Collaboration with the IMF

Given the IMF had started their study on exchange rate policy solutions, Machlup planned a Joint Conference of officials, practitioners and academics at Arden House in upstate New York on 4–6 January 1970. All those who had participated in the Oyster Bay and Bürgenstock conferences were invited. Invitations were also sent to a number of officials. In a letter of 22 October 1970, Machlup would write to his Ford Foundation funders, 'The meeting was attended by forty-five persons – eighteen officials, seventeen practitioners and ten academic economists. That there was a plurality of officials testifies to the importance they attached to our discussions. Five central banks were represented, two of them by their governors, and three ministries of finance, all by high officials. The International Monetary Fund was represented by six directors and staff members'.[24]

A follow-up meeting was held in Tarrytown, New York on 4–6 February 1971, after the publication of the 1970 IMF study.

A Comparison of the Bürgenstock and IMF Study Results

The IMF Report entitled 'The Role of Exchange Rates in the Adjustment of International Payments', published 12 August 1970, reaffirmed the contribution of the existing par value system to monetary system stability. The main elements of Part II, titled 'Implications for Policy', included two statements about changes in the system. The executive directors rejected three alternative exchange rate regimes that had been proposed, including fluctuating exchange rates, wider margins and adjustment of par values at fixed intervals based on an automatic application of a predetermined formula. The directors thought the positive contributions of these regimes would be negligible and the disadvantages would outweigh any advantages.[25] However, the executive directors had also considered three ways in which additional flexibility might be introduced into the system, all of which would require amendment of the IMF Articles of Agreement: 1) prompt and small adjustments in par values in appropriate cases, say, 3 per cent in any 12-month period, or a cumulative amount of 10 per cent in any 5-year period, without the concurrence of the Fund; 2) a slight widening of the margins around par values from 1 to 2 or 3 per cent; and 3) temporary deviations from par values. Amendment of the Articles remained an open issue. In effect, the directors set forth the options for the IMF governors and left them to respond.[26]

At the IMF Annual Meeting in Copenhagen, 21–5 September 1970, the governors were not responsive to the suggested changes for more flexibility. Giscard D'Estaing argued for 'minimum flexibility and maximum stability', referring both to the world monetary situation and to the EEC's plan to move closer to economic and monetary union.[27]

In May 1971 six European countries took exchange rate action, including resorting to floating rates by the Federal Republic of Germany and the Netherlands. In August 1971, US authorities suspended the convertibility into gold or other reserve assets of dollars held by the monetary authorities of other countries.

Conclusions

This chapter focused on Machlup's expansion of the Bellagio Group approach to an audience of business leaders and bankers. For a methodologist like Fritz Machlup, methods shaped thinking and provided a lens for interpreting and making sense of data, and scenario analysis was a method that makes sense of alternative versions of events. Because Machlup redirected his Bellagio and Bürgenstock audiences to think of the adjusting changes in his model as the desired big picture outcomes – payments balance adjustment, liquidity and confidence – conferees left with a consensus view of reaching these desirables as quickly and painlessly as possible.

The absence of an adjustment mechanism and the failure to control international liquidity seemed to rule out multiple currencies and the semi-automatic gold standard for the Bellagio Group conferees, just as unlimited, unmanaged flexibility of exchange rates were effectively ruled out by the Bürgenstock conferees. Nevertheless, the dramatic reversal of thinking among the corporate executives at the Bürgenstock conferences – after rigorous discussion and commitment to research, write, present and re-edit for publication – is telling: 100 per cent against any change to the existing exchange rate regime at the start of the conference, and more than 75 per cent for flexible rates at its conclusion.

The disciplined exploration of alternative scenarios and their consequences for policy, management and institutional decisions prepared conferees for a range of contingencies – and the extent that conferees shared their experience with home audiences in academia, public policy and management assured the diffusion of scenario analysis based on assumptions about adjusting mechanisms.

Appendix

Table 10.2: Participants and their Affiliations, Five Bürgenstock Conferences

Participants	Affiliation	First Two Bürgenstock Conferences (Jan and Jun 1969)	Washington, DC (Oct 1969)	Tarrytown, NY (Jan 1970)	Arden House, NY (Feb 1971)
Nils E. Astrom	Skandinaviska Bank			•	•
Ludovico Barattieri	IMF				•
Francis M. Bator	Harvard University				•
W. F. J. Batt	Westminster Bank Ltd	•			
Paul Berger	Austrian National Bank			•	•
James Bergford	Chase Manhattan Bank	•		•	
C. Fred Bergsten	National Security Council	•	•	•	•
Carlos Bustelo	IMF				•
George Chittenden	Morgan Guaranty Trust	•		•	•
Richard Cooper	Yale University	•		•	•
J. Dewey Daane	Federal Reserve Board			•	
William Dale	IMF			•	
Tom De Vries	IMF				•
William Fellner	Yale University	•			
F. E. Figgures	UK Treasury			•	•
Richard G. Fisher	Brown Brothers Harriman				•
J. Marcus Fleming	IMF			•	
Michel Fribourg	Continental Grain	•			
Edward Fried	Brookings Institution	•	•	•	
Milton Friedman	University of Chicago	•			•
Genso Fujimoto	Bank of Japan			•	
Herbert Giersch	University of Kiel	•			•
Milton Gilbert	BIS			•	
Florio Gradi	Banca D'Italia			•	•
Armin Gutowski	Kreditanstalt fur Wieder-aufbau				•
David L. Grove	IBM	•		•	•
Pierre Haas	Banque de Paris et des Pays-Bas	•		•	
Gottfried Haberler	Harvard University	•		•	•
George Halm	Fletcher School, Tufts University	•	•		•
Fred Hirsch	IMF			•	•

Participants	Affiliation	First Two Bürgenstock Conferences (Jan and Jun 1969)	Washington, DC (Oct 1969)	Tarrytown, NY (Jan 1970)	Arden House, NY (Feb 1971)
Erik Hoffmeyer	Danmarks National Bank			•	
Marius Holtrop	Nederlandsche Bank	•		•	
Tadashi Iino	Mitsui Bank Ltd	•			
Max Ikle	Eidgenossische Bank	•			•
Harry G. Johnson	London School of Economics	•		•	
David J. Jones	Standard Oil of New Jersey	•		•	•
Alexandre Kafka	IMF			•	
Wolfgang Kasper	University of Kiel			•	
Peter Kenen	Columbia University	•			
Albert Kervyn	Universite catholique de Louvain	•			
John A. Kirbyshire	Bank of England				•
Lawrence Krause	Brookings Institution		•		•
Emil J. Kuster	J. H. Schroeder Banking Corp.	•		•	
Arthur B. Laffer	University of Chicago			•	•
Alexandre Lamfalussy	Banque de Bruxelles			•	
Rene Larre	Ministere des Finances, France			•	
Helmut Lipfert	Westdeutsche Landsbank Girozentrale	•			
Erik Lundberg	Stockholm School of Economics	•		•	•
Ake Lundgren	Scandinaviska Banken	•			
Friedrich Lutz	University of Zurich	•			
Fritz Machlup	Princeton University	•	•	•	•
Robert Marjolin	University of Nancy	•			
Stephen N. Marris	Brookings Institution	•	•	•	
Donald B. Marsh	Royal Bank of Canada	•	•	•	
Ronald I. McKinnon	Stanford University				•
James E. Meade	Cambridge University	•			
Derek Mitchell	IMF				•
D. H. McDonald	BIS			•	
Robert Mundell	University of Chicago	•	•	•	•
Maurice P. Omwony	IMF				•
Peter Oppenheimer	Oxford University	•			
Rinaldo Ossola	Bank of Italy				•

Participants	Affiliation	First Two Bürgenstock Conferences (Jan and Jun 1969)	Washington, DC (Oct 1969)	Tarrytown, NY (Jan 1970)	Arden House, NY (Feb 1971)
Francesco Palamenghi-Crispi	IMF				•
G. Pelli	Swiss Bank Corp.	•		•	
Edwin Reichers	First National City Bank	•	•	•	
Paolo N. Rogers	Olivetti	•	•	•	•
Robert Roosa	Brown Brothers Harriman	•	•	•	•
Wolfgang Schmitz	Austrian National Bank			•	•
David M Slater	Queen's University, Canada	•			
Egon Sohmen	Heidelberg University	•			•
Robert Solomon	Federal Reserve Board			•	•
Hideo Suzuki	IMF			•	•
Lars-Erik Thunholm	Scandinaviska Banken	•			
Merlyn N. Trued	Inter-American Development Bank	•			
Constant M. Van Vlierden	Bank of America	•		•	
Paul Volcker	US Treasury			•	
John H. Watts	Brown Brothers Harriman	•		•	•
Thomas D. Willett	Harvard University	•	•	•	

Source: Author's own research.

11 FROM THE BELLAGIO GROUP AND JOINT CONFERENCES OF OFFICIALS AND ACADEMICS TO THE GROUP OF THIRTY

Introduction

The last Basle meeting of officials and academics in 1977, funded by the Bank for International Settlements, was the final group meeting organized by Machlup, Triffin and Fellner. On several occasions in the early 1970s, there had been discussions at the Ford Foundation of the wisdom of continuing to fund Machlup's meetings after so many years.

In some important ways, including the early membership, the Group of Thirty (as the group would be called) was an extension of the Joint Meetings of Officials and Academics established by Fritz Machlup in 1964, but it was not a similar forum for private discussion.

In a paper written on the thirtieth anniversary of the Group of Thirty, Peter Kenen confirmed that the Bellagio Group so named would not meet again until 1996, when Andrew Crockett, the general manager of the Bank for International Settlements (BIS), asked Kenen to put together a meeting of academics, central bankers and officials from the finance ministries of the major industrial countries, as well as the chief economists of the BIS, the International Monetary Fund and the Organisation for Economic Co-operation and Development (OECD). The group continues under the leadership of Barry Eichengreen, professor of economics and politics at the University of California, Berkeley. It meets once each year and is financed by the participating central banks.[1] The Rockefeller Foundation, owner of the Bellagio estate, also uses the name Bellagio Group for the varied conferences and activities conducted there.

This chapter explores the creation of the Group of Thirty as the successor of the Joint Meetings of Officials and Academics, the assessment of its work by contemporaries, and the differences between the original Joint Meetings and the Group of Thirty.

Establishment of the Group of Thirty

Robert Roosa, formerly under-secretary of the US Treasury and now at Brown Brothers Harriman, had also become vice chair of the Rockefeller Foundation Board of Trustees. Roosa had been an active participant in the Bürgenstock conferences and had attended a few of the Joint Meetings of Officials and Academics. He was influential in steering a three-year grant to a new Consultative Group on International Economic and Monetary Affairs. Roosa's background and interests had focused on the US role and confidence in the dollar. The purpose of the Consultative Group (soon to be called the Group of Thirty or G30) was to explore basic problems involving the structure and functioning of the international economic system. The Group would commission a series of position papers on selected topics to be produced both by academics and by members of study groups, including Group members as well as outside experts. On the basis of these papers, the Group would hold discussions and clarify issues, leading to further analysis. By so doing, the Group hoped to help governments come to a better understanding of the means at their disposal to resolve some major international economic issues. Over the first three-year grant period, the Group planned to publish a series of papers from the commissioned studies and study group reports. The mission of the Consultative Group had expanded to the economy as a whole. In his feasibility study, Geoffrey Bell cited problems of slow growth around the world combined with high inflation, widely fluctuating exchange rates, growing scepticism about the effectiveness of exchange rates in correcting balance of payment imbalances and increasing fears of protectionism.

Johannes Witteveen, who had been managing director of the IMF until June 1978, was appointed chair of the Consultative Group. Peter Kenen, Marina von Neumann and Herbert Stein led the academic panel, which also included Carlos Diaz-Alejandro (Yale), Assar Lindbeck (Stockholm), Alan Deardorff (Michigan), Rudiger Dornbusch (MIT) and Alexander Swoboda (Geneva). Geoffrey Bell was elected executive secretary.

Six scholars were separately asked to develop a research agenda for the Group of Thirty. They were Ralph Bryant of Brookings, Robert Solomon of Brookings, Alexander Swoboda of Harvard, Armin Gutowski of Kreditantalt fur Wiederaufbau, Richard Erb of the American Enterprise Institute, Albert Fishlow of Yale and John Williamson of Pontificia Universidade Catolica do Rio de Janeiro.

A small group was formed around the experience to date of floating exchange rates using empirical data, with Dennis Weatherstone of Morgan Guaranty Trust agreeing to chair. Members were largely drawn from outside the G30, in the spirit of most study groups, and included Hubert Baschnatel of Swiss National Bank, Scott Pardee of the Federal Reserve Bank of New York, Herbert Evers of Marine Midland, Geoffrey Bardsley of Xerox, Richard Goeltz of Seagram,

Richard Fischer of the US Treasury, Richard Levitch of NYU and Geoffrey Bell. The study group's report 'Foreign Exchange Markets under Floating Rates' was published in 1980.

A study group on reserve assets, chaired by Johannes Witteveen, published a paper in 1980 on the substitution account, an account in the IMF wherein members could deposit their US dollars in exchange for SDRs. The paper was entitled 'Towards a Less Unstable International Monetary System'.

Another group was established within the first three years on the European Monetary System, with Alexandre Lamfalussy as chair. Members included Conrad Oort, treasurer-general of Holland, and Professors Peter Oppenheimer, Robert Triffin, Alexander Swodoba, Niels Thygesen and Ronald Vaubel.

Early Structure, Membership and Functioning of the Group of Thirty

In his paper 'The Group of Thirty at Thirty', Peter Kenen (2008) wrote that at the beginning 'the Group was managed by three bodies: ... a Board of Trustees, responsible formally to the Foundation for the proper use of its generous grant ... a Steering Committee, responsible for choosing the site and setting the agenda for the Group's meetings ... and an Academic Panel'.[2]

The full Group of Thirty met twice a year for two or three days at a time. Between the main meetings, study groups arranged for analysis and information to be collected for the main meetings. Special papers were commissioned, most with eventual publication in mind. With the Group's office in New York, executive director Robert Pringle, former editor of *The Banker* magazine, was the main organizer and a member of all the study groups. The general direction of the Group's activities was decided by a steering committee chaired by Geoffrey Bell. The early steering committee had eight members, all of whom were either Americans or Europeans (three Americans, three Englishmen).

Members of the group were handpicked in an informal way. Of the original thirty, seven were Americans and another three worked in the United States. 'Twelve were European, two were Japanese and six were from developing countries'.[3] Three international institutions – the OECD, IMF and BIS – were also represented among the early members. All the private bankers in the Group, with the exception of Dennis Weatherstone of Morgan Guaranty, had served in finance ministries or central banks at some time. This was considered to be an advantage in working with policymakers. In the early Group of Thirty, there were only two corporate leaders. Six members of the group were economists and five of these were American.

Over time the membership has grown to include members from all G20 nations. See Appendix: Table 11.1. The movement from central bank to private banking conglomerate remains a typical career track of Group of Thirty members.

Study groups opened up membership to non-Group members, often corporate executives in finance or economics. A decision was taken in the summer of 1979 that as a general rule authors of commissioned papers should not be invited to attend meetings, even though their papers were to be discussed. The reasoning presumably was that so many outside academic papers had been commissioned that initiations would have been too numerous. For the first three years there were four study groups:

Reserve assets and a multicurrency reserve system
Capital movements and LDC debts
International banking supervision and risk
Energy.

Early Assessment of the Work of the Group of Thirty

Three years after the Group of Thirty began (and likely prior to any decision to fund another three years), the Rockefeller Foundation asked Anthony Solomon, president of the Federal Reserve Bank of New York, and financial journalist Marjorie Deane to conduct independent assessments of the work of the Group of Thirty. In both cases, the reports drew on interviews with current group members.[4]

Among the key issues raised by Solomon's work were two distinct points of view held by members of the Group about the relationship between the Group of Thirty and the Bellagio Group. Some interviewees argued that the Group of Thirty should be in the tradition of the former Bellagio Group, where officials and academics spoke privately, intimately and in depth about questions of the organization of the international monetary system. From this viewpoint, the Group would be primarily a vehicle for informing and educating the members of the Group on major issues. The impact of the Group would be visible through the subsequent efforts and contacts the members would make in their normal jobs. Like the earlier Bellagio Group, the Group of Thirty would not seek to develop or publish a consensus view. Other interviewees saw the need for a Group consensus if there was to be an impact on the outside world, either on the public at large or on policymakers directly. The broad public impact could be achieved either by publications targeted to major issues and publicized fully in the press and elsewhere, or by direct and structured contacts with key policymakers in official positions.

There was some difference of opinion about the selection of issues. It made sense to start with international money issues, because that was the natural comparative advantage of many of the Group's members. After three years, and in a different world, should the Group 'stick to its knitting' or explore a broader range of issues? After all, the mission of the Group of Thirty had suggested the topics would include economic and financial issues. Closely related to issue selection was the time horizon of the Group's focus: should members focus on current topics under consideration in official circles, or pursue a longer-term focus? A case could be made that the Group had a unique opportunity to influence current discussions and negotiations, and should not dilute that position by becoming too much of a think tank. A third viewpoint stressed the importance of focusing on practical problems and practical solutions. The longer the time horizon, the more theoretical and less practical.

The Deane report also compared the Group of Thirty to the original and extended Bellagio Group (that is, the Joint Meetings of Officials and Academics). Interviewees acknowledged the value of lively discussions between the officials and academics to their own deliberations. Because there were no officials in the original Bellagio Group (the 1963–4 conferences composed of academics only), there was not the agonizing over wording of its report as there has been over Group of Thirty policy statements. The Joint Meetings of Officials and Academics were designed to get a two-way debate going between public and private sectors. But times had changed and the Group of Thirty was not just representative of the Group of Ten, but also of the third world. This is essential in today's changed conditions, but obviously makes policy statements more difficult. While the Bellagio Group's discussions were about fundamental international monetary reform, the Group of Thirty's task was less obvious, but even more challenging: how to live with the current system and make the best of it.

Furthermore, the Group of Thirty was broader than the Bellagio Group, including industrialists and private bankers – those who actually have to use the system or act as intermediaries; an advantage, if the Group of Thirty were to make use of their expertise.

The Deane report acknowledged many more opportunities in the 1980s than in the 1960s for officials and policymakers to get together with academics and businessmen. While most conferences and meetings were one-off affairs, even those that occurred more regularly were profit centres for their organizers or promotional vehicles for sponsors. The interviewees saw a distinct advantage for the Group of Thirty in conducting research studies on a continuing basis. Importantly, the second oil price shock had intensified problems in the world's economic and monetary systems. Could the Group of Thirty help identify and solve some of these problems?

Some members interviewed by Deane for her report said they feared the Group's discussions would parallel the official debate, with officials and ex-officials dominating them. Others – particularly the bankers – wanted more attention paid to the 'real' side of world economic development, such as the implications of the rapid growth in the trade of advanced developing countries, trade barriers or technology transfers. The latter suggested that the Group's potential seemed to lie in addressing itself to two types of questions: 1) What is actually happening in the financial markets and the recycling processes, what really is going on? 2) How should multinational institutions like the World Bank and IMF be re-shaped to serve the monetary system best over the next five to ten years?

All agreed that early reports had produced excellent results – the Weatherstone poll on how banks and multinational corporations cope with floating exchange rates was a good example of how the Group can put its resources to work to build a reputation for itself and its publications. Few if any members of the Group were interested in its visible profile. All felt that the chief usefulness of the Group was in the discussions rather than the publications.

The Solomon and Deane reports made some recommendations for change and continuance. While there was obvious merit to the concern about diluting the intimacy of the discussions, there was a responsibility, recognized in the original prospectus, that the Group share its thinking with others. With the public, this might be accomplished through published reports including minority reports to show the full sweep of members' thinking. With relevant officials in finance ministries and other official bodies, it can be done by seminars or informal meetings with members of the Group.

Study groups were recognized as central to the Group of Thirty. Different kinds of study groups should be supported. Study groups might be devoted to a specific issue with a short timetable for research and publication. Others might be a forum for continuing interchange between private and public sector professionals with an aim toward publishing policy analyses or statements. Still others might be deep dives into complex issues where publication was a lesser objective.

The Group had a definite advantage, particularly in the study groups, of promoting the information-gathering questionnaire approach that characterized the Weatherstone survey of foreign exchange market attitudes, and that was also central to other efforts already underway (in the areas of bank attitudes towards country lending and the currency denomination of international trade). By contrast, the Group did not have a strong advantage in commissioning academic papers and survey articles. There are other convenient outlets for papers on these issues to be published. Any academic commissioned work might well be made more empirical rather than general in their focus and closely tied to a specific issue of the Group's concern on which academic work does not exist.

Rotation of members was another recommendation, as was the inclusion of more observers to the core group meetings.

Solomon and Deane also recommended redefining the role of the executive director and questioned the ongoing need for a steering committee.

The Group of Thirty – Change and Renewal

Within the first three years, the Academic Panel had been abandoned. As a result of the consultants' reports, the Steering Committee was also abandoned, and its work transferred to the trustees, the executive director and the chairman of the Group.[5] Discussions in the Group's plenary sessions and in its publications showed an increasingly broad agenda – from the Latin American debt crisis and the Plaza Agreement of 1985, to the reunification of Germany, the collapse of the Soviet Union and further movements toward European Monetary Union.[6] Some thirty-four publications were issued between 1980 and 1985, some ten of these the work of G30 working groups. Sir Gordon Richardson replaced Johannes Witteveen as chairman of the trustees and chairman of the Group in 1985. Richardson was replaced by Paul Volcker in 1991 and Jacob Frenkel in 2001. Jean-Claude Trichet, former president of the European Central Bank from 2003 to 2011, was elected chairman of the Group of Ten in 2003. After 1985, the Group's funding no longer came from the Rockefeller Foundation, but was raised from financial institutions.

From 1985 to 2012, the Group of Thirty has published over a hundred studies, thirty-eight of these the products of G30 working groups. The study groups have included topics on the reform of the International Monetary Fund, financial reform, regulatory supervision and greater accounting standards. Papers prepared by members and outside experts have ranged from derivatives to debt, economic reform, the European Union, foreign direct investment, governance and trade, among others.

Conclusion

The Group of Thirty was a de facto successor to the Joint Meetings of Officials and Academics, but operating with a more formal structure and a larger budget. Unlike the Joint Meetings of Officials and Academics, where the focus was on the Group of Ten countries, the intention of the Consultative Group was to draw developing countries into the membership. Like the Joint Meetings of Officials and Academics, members of the core Group of Thirty included central banks and public officials. These included Otmar Emminger, president of the Bundesbank; Henry Wallich, governor, Federal Reserve Bank; Christopher McMahon, executive director, Bank of England; I. G. Patel, governor, Reserve Bank of India; Michiya Matsukawa, special adviser to the minister of finance, Japan; Jose Antonio Mayobre, former minister of finance, Venezuela; and Janus Fekete, deputy governor, National Bank of Hungary. International institutions were also represented: Alexandre Lamfalussy, economic adviser, Bank for International Settlements; Jacques Pollak, director of research, IMF; and Jawad Hashim, managing director, Arab Monetary Fund.

Unlike the Bellagio Group and the Joint Meetings of Officials and Academics, the academic cadre was limited. Core members included: Peter Kenen, professor of economics, Princeton; Fritz Machlup, professor of economics, New York University; and Marina Whitman, professor of economics, University of Pittsburgh. Members of research institutions were also included: Robert Soloman, Brookings Institution; Herbert Stein, American Enterprise Institute; Armin Gutowski, Kreditansdtalt fur Wiederaufbau, Frankfurt; Saburo Okita, chair, Japan Economic Research Centre.

Like the Bürgenstock meetings, bankers and corporate executives were part of the core group, including: Robert Roosa, Brown Brothers Harriman; Geoffrey Bell, director, Schroders; Claude Pierre-Brossolette, chairman, Credit Lyonnais; Andre de Lattre, president, Credit National; and Johannes Witteveen, adviser, Amsterdam-Rotterdam Bank. Dirk de Bruyne, vice chair of Shell International Petroleum and Jacque Maisonrouge, president of IBM World Trade completed this group.

Appendix

Table 11.1: All Group of Thirty Members, 1978–2012

Academic/Official	Title	Institution	Prior Bellagio Group Meetings (1963-77)
Ackermann, Josef	Chairman of the Management Board and the Group Executive Committee	Deutsche Bank AG	
Ahluwalia, Montek	Deputy Chairman, Planning Commission of India; Former Director, Independent Evaluation Office, International Monetary Fund	Government of India; formerly IMF	
Al-Hamad, Abdulatif	Chairman, Arab Fund for Economic and Social Development		
Aspe, Pedro	Former Minister of Finance	Government of Mexico	
Al Quraishi, Abdul Aziz	Former Governor	Saudi Arabian Monetary Agency	
Balcerowicz, Leszek	Professor, Warsaw School of Economics; Former President	Warsaw School of Economics, formerly Bank of Poland	
Bell, Geoffrey	Executive Secretary, Group of Thirty' President; Former Adviser	Group of Thirty; President, Geoffrey Bell & Company, Inc.; Banque of Venezuela	
Campos, Roberto	Former Brazilian Ambassador to the United Kingdom	Formerly Government of Brazil	
Carnegie, Sir Roderick	Former Chairman & Chief Executive	CRA Limited	
Carney, Mark J.	Governor and Chairman; Chairman	Bank of Canada; Financial Stability Board; Board of Directors, BIS	
Caruana, Jaime	General Manager; Former Governor	Bank for International Settlements; formerly Banco de Espana	
Cavallo, Domingo	Chairman and CEO; Former Minister of Economy	DFC Associates, LLC; formerly Government of Argentina	

Academic/Official	Title	Institution	Prior Bellagio Group Meetings (1963-77)
Corden, W. Max	Professor of International Economics Emeritus, School of Advanced International Studies	The Johns Hopkins University; also Professorial Fellow of Economics, University of Melbourne	
Corrigan, E. Gerald	Managing Director; Former President	Goldman Sachs Group, Inc; formerly Federal Reserve Bank of New York	
Crockett, Andrew D.	President; former General Manager,	JPMorgan Chase International; formerly Bank for International Settlements	
Debs, Richard	Former President; former CEO	Morgan Stanley International; formerly Federal Reserve Bank of New York	
de Bruyne, Dick	Former President	Formerly Royal Dutch Petroleum Co, London	
Martínez de Hoz, Jose **de la Dehesa Romero, Guillermo**	Former Minister of Economy Director; Former Deputy Director	Government of Argentina Grupo Santander; formerly Banca d'Espana	
Draghi, Mario	President; Former Governor; Former Chairman, FSB	European Central Bank; formerly Banca d'Italia; formerly FSB	
Dudley, William C.	President; Former Managing Director	Federal Reserve Bank of New York; formerly Goldman Sachs	
Emminger, Otmar	Former President; former chair of the deputies of the Group of Ten	Deutsche Bundesbank	Joint Meetings
Fekete, Janos	Former Vice President	National Bank of Hungary	
Feldstein, Martin	Professor of Economics, Harvard University; President Emeritus,	Harvard University; Formerly National Bureau of Economic Research	

Academic/Official	Title	Institution	Prior Bellagio Group Meetings (1963-77)
Fels, Gerhard	Former Director	Institut der Deutschen Wirtschaft	
Ferguson, Roger W.	President and CEO; Former Chairman, Swiss Re America Holding Corporation	TIAA-CREF; formerly Swiss Re; formerly Swiss Re America Holding Corporation	
Fischer, Stanley	Governor; Former First Managing Director	Bank of Israel; formerly IMF	
Fraga Neto, Arminio	Founding Partner; Former Governor	Gavea Investimentos; formerly Banco Central do Brasil	
Frenkel, Jacob	Chairman of the Board of Trustees, Group of Thirty; Chairman; Former Vice Chairman; Former Economic Counsellor and Head of Research Department	JPMorgan Chase International; formerly AIG; formerly Bank of Israel; formerly IMF	
Fung, Victor K.	Group Chair	Li & Fung	
Geithner, Timothy	President and Chief Executive Officer; Former US Under-Secretary of Treasury for International Affairs	Federal Reserve Bank of New York; US Treasury	
Greenspan, Alan	Former Chair	Board of Governors of the Federal Reserve	
Guth, Wilfried	Former Spokesman of the Board of Managing Directors	Deutsche Bank AG	Bürgenstock Joint Meetings
Gutowski, Armin	Former Professor of Political Economy,	University of Frankfurt, Germany	
Gyohten, Toyoo	President; Former Chair	Institute for International Monetary Affairs; formerly Bank of Tokyo	
Hashim, Jawad	Former Managing Director	Arab Monetary Fund, Abu Dhabi	
Häusler, Gerd	CEO, Bayerisch Landesbank; Former Managing Director and Member of the Advisory Board	Bayerisch Landesbank RHJ International; formerly Lazard and Company	
Heimann, John	Senior Adviser; Former US Comptroller of the Currency	Financial Stability Institute; US Treasury	

Academic/Official	Title	Institution	Prior Bellagio Group Meetings (1963-77)
Hildebrand, Philipp	Senior Visiting Fellow, Blavatnik School of Government, Oxford University; Former Chairman of the Governing Board, SNB	Blavatnik School of Government, Oxford University; formerly Swiss National Bank	
Hoffmeyer, Erik	Former Chair	Danmarks Nationalbank	Joint Meetings
Johnson, Thomas S.	Former Chair and CEO; Former President and Director	GreenPoint Financial Corp; formerly Chemical Bank	
Kenen, Peter B.	Professor of Economics and International Finance, Emeritus; Former Senior Fellow in International Economics	Princeton University; formerly Council on Foreign Relations	Bellagio; Bürgenstock; Joint Meetings
King, Mervyn	Governor; Former Professor; Fellow	Bank of England; formerly London School of Economics; The British Academy	
Krugman, Paul	Professor of Economics, Former Member	Princeton University; formerly Council of Economic Advisers	
Kurosawa, Yoh	Former Chair and CEO	Industrial Bank of Japan	
Lamfalussy, Alexandre	Former General Manager; Former General Manager	Bank for International Settlements; Banque de Bruxelles	Bellagio; Bürgenstock; Joint Meetings
Larosière, Jacques de	Conseiller; Former President; Former Managing Director; Former Governor	BNP Paribas; formerly European Bank for Reconstruction and Development; formerly IMF; formerly Banque de France	Joint Meetings
Lattre, Andre de	Former Deputy Governor; Former Finance Minister	Banque de France; Government of France	Joint Meetings
Loehnis, Anthony	Former Executive Director	Bank of England	
Machlup, Fritz	Former Professor, Department of Economics; Former Professor of Economics	New York University; formerly Princeton University	Bellagio; Bürgenstock; Joint Meetings

Academic/Official	Title	Institution	Prior Bellagio Group Meetings (1963-77)
Maisonrouge, Jacques	Former Chairman of the Board	IBM World Trade Corporation, Paris	Bürgenstock
Marris, Stephen	Senior Economist	Institute for International Economics; formerly OECD	Joint Meetings
Matsukawa, Michiya	Former Special Adviser to the Minister of Finance	Government of Japan	
Mayobre, Jose Antonio		Formerly Banco Central de Venezuela	
McDonough, William	Vice Chairman and Special Adviser to the Chair; Former Chair; Former President	Merrill Lynch; formerly Public Company Accounting Oversight Board; formerly Federal Reserve Bank of New York	
McMahon, Christopher	Former Executive Director	Bank of England	Joint Meetings
Ogata, Shijuro	Former Deputy Governor; Former Deputy Governor	Bank of Japan; formerly Japan Development Bank	
Okita, Saburo	Former Japanese Minister of Foreign Affairs	Government of Japan	
Olayan, Suliman S.	Former Chair	The Olayan Group	
Ortiz, Guillermo	President and Chairman; Former Governor; Chairman of the Board	Grupo Financiero Banorte; formerly Banco de Mexico; formerly Bank for International Settlements	
Ostry, Sylvia	Distinguished Research Fellow; Former Ambassador for Trade Negotiations; Former Head	Munk Centre for International Studies, Toronto; formerly Government of Canada; formerly OECD Economics and Statistics Department	
Pohl, Karl Otto	Partner; Former President and Chairman of the Central Bank Council	Sal. Oppenheim Jr. & Cie. KgaA; formerly Bundesbank, Germany	

Academic/Official	Title	Institution	Prior Bellagio Group Meetings (1963-77)
Padoa-Schioppa, Tommaso	Former Minister of Economy and Finance; Chairman; Former Member of the Executive Board; Former Chairman	Government of Italy; International Accounting Standards Committee; European Central Bank; formerly Commissione Nazionale per le Società e la Borsa	
Patel, I. G.	Former Governor	Reserve Bank of India	Joint Meetings
Pennant-Rea, Rupert	Former Deputy Governor	Bank of England	
Pierre-Brossolette, Claude	Former Chairman; Former Secretary General; Former Director of the Treasury	Credit Lyonnais; formerly Presidency of France; formerly Government of France	Joint Meetings
Polak, Jacques	Former Economic Counseller and Director of Research	IMF	Joint Meetings
Rajan, Raghuram G.	Professor of Economics; Economic Adviser to Prime Minister of India	Chicago Booth School of Business; Government of India	
Rhodes, William	Senior Vice Chairman; Chairman, President and CEO	Citigroup; Citicorp and Citibank	
Gordon, Lord Richardson of Duntisbourne, K. G.	Honorary Chairman, Group of Thirty; Former Governor	Bank of England	
Rogoff, Kenneth	Professor of Public Policy and Economics; Former Chief Economist	Harvard University; IMF	
Roosa, Robert V., Esq.	Former Partner; Former Undersecretary of the Treasury for Monetary Affairs	Brown Brothers Harriman; US Treasury	Bürgenstock
Ryrie, Sir William	Former Executive Vice President; Former Second Permanent Secretary of the HM Treasury	International Finance Corporation; formerly UK Treasury	Joint Meetings

Academic/Official	Title	Institution	Prior Bellagio Group Meetings (1963-77)
Shanmugaratnam, Tharman	Deputy Prime Minister and Minister for Finance and Manpower, Singapore; Chairman	Government of Singapore; formerly Monetary Authority of Singapore	
Shirakawa, Masaaki	Governor; Former Professor	Bank of Japan; Kyoto University School of Government	
Solomon, Robert	Senior Fellow; Former Member	Brookings Institution; Federal Reserve Board	Bürgenstock; Joint Meetings
Solomon, Anthony	Former President; Former Undersecretary of the Treasury for Monetary Affairs	Federal Reserve Bank of New York; formerly US Treasury	
Stein, Herbert	Former Senior Fellow; Former Chairman	American Enterprise Institute; Council of Economic Advisers, United States	
Stern, Ernest	Partner and Senior Adviser; Former Managing Director; Former Managing Director	The Rohatyn Group; formerly JPMorgan Chase; formerly World Bank	
Summers, Lawrence	Charles W. Eliot University Professor; Former Director; Former President; Former Secretary of the Treasury	Harvard University; formerly National Economic Council; formerly Harvard University; US Government	
Takagaki, Tasuku	Senior Adviser; Former Chairman of the Board	Bank of Tokyo-Mitsubishi, Ltd; Bank of Tokyo	
Trichet, Jean Claude	Chairman, Group of Thirty; Former President, ECB; Honorary Governor	Group of Thirty; formerly ECB; Banque de France	
Turner, Lord Adair	Chair; Member House of Lords	Financial Services Authority; UK Government	
Walker, David	Senior Adviser; Former Chair	Morgan Stanley International; formerly Securities and Investments Board	
Wallich, Henry	Member; Member; Professor	Federal Reserve Board; Council of Economic Advisers; Yale University	Joint Meetings

Academic/Official	Title	Institution	Prior Bellagio Group Meetings (1963-77)
Weatherstone, Dennis	President and Chief Executive	JPMorgan Chase	
Weber, Axel A.	Chair; Former Visiting Professor of Economics	UBS; formerly Chicago Booth School of Business	
Whitman, Marina v. N.	Professor; former member	University of Michigan; Council of Economic Advisers	Joint Meetings
Witteveen, Johannes	Former Managing Director; former Minister of Finance an member of Parliament; Economic consultant	IMF; Netherlands	
Volcker, Paul A.	Chairman Emeritus, Group of Thirty; Former Chair	Federal Reserve System	Bürgenstock
Virata, Cesar	Former Prime Minister; Former Finance Minister	Philippines	
Yamaguchi, Yutaka	Former Deputy Governor; Former Chair	Bank of Japan; formerly Euro Currency Standing Commission	
Yellen, Janet L.	Vice Chair, Board of Governors; Former President and CEO; Former Chair; Professor Emeritus	Federal Reserve; Federal Reserve of San Francisco; Council of Economic Advisers; University of California, Berkeley – Haas School of Business	
Zedillo, Ernesto	Director; Former President	Yale Center for the Study of Globalization; formerly Government of Mexico	
Xiaochuan, Zhou	Governor; Former President; Former Assistant Minister of Trade	People's Bank of China; Chinese Construction Bank; Foreign Economic Relations and Trade	

Source: Author's research based on Kenen (2008), Group of Thirty Website and other sources. Current members in **bold**.

Table 11.2: Publications of the Group of Thirty, 1980–2012

Year	Author	Title
1980	Alexander K. Swoboda	Credit Creation in the Euromarket: Alternative Theories and Implications for Control
	G30 Working Group	Exchange Rates, Domestic Prices and the Adjustment Process
	G30 Working Group	Foreign Exchange Markets Under Floating Rates
	Peter Kenen, Clare Pack	Towards a Less Unstable International Monetary System
	Alexander K. Swoboda	Views of Inflation in the United States
1981	G30 Working Group	Balance-of-Payments Problems in Developing Countries
	Jacques Polak	Coordination of National Economic Policies
	Edwin A. Deagle Jr, Bijan Mossavar-Rahmani, Richard Huff	Energy in the 1980s: An Analysis of Recent Studies
	Richard M. Levich	'Overshooting' in the Foreign Exchange Market
	Michael Mussa	The Role of Official Intervention
	William Fellner	Shock Therapy or Gradualism? A Comparative Approach to Anti-Inflation Policies
1982	Richard Dale	Bank Supervision Around the World
	Otmar Emminger	Exchange Rate Policy Reconsidered
	G30 Working Group	How Bankers See the World Financial Market
	G30 Working Group	How Central Banks Manage Their Reserves
	Courtney Blackman	Managing Foreign Exchange Reserves in Small Developing Countries
	G30 Working Group	Policy Choice and Economic Structure
	Robert V. Roosa	Reserve Currencies in Transition
	G30 Working Group	Risks in International Bank Lending
1983	M.S. Mendelsohn	Commercial Banks and the Restructuring of Cross-Border Debt
	Edwin A. Deagle, Jr	The Future of the International Oil Market
	G30 Working Group	The International Monetary Fund and Private Markets
	Henry C. Wallich, Otmar Emminger, Peter B. Kenen, Robert V. Roosa	World Money and National Policies

Year	Author	Title
1984	Robert V. Roosa	World Money and National Policies
	Marjorie Deane, Robert Pringle	Economic Cooperation from the Inside
	Henry C. Wallich	Insurance of Bank Lending to Developing Countries
	Joseph Kraft	The Mexican Rescue
	W. M. Corden	The Revival of Protectionism
	Peter B. Kenen	The Role of the Dollar as an International Currency
1985	Otmar Emminger	The Dollar's Borrowed Strength
	G30 Working Group	The Foreign Exchange Market in the 1980s
	Masaru Yoshitomi	Japan as Capital Exporter and the World Economy
	Hamish McRae	Japan's Role in the Emerging Global Securities Markets
	Helen Hughes	Policy Lessons of the Development Experience
1986	Polly Reynolds Allen	ECU: Birth of a New Currency
	R. H. Carnegie	Outlook for Mineral Commodities
	Robert V. Roosa	The United States and Japan in the International Monetary System 1946–1985
1987	Paul Krugman	Adjustment in the World Economy
	Richard A. Debs, David L. Roberts, Eli M. Remolona	Finance for Developing Countries
	Rudiger Dornbusch, Mario Henrique Simonsen	Inflation Stabilization with Income Policy Support
	Michiya Matsukawa	The Japanese Trade Surplus and Capital Outflow
	J. A. Kay	The State and the Market: The UK Experience of Privatization
1988	G30 Working Group	Clearance and Settlement Systems in the World's Securities Markets
	G30 Working Group	International Macroeconomic Policy Coordination
1989	David Henderson	1992: The External Dimension
	Masaru Yoshitomi	Japan's Savings and External Surplus in the World Economy
	John P. Hardt, Sheila N. Heslin	Perestroika: A Sustainable Process for Change

Year	Author	Title
1990	Douglas Croham	Reciprocity and the Unification of the European Banking Market
	G30 Working Group	Clearance and Settlement Systems: Status Reports, Spring 1990
	G30 Working Group	Conference on Clearing and Settlement Systems; London, March 1990, Speeches
	Wilfried Guth	Europe in the Nineties: Problems and Aspirations
	Tommaso Padoa-Schioppa	Financial and Monetary Integration in Europe: 1990, 1992 and Beyond
	Benjamin M. Friedman	Implications of Increasing Corporate Indebtedness for Monetary Policy
	Stephen H. Axilrod	Interdependence of Capital Markets and Policy Implications
	Hans Tietmeyer, Wilfried Guth	Two Views of German Reunification
1991	G30 Working Group	Clearance and Settlement Systems: Status Reports, Year-End 1990
	Gerhard Fels, Claus Schnabel	The Economic Transformation of East Germany: Some Preliminary Lessons
	Richard A. Debs, Harvey Shapiro, Charles Taylor	Financing Eastern Europe
	DeAnne Julius	Foreign Direct Investment: The Neglected Twin of Trade
	Sydney J. Key, Hal S. Scott	International Trade in Banking Services: A Conceptual Framework
	Guillermo de la Dehesa	Privatization in Eastern and Central Europe
	G30 Working Group	The Risks Facing the World Economy,
	G30 Working Group	The Summit Process and Collective Security: Future Responsibility Sharing
1992	Raymond Vernon	Are Foreign-Owned Subsidiaries Good for the United States?
	G30 Working Group	Clearance and Settlement Systems: Status Reports, Autumn 1992
	Peter B. Kenen	EMU After Maastricht
	Guillermo de la Dehesa, Paul Krugman	EMU and the Regions
	Geza Feketekuty	The New Trade Agenda
	Andres Bianchi, Domingo Cavallo	Sea Changes in Latin America
	Lawrence J. White	Why Now? Change and Turmoil in US Banking
1993	G30 Working Group	Derivatives: Practices and Principles
	G30 Working Group	Derivatives: Practices and Principles, Appendix I: Working Papers

Year	Author	Title
	G30 Working Group	Derivatives: Practices and Principles, Appendix II: Legal Enforceability, A Survey of Nine Jurisdictions
	E. Gerald Corrigan	The Financial Disruptions of the 1980s: A Central Banker Looks Back
	James A. Leach, William J. McDonough, David W. Mullins, Brian Quinn	Global Derivatives: Public Sector Responses
	Vaclav Klaus	The Ten Commandments of Systemic Reform
	Sylvia Ostry	The Threat of Managed Trade to Transforming Economies
	Tommaso Padoa-Schioppa	Tripolarism: Regional and Global Economic Cooperation
1994	Linda M. Hooks	Capital, Asset Risk and Bank Failure
	G30 Working Group	Derivatives: Practices and Principles Appendix III: Survey of Industry Practice
	G30 Working Group	Derivatives: Practices and Principles: Follow-up Surveys of Industry Practice
	G30 Working Group	Defining the Roles of Accountants, Bankers, and Regulators in the United States
	Robert Z. Lawrence	The Impact of Trade on OECD Labor Markets
	Hal S. Scott, Shinsaku Iwahara	In Search of a Level Playing Field: The Implementation of the Basle Capital Accord in Japan and the United States
	G30 Working Group	Latin American Capital Flows: Living with Volatility
	Erik Hoffmeyer	Thirty Years in Central Banking
1995	Guillermo de la Dehesa, Peter B. Kenen	EMU Prospects
	Sylvia Ostry	New Dimensions of Market Access
1996	Gerd Hausler	Derivatives and Monetary Policy
	Ulrich Cartellieri, Alan Greenspan	Global Risk Management
	David Folkerts-Landau, Peter Garber, Dirk Schoenmaker	The Reform of Wholesale Payment Systems and its Impact on Financial Markets
1997	Sylvia Ostry	A New Regime for Foreign Direct Investment
	Sydney J. Key	Financial Services in the Uruguay Round and the WTO

Year	Author	Title
	G30 Working Group	Global Institutions, National Supervision and Systemic Risk
1998	Andrew Crockett	Banking Supervision and Financial Stability
	Sir Andrew Large	The Future of Global Financial Regulation
	G30 Working Group	International Insolvencies in the Financial Sector
	Akio Mikuni	Japan: The Road to Recovery
	Sylvia Ostry	Reinforcing the WTO
1999	Ernest Preeg	Charting a Course for the Multilateral Trading System: The Seattle Ministerial Meeting and Beyond
	G30 Working Group	The Evolving Corporation: Global Imperatives and National Responses
	Felipe Larrain, Andrés Velasco	Exchange Rate Arrangements for the Emerging Market Economies
	Richard Clarida	G3 Exchange Rate Relationships: A Recap of the Record and a Review of Proposals for Change
	Richard Herring, Susan Wachter	Real Estate Booms and Banking Busts: An International Perspective
2000	Ruth de Krivoy	Collapse: The Venezuelan Banking Crisis of 1994
	Erik Hoffmeyer	Decisionmaking for European Economic and Monetary Union
	Charles Wyplosz	Exchange Rate Regimes: Some Lessons from Postwar Europe
	Tomasso Padoa-Schioppa	Licensing Banks: Still Necessary?
	G30 Working Group	Reducing the Risks of International Insolvency
2001	Tomasso Padoa-Schioppa	Explaining the Euro to a Washington Audience
	Lee Hsien Loong	Post Crisis Asia: The Way Forward
2002	Jaime Caruana, Andrew Crockett, Douglas Flint, Trevor Harris, Tom Jones	Enron et al: Market Forces in Disarray
	G30 Working Group	Key Issues in Sovereign Debt Restructuring
	Guillermo de la Dehesa	Venture Capital in the United States and Europe
2003	Marina V. N. Whitman	American Capitalism and Global Convergence

Year	Author	Title
	G30 Working Group	Global Clearing and Settlement: A Plan of Action
	Stanley Fischer	Implications of Basel II for Emerging Market Countries
	William J. McDonough	Issues in Corporate Governance
2004	Jacques de Larosiere	The Critical Mission of the European Stability Growth Pact
	Guillermo de la Dehesa	Is it Possible to Preserve the European Social Model?
	G30 Working Group	Enhancing Public Confidence in Financial Reporting
	Sylvia Ostry	External Transparency in Trade Policy
	G30 Working Group	Sharing the Gains from Trade: Reviving the Doha Round
2005	NONE	
2006	G30 Working Group	Global Clearing and Settlement: Final Monitoring Report
	Barry Eichengreen	International Currencies and National Monetary Policies
	Linda Goldberg, Cédric Tulle	The International Role of the Dollar and Trade Balance Adjustment
	G30 Working Group	Reinsurance and International Financial Markets
	Howard Davies	Two Cheers for Financial Stability
2007	Jacques de Larosiere	The Achievements and Challenges of European Union Financial Integration and Its Implications for the United States
	Liu Mingkang, Roger Ferguson, Guillermo Ortiz Martinez	Banking, Financial and Regulatory Reform
2008	Guillermo de la Dehesa	Nine Common Misconceptions About Competitiveness and Globalization
	E. Gerald Corrigan	The Credit Crisis: The Quest for Stability and Reform
	Thomas A. Russo	Credit Crunch: Where Do We Stand?
	Domingo Cavallo, Joaquin Cottani	Distorting the Micro to Embellish the Macro: The Case of Argentina
	Peter B. Kenen	The G30 at Thirty
	Eugene A. Ludwig	Lessons Learned from the 2008 Financial Crisis
	G30 Working Group	The Structure of Financial Supervision: Approaches and Challenges in a Global Marketplace

Year	Author	Title
2009	G30 Working Group	Financial Reform: A Framework for Financial Stability
	Stefan Ingves, Goran Lind, Masaaki Shirakawa, Jaime Caruana, Guilllermo Ortiz Martinez	Lessons Learned from Previous Banking Crises: Sweden, Japan, Spain, and Mexico
	G30 Working Group	Reform of the International Monetary Fund
2010	Guillermo de la Dehesa	Twelve Market and Government Failures Leading to the 2008–09 Financial Crisis
	G30 Working Group	Enhancing Financial Stability and Resilience: Macroprudential Policy, Tools and Systems for the Future
2011	Paul Volcker	Three Years Later: Unfinished Business in Financial Reform
	Alastair Clark, Andrew Large	Macroprudential Policy: Addressing the Things We Don't Know
	Thomas A. Russo, Aaron J. Katzel	The 2008 Financial Crisis and Its Aftermath: Addressing the Next Debt Challenge
	Thomas M. Hoenig	It' Not Over 'Til It's Over: Leadership and Financial Regulation
	Mark Carney, Paul Tucker, Philipp Hildebrand, Jacques de Larosière, William Dudely, Adair Turner, Roger W. Ferguson, Jr.	Regulatory Reforms and Remaining Challenges
2012	G30 Working Group	Toward Effective Governance of Financial Institutions

Source: Author's research, based on Group of Thirty website. Publications updated through July 2012.

12 REASSESSING THE BELLAGIO GROUP'S IMPACT ON INTERNATIONAL MONETARY REFORM

Introduction

There are significant parallels between the calls for monetary system reform in the 1960s and those for reform following the financial crisis of 2008–9. Efforts at reform continue into 2012. The system attributes (gold versus fiat, fundamentally fixed versus managed floating) are different, as is the size of the deficits, from 1 per cent or less in 1960 to over 10 per cent of GDP in the aftermath of the 2008–9 financial crisis. While no attempt has been made to revisit the numbers, the question of confidence in the system and the credibility of policymaker response has been everywhere in this book.

Whatever the value of hindsight provided by ex post analysis, there is no question that many policymakers and academic economists in the UA and Europe perceived a potential crisis for the dollar. Europe was already deeply engaged in building an external monetary policy to end dependency on the USA and the US dollar as the pivotal international currency, which involved reforming the international monetary system to base it on a neutral, non-dollar standard.[1] Some of the same economists who would become important to international monetary system reform as members of the so-called Group of thirty-two non-governmental economists (the Bellagio Group) were also involved in European integration, including Jacques Rueff, monetary economist and close adviser to French President Charles de Gaulle, and Pierre Uri, among the French; German economists Herbert Giersch, member of the Kiel Institute of World Economics, and Egon Sohmen; Belgian economists Alexandre Lamfalussy and Robert Triffin. Fourteen of the economists invited to join the Bellagio Group were émigrés from countries annexed or occupied by Germany in World War II. As Bellagio Group members Dupriez (1947) and Dieterlen (1948) would write in monographs published by the Carnegie Foundation for Peace, countries like Belgium and France literally had to pay fees to the National Socialists for 'administering' the occupation.[2] Did experience with authoritarian regimes influence their thinking about the USA, 'exorbitant privilege', adjustment policies and European integration?

By 1963, all of the Bellagio Group members were living and working in the Group of Ten countries, the countries that had signed the General Arrangements to Borrow, which committed them to protecting IMF member countries from financial crisis. Additionally, a number of the policy officials important to international monetary system discussions played key roles in European integration as well as in the extended Bellagio Group meetings (called Joint Meetings of Officials and Academics). Most significant among these was Otmar Emminger, chair of the deputies of the Group of Ten and president of the European Monetary Committee.

That every economist had a plan for monetary system reform – and that European policymakers were especially open to the potential contribution of academic economists – is not surprising given the high stakes and a European tradition that embraced academics. Chapter 12 seeks to evaluate the contributions to monetary system reform of Fritz Machlup and the Bellagio Group. It begins with the assessment of contemporaries engaged in the reform process, including Bellagio Group members and the chair of the deputies of the Group of Ten, and continues with an evaluation of the group by theorists and economic historians today, before turning to a self-assessment by the Bellagio Group founders. The chapter concludes with a review of the Bellagio Group's unresolved issues in light of today's financial crises.

Eyewitnesses to Reform and Recent Scholarship

Eyewitnesses to Machlup's efforts to bringing competing exchange rate policy advocates together for debate attribute both power and influence to his approach. Robert Triffin (1960) said that it was Machlup's influence over economists that turned the tide towards flexible rates.[3] Former historian of the IMF Margaret DeVries (1987) said that that it was Machlup and the Bellagio Group's focus on adjustment, liquidity and confidence that distinguished their arguments and made them so persuasive.[4] Machlup's contribution to framing the discussion in terms of adjustment, liquidity and confidence is echoed by Otmar Emminger:

> Machlup belonged to the group of economists who simplified the discussion on reform by clearly isolating three problems; 'adjustment', 'liquidity', and 'confidence', that is, 1) what to do in order to improve, and facilitate, the adjustment of persistent payments imbalances, 2) what to do in order to provide for an orderly increase in needed monetary reserves in the world and 3) what to do to prevent currency crises and massive destruction of international liquidity due to a loss of confidence in the reserve currencies.[5]

Emminger also noted that Machlup, like many other academic economists, thought that solutions to the problems of confidence and adjustment were more urgent than the problem of liquidity.

Richard Cooper, senior economist for the US Council of Economic Advisers and deputy assistant secretary of state for international monetary affairs, wrote: 'The "Bellagio Group" … exposed key central bankers to the evolution in academic thinking, and may have played some role in persuading central bankers that flexible exchange rates were workable, or at least would not be more troublesome than the fixed exchange rate system with which they were then having to cope'.[6] Robert Solomon, a member of the Federal Reserve and American representative on the Ossola Group of the Group of Ten, said of the work of the thirty-two economists of the Bellagio Group, 'One can discern [in their work] two areas of divergence from the content of the reports of the Group of Ten and the IMF. More stress was placed on the desirability of changing exchange rates as a means of balance of payments adjustment. And more concern was expressed about the instability that could arise from the "overhang" of foreign exchange reserves. (In general the report of the Bellagio Group holds up well in the light of subsequent developments)'.[7] Peter Kenen, a member of the Bellagio Group, recalled: 'At Robert Triffin's suggestion, I was invited to participate in the first meeting of what later came to be known as the Bellagio Group of officials and academics, chaired by Fritz Machlup of Princeton on the academic side and Otmar Emminger of the Bundesbank on the official side. The group met once or twice each year for more than a decade to discuss international monetary issues in an informal setting. The academics included William Fellner, Roy Harrod, Harry Johnson and Robert Mundell; the officials included Andre de Lattre, Kitt McMahon, Robert Roosa and Emile van Lennep. It was the most successful endeavour of its kind – I have been involved in several since – and contributed greatly to my education … In 1964, at a meeting in Bellagio, a group of economists prepared a report on the international monetary system. It identified three issues: adjustment, liquidity and confidence'.[8]

Triffin (1978) acknowledged the strong appeal of the ferreting out of assumptions (and values) underlying policy recommendations, as well as the defence and cross-examination approach of the Bellagio Group meetings:

> The assumptions and 'hunches about the future' brought out to explain and justify our recommendations were unsurprisingly predictable. Proponents of a semiautomatic gold standard or of unmanaged floating rates both distrusted government interference in economic life, but the former felt confident that downward price and wage adjustments could be enforced by proper monetary policies 'without undue hardship', while the latter stressed that downward price and wage adjustments would entail wasteful and intolerable levels of unemployment. National 'monetary sovereignty' was a favourite argument of the opponents of radical reforms as well as of the

proponents of flexible rates. Those favouring a centralization of reserves were more sceptical of the virtues of national sovereignty in an interdependent world, and more concerned about the ability of reserve currency centres to export their own inflation to the rest of the world.[9]

Importantly, Triffin, like Machlup, saw the Bellagio Group as advisers to policy-makers: 'Politics as the "art of the possible" should be left to them, but we should be particularly anxious to help those statesmen who view it also as the "art of making possible tomorrow what may still be impossible today"'.[10] Machlup's use of framing, scoping, scenarios and collaboration in all aspects of the conferences from discussion to drafting definitional statements and papers for publication are the elements in the strategic adviser's tool kit.

Emminger attributed to Machlup the consideration as early as 1968 of a scenario in which the United States might unilaterally sever the link between the dollar and gold in order to avert the threat of confidence crises. The scenario Emminger referred to appeared in Machlup's essay 'Remaking the International Monetary System: The Rio Agreement and Beyond', published as a book in 1968.[11] While Emminger saw the catalyst as the SDR, the catalyst for tabling the SDR in 1968 was the imposition by the US of mandatory capital movements and purchases of foreign services.[12] According to Emminger, such unilateral action by the United States was 'the most disconcerting thought' that might ruin or table the SDR as a solution to the liquidity problem. Emminger noted:

> The discussion in the deputies of the Group of Ten had from the beginning been under an injunction from the Americans that flexible exchange rate and a change in the official price of gold were "off limits". However, it was precisely these two problems that came back with a vengeance during the currency crises from 1971 to 1973.[13]

As Emminger saw it, despite the dollar's inconvertibility into gold and the introduction of floating, the world's holdings of dollar reserves increased more than fivefold after 1969, hence the SDR had no chance to become the principal reserve asset, the declared goal of the Jamaica decision of January 1976. Nevertheless, the SDR replaced gold as the unit of account in the transactions of the IMF. Discussions continue about an enhanced role for the SDR.

Henry Reuss, head of the House Subcommittee on International Exchange and Payments, had participated in the Joint Meetings of Officials and Academics on eight occasions. He considered himself a member and valued both its European orientation and the diversity of viewpoint. Reuss recalls the originality of the group's recommendations. Importantly, he saw the discussion of an international monetary unit more immediately applicable for members of the European Union, but thought a single North American currency and coordinated fiscal policies would provide considerable trade, investment and tourism gains with manageable risks. 'If the time for such consideration arrives, the minutes of the Bellagio Group would be helpful'.[14] He thought Europe's experience in pursuit of a common currency would require a strong European Parliament and a strong European Bank to provide control and fiscal policy coordination – and he thought that experience would provide valuable lessons.

Reuss considered US pleas to creditor countries not to convert their dollars into gold 'disingenuous ... If the dollar were ever to be devalued by a closing of the gold window, they would stand to lose heavily for their friendly cooperation'.[15]

Recent scholarship on the Bellagio Group has been very limited, but also points to the group's impact on the acceptance of exchange rate flexibility (Leeson 2003) and the creation of the SDR. Bordo and Eichengreen (1998) attributed to the Bellagio Group the advocacy of the creation of a special reserve asset before the publication of the 1963 IMF Annual Report and the 1964 report of the Group of Ten study group.[16] An amendment to the IMF Articles of Agreement creating the special drawing rights (SDRs) finally came in 1968. In his essay 'Le groupe de Bellagio: origins et premiers pas (1960–1964)', Jerome Wilson also found that the Bellagio Group anticipated the work of the Ossola Group on SDRs.[17] The published papers of Fritz Machlup and his contemporaries, as well as Machlup's personal papers housed in the Hoover Institution and the Robert Triffin Papers at Yale University, support these conclusions. The research findings presented here in Chapters 5, 8, 9 and 10 demonstrate the Bellagio Group's focus on outcomes, specifically adjustment, liquidity and confidence; its stress on exchange rate regimes for payments adjustment; its exposure of audiences of academics, policymakers and bankers to an exploration of alternative exchange rate scenarios; and its exploration of flexible exchange rates at a time when policymakers as well as bankers were against (or at least very uncomfortable with) a move to exchange rate flexibility.

Powerful Platforms for Discussion and Dissemination

With the support of the Ford and Rockefeller foundations, as well as Princeton University and the Bank for International Settlements, Machlup, Triffin and Fellner led twenty-eight conferences – four original Bellagio Group conferences, eighteen Joint Meetings of Officials and Academics and five Bürgenstock conferences. In addition to these platforms, the Bellagio Group had access to conferences organized by others, like the American Enterprise Institute, the American Bankers Association and the Claremont-McKenna conferences, which provided access to larger and more international audiences of policymakers, business leaders and academics in both the developed and developing worlds.

In addition to the conferences, as senior editor of the Princeton Finance Section at Princeton University, Machlup was able to publish many dozens of papers on the international monetary system, including his own papers and those submitted by economists associated with the Bellagio and Bürgenstock group conferences. Table 12.1 depicts the publications of the Princeton Finance Section under Machlup's leadership.

Just as Machlup had invited Robert Triffin and William Fellner to be co-leaders of the first four Bellagio Group conferences, he continued to extend invitations to academics and former policymakers – including those with very different policy prescriptions from his own – to be co-leaders of Bellagio and Bürgenstock conferences, extending the policy and intellectual reach of the conferences and, equally importantly, ensuring that policy rivals had the opportunity to put their arguments through the same rigorous methodological analysis to determine impact on payments adjustment, liquidity and confidence.

Assessment of Monetary Reform by Bellagio Group Founders and Members

By 1968, Machlup was already fearful that the SDR embedded in the Rio Agreement would not become the universal asset it was planned to be and that unilateral actions of the USA (whether import restrictions, restrictions on foreign investment or service purchase, or termination of gold convertibility) would 'have the hard work of several years come to naught'.[18]

In fact Machlup and Triffin were both disappointed in the Jamaica Agreement (1976) and hence in the outcome of the reform efforts. In 1976 Triffin would ask, 'Can the Jamaica agreement really be accepted as the final outcome of more than twelve years of nearly continuous official debates and negotiations on international monetary reform? The question is worth asking, since it embodies a 180-degree turnaround in relation to the main analysis and conclusions that had emerged in previous discussions'.[19] Two years later Triffin would argue that all the Bellagio Group founders could claim that their discussions helped them to explain and understand the collapse of the system as well as any hopes and dreams they had for it. He wrote:

Few, if any, of the conclusions most generally shared by us about the major needs for reform ever led to negotiated agreements, and the officials theoretically in charge increasingly lost control, or even relinquished it, under the new philosophy and economic policies initiated in the United States by Messrs Nixon and Connelly and their successors: 'benign neglect' at first, soon followed by the unilateral repudiation of Bretton Woods commitments and the generalized adoption of nationally managed, mismanaged or unmanaged flexible rates of exchange, the abandonment of any attempt to control overall reserve creation, and an increasing switch of actual responsibilities for balance of payments credit assurance from the official authorities to the private sector ...[20]

In 'Between Outline and Outcome the Reform was Lost' (1976), Machlup wrote with chagrin that the problems and potential answers were all revealed in the work and final report of the Bellagio Group. The Group of Ten officials knew the options and agreed on the fundamental needs of a workable system. 'Their statements released over a period of eleven years, emphasized the importance of building into the system an effective adjustment mechanism and international control and management of international liquidity'.[21] In his comments on the Jamaica Agreement, Machlup noted that managed floating of exchange rates was accommodated, but what about the adjustment mechanism? What about the substitution of SDRs for currency reserves and gold? Which of these well-considered provisions had been retained in the Jamaica Agreement? 'Almost nothing', Machlup concluded, but empty words: 'The alleged objective of making SDRs the "principal reserve asset" is shown to be a sham by the absence of any attempt to reduce the role of foreign exchange reserves and by the ... new agreement about gold – to allow an increase in the physical amounts of gold in the members' official reserves, to allow increases in the book value of gold held by the monetary authorities, and to enhance the liquidity of gold reserves by making them more usable in official transactions'.[22] To make the SDR the principal reserve asset, it must be given the role of determining the gradual increase in global liquidity and of ensuring an improved adjustment mechanism.[23]

Some Bellagio Group members may have had lower expectations. Edward Bernstein acknowledged that one of the major issues on which agreement had been difficult was resolved by the Jamaica Agreement: 'It may seem that the amended Article on the exchange rate regime has no practical significance because it does no more than legalize the existing exchange system and recognize the need for greater exchange rate flexibility. But even that is of considerable importance'.[24] Charles Kindleberger took an evolutionary view: 'The fact is, of course, that the system is evolving subject to two sets of forces, long-run and short. In the long-run, the reduction of costs of communication and transport has increased the efficient scale of economic operation in production, consumption, commerce, and finance and requires international harmonization of institutions in the fields of taxation, economic regulation, and the adoption of international money. The optimum economic area ... is rapidly becoming the world'.[25] Bürgenstock and Joint Meetings of Officials and Academics participants John Williamson and Robert Roosa saw benefits in Jamaica's recognition of floating rates. As Williamson put it, 'A central fact of international monetary life is that the development of capital mobility has rendered the continued use of the adjustable peg impracticable'.[26]

The Bellagio Group's Unresolved Issues Today

In an article in *Foreign Affairs* (1969), Triffin asked, 'Is our international monetary system heading towards a sudden collapse as in 1931, or towards the fundamental reforms needed to cure its most glaring and universally recognized shortcomings? Or will it continue to drift precariously from crisis to crisis, each one dealt with by belated rescue operations and the spread of restrictions and currency devaluations?'[27] As Fabrizio Saccomanni, director general of the Bank of Italy, said at the Conference on the International Monetary System: Sustainability and Reform Proposals, marking the 100th anniversary of Robert Triffin (1911–93), at the Triffin International Foundation, Brussels, 4 October 2011:

> I have no doubt that Robert Triffin would be equally infuriated, if not more, by the current state of the international monetary and financial system, still beset by the global crisis set in motion by the seizure of the US subprime mortgage market in August 2007. The fact that the crisis has now moved to Europe and is destabilizing the eurozone would certainly be a cause of deep regret for Triffin, who firmly believed that regional monetary integration in Europe could contribute to fostering stability in the world's monetary system. In the age of financial globalization, unfortunately, this assumption no longer holds true.[28]

Triffin might be disappointed, but he would have ample demonstration in both the 2008 crisis and current European debt crisis of the interdependence of the monetary system and the importance of adjustment to confidence and the health of the system. Lorenzo Bini Smaghi, member of the Executive Board of the European Central Bank, said in a speech on the 100th anniversary of Triffin's birth:

> The IMS is not in a better situation today. The quandary under the BW system – the lack of a credible anchor for international monetary and financial stability – continues to exist. Key issuers and holders of reserve currencies pursue domestic objectives independently of what would best serve the global system and even their longer-run interest ... All in all, as in Triffin's time, there is not a credible mechanism for symmetric adjustment of imbalances at work today, even though we now have more flexible exchange rates, more financial innovation, more capital mobility and more private international liquidity.[29]

Even under a system of floating exchange rates, in the absence of systemic reforms, a response to the question would be pessimistic. There continue to be crises verging close to Great Depression stature. The financial crisis that began in August 2007 was fuelled by rising real estate values, cheap credit, booming debt and current account deficits, and $50 trillion in investment vehicles called credit default swaps traded between banks, insurance companies and other financial institutions, countries as well as individual institutions. A total crisis in confidence and withdrawal of credit brought the monetary system to a near collapse. Forty years after Triffin's *Foreign Affairs* article, Fred Bergsten (2009) urged a USA climbing out of the financial crisis to launch new policies to avoid large external deficits, balance the budget, and adapt to a global currency system less centred on the dollar to bolster confidence in the recovery and to build the foundation for a sustainable US economy over the long haul. He saw these actions as an economic imperative and as a foreign policy and national security one as well. He argues that the dollar's role as the dominant international currency has made it much easier for the United States to finance, and thus run up, large trade and current account deficits with the rest of the world over the past thirty years. These huge inflows of foreign capital, however, turned out to be an important cause of the current economic crisis, because they contributed to the low interest rates, excessive liquidity and loose monetary policies that – in combination with lax financial supervision – brought on the overleveraging and underpricing of risk that produced the meltdown.[30]

Richard Cooper (2010), like Bergsten, both at the Peterson Institute, did not see the euro or the yuan as an immediate viable substitute for the dollar. Despite great progress over the decade of its existence, the euro capital market is still quite fragmented, with varying degrees of liquidity depending on the security. Similarly, the Chinese capital market, including that for government securities, is not well developed. Foreigners at present do not have access to Chinese government securities, and the Chinese currency is not convertible for capital account transactions.[31]

What about the SDR as a substitute? While distributions had been limited until 2009, SDR holdings/allocations rose from 21 billion to 204 billion or about US $316 billion. Based on the discussions in Chapter 9, it is clear that the distribution of the SDR was intentionally limited to discourage its abuse by the USA, primarily, either as a means of financing its continued deficits or as a political carrot to dangle before developing countries. The possibility of moral hazard remains a consideration. According to Saccomani, 'The SDR is seen as an unconditional form of credit, giving rise to moral hazard. And central banks see the risk of politically-driven SDR allocations stoking global inflation'.[32] Perhaps the future of the SDR as a credible reserve asset may be found in the European unit of account (as discussed in Chapter 6) or in its successor, the ECU. As Saccomanni has said of the ECU, 'a key factor of its success was the link to the long-term process of European monetary integration, which provided not only a legal, economic and institutional frame of reference but also a strong political constituency. By analogy, making the SDR a credible reserve asset and unit of account for both official and private agents would probably require a commitment to eventually transform it into something more than a basket, i.e. a currency in its own right'.[33]

Augmenting the role of this synthetic unit account of the International Monetary Fund, defined in terms of four currencies (the USD, the euro, the Japanese yen, and the British pound), avoids the issue of dependency on a national currency (or currencies) and fulfils the official objective of the international community since 1978 – to make the SDR the principal reserve asset. SDR creation under existing IMF arrangements involves an evaluation of whether the world economy needs additional liquidity, and a decision by IMF governors (essentially the finance ministers of the world) by an 85 per cent weighted vote (which gives the European Union taken together and the USA power to block such a decision) concerning when and how much. Such evaluations have typically taken place every five years. The fact that the volume of SDRs has been increased in response to recent financial crises is a recognition of the shared responsibility of the world's central bankers for an increasingly interdependent economic system.

Conclusions

Contemporaries and insiders testify to the Bellagio Group's impact, noting its focus on outcomes, specifically adjustment, liquidity and confidence; its stress on exchange rate regimes for payments adjustment; its exposure of audiences of academics, policymakers and bankers to an exploration of alternative exchange rate scenarios; its exploration of flexible exchange rates at a time when policymakers as well as bankers were against a move to exchange rate flexibility; and most particularly its work on 'the pretty solution that was found for the liquidity problem' – Machlup's words in 1968 for the SDR. His fear: that the Bellagio Group had made a mistake in giving priority to the problem of liquidity and disregarding the problems of confidence and adjustment. 'Responsible governments may reflect on the possible developments and realize that a failure to negotiate collective actions solving the problems of confidence and adjustment might jeopardize the successful solution of the liquidity problem.'[34]

From the vantage point of the near collapse of the global financial system in 2008–9, and the current European debt crisis, we recognize that confidence depends on both liquidity and adjustment – but these alone may be insufficient given geopolitical events. We need a collaborative process for both liquidity (SDR creation) and adjustment (equal consideration of the responsibilities of surplus and deficit countries). We need the kind of cooperation and coordination that central banks gave to the financial crisis, with a similar sense of urgency, from national governments. There is serious disbelief in the willingness of national governments to commit to a process and follow it. Nevertheless, the 'fragility' and interdependence of the international monetary system demand collaborative action and transparency.

Would the relative informality of a Bellagio Group setting provide the necessary conditions for frank unscripted discussion, the exploration of hypotheses and assumptions, and an exploration of alternative solutions? The Bellagio Group had a singular ability to expose participants to 'original ideas' (in the words of Henry Reuss), an opportunity to 'try on new masks', as Machlup would say. Remember that the largely European membership of the Joint Meetings of

Officials and Academics coalesced around their shared perception that the problem with the international monetary system was the USA, as well as their need to build a European point of view. Are conditions right for a Bellagio Group exploration with a more diverse membership, the G20 for example? Just as in the 1960s, problems facing the system as a whole are also facing Europe as it strives to pursue growth and rein in (or consolidate) the fiscal policies of its member states. There is sufficient difference between the countries of Europe to provide significant lessons for the international monetary system.

Today, policymakers and academics, in the spirit of the Bellagio Group, are working towards that end. Chapter 13 introduces some of the scholars who have worked and are working under the influence of the Bellagio Group.

**Table 12.1: Publications of the Princeton Finance Section under
Fritz Machlup's Leadership**

Author	Title	Year
Robert W. Oliver	*Early Plans for a World Bank*	1971
Arnold Collery	*International Adjustment, Open Economies, and the Quantity Theory of Money*	1971
M. June Flanders	*The Demand for International Reserves*	1971
Fritz Machlup	*The Book Value of Monetary Gold*	1971
John Williamson	*The Choice of a Pivot for Parities*	1971
Franco Modigliano and Hossein Askari	*The Reform of the International Payments System*	1971
Giovanni Magnifico	*European Monetary Unification for Balanced Growth: A New Approach*	1971
Rinaldo Ossola	*Towards New Monetary Relationships*	1971
Richard N. Cooper	*Currency Devaluation in Developing Countries*	1971
Robert A. Mundell	*The Dollar and the Policy Mix: 1971*	1971
Ronald I. McKinnon	*Monetary Theory and Controlled Flexibility in the Foreign Exchanges*	1971
George N. Halm	*The International Monetary Fund and Flexibility of Exchange Rates*	1971
Norman S. Fieleke	*The Welfare Effects of Controls over Capital Exports from the United States*	1971
Fritz Machlup	*The Book Value of Monetary Gold*	1971
Stanley W. Black	*An Econometric Study of Euro-Dollar Borrowing by New York Banks and the Rate of Interest on Euro-Dollars* [reprinted from *The Journal of Finance*, vol. 26, March 1971]	1971
Marina von Neumann Whitman	*Policies for Internal and External Balance*	1970
A. F. Wynne Plumptre	*Exchange-Rate Policy: Experience with Canada's Floating Rate*	1970
Stephen Marris	*The Bürgenstock Communiqué: A Critical Examination of the Case for Limited Flexibility of Exchange Rates*	1970
Helmut W. Mayer	*Some Theoretical Problems Relating to the Euro-Dollar Market*	1970
Thomas D. Willett, Samuel I. Katz and William H. Branson	*Exchange-Rate Systems, Interest Rates, and Capital Flows*	1970
Klaus Friedrich	*A Quantitative Framework for the Euro-Dollar System*	1970
Ralph C. Bryant and Patric H. Hendershott	*Financial Capital Flows in the Balance of Payments of the United States: An Exploratory Empirical Study*	1970
Fritz Machlup	*Euro-Dollar Creation: A Mystery Story* [reprinted from *Banca Nazionale del Lavoro Quarterly Review*, no. 94, September 1970]	1970
Benjamin J. Cohen	*The Benefits and Costs of Sterling* [reprinted from *Euromoney*, vol. 1, nos. 4 and 11, September 1969 and April 1970]	1970

Author	Title	Year
Fritz Machlup	*On Terms, Concepts, Theories and Strategies in the Discussions of Greater Flexibility of Exchange Rates* [reprinted from *Banca Nazionale del Lavoro Quarterly Review*, no. 92, March 1970]	1970
Benjamin J. Cohen	*Sterling and the City* [reprinted from *The Banker*, vol. 120, February 1970]	1970
Fritz Machlup	*Speculations on Gold Speculations* [reprinted from *American Economic Review, Papers and Proceedings*, vol. 56, May 1969]	1969
Peter H. Lindert	*Key Currencies and Gold, 1900–1913*	1969
Benjamin J. Cohen	*The Reform of Sterling*	1969
Albert O. Hirschman	*How to Divest in Latin America, and Why*	1969
Jack L. Davies	*Gold: A Forward Strategy*	1969
Ronald I. McKinnon	*Private and Official International Money: The Case for the Dollar*	1969
George N. Halm	*Toward Limited Exchange-Rate Flexibility*	1969
Anthony Lanyi	*The Case for Floating Exchange Rates Reconsidered*	1969
Henry G. Aubrey	*Behind the Veil of International Money*	1969
Samuel I. Katz	*External Surpluses, Capital Flows, and Credit Policy in the European Economic Community*	1969
Benjamin J. Cohen	*The Reform of Sterling*	1969
Hans Aufricht	*The Fund Agreement: Living Law and Emerging Practice*	
		1969
Fritz Machlup	*The Transfer Gap of the United States* [reprinted from *Banca Nazionale del Lavoro Quarterly Review*, no. 86, September 1968]	1968
Fritz Machlup	*The Price of Gold* [reprinted from *The Banker*, vol. 118, September 1968]	1968
Benjamin J. Cohen	*Reparations in the Postwar Period: A Survey* [reprinted from *Banca Nazionale del Lavoro Quarterly Review*, no. 82, September 1967]	1968
Jagdish Bhagwati	*The Theory and Practice of Commercial Policy: Departures from Unified Exchange Rates*	1968
Milton Gilbert	*The Gold-Dollar System: Conditions of Equilibrium and the Price of Gold*	1968
Albert O. Hirschman and Richard M. Bird	*Foreign Aid––A Critique and a Proposal*	1968
George N. Halm	*International Financial Intermediation: Deficits Benign and Malignant*	1968
J. Marcus Fleming	*Guidelines for Balance-of-Payments Adjustment under the Par-Value System*	1968
Eugene A. Birnbaum	*Gold and the International Monetary System: An Orderly Reform*	1968
Fred H. Klopstock	*The Euro-Dollar Market: Some Unresolved Issues*	1968
Alexander K. Swoboda	*The Euro-Dollar Market: An Interpretation*	1968

Author	Title	Year
Arthur I. Bloomfield	*Patterns of Fluctuation in International Investment Before 1914*	1968
Fritz Machlup	*From Dormant Liabilities to Dormant Assets* [reprinted from *The Banker*, vol. 117, September 1967]	1967
Fritz Machlup	*Credit Facilities or Reserve Allotments?* [reprinted from *Banca Nazionale del Lavoro Quarterly Review*, no. 81, June 1967]	1967
Benjamin J. Cohen	*Voluntary Foreign Investment Curbs: A Plan that Really Works* [reprinted from *Challenge: The Magazine of Economic Affairs*, March/April 1967]	1967
Eugene A. Birnbaum	*Changing the United States Commitment to Gold*	1967
Delbert A. Snider	*Optimum Adjustment Processes and Currency Areas*	1967
Charles P. Kindleberger	*The Politics of International Money and World Language*	1967
Miroslav A. Kriz	*Gold: Barbarous Relic or Useful Instrument?*	1967
N. T. Wang	*New Proposals for the International Finance of Development*	1967
J. Marcus Fleming	*Toward Assessing the Need for International Reserves*	1967
Gunther Ruff	*A Dollar-Reserve System as a Transitional Solution*	1967
Fred R. Glahe	*An Empirical Study of the Foreign-Exchange Market: Test of A Theory*	1967
Marina von Neumann Whitman	*International and Interregional Payments Adjustment: A Synthetic View*	1967
John Parke Young	*United States Gold Policy: The Case for Change*	1966
Robert Triffin	*The Balance of Payments and the Foreign Investment Position of the United States*	1966
Robert V. Roosa and Fred Hirsch	*Reserves, Reserve Currencies, and Vehicle Currencies: An Argument*	1966
Milton Gilbert	*Problems of the International Monetary System*	1966
Raymond F. Mikesell	*Public Foreign Capital for Private Enterprise in Developing Countries*	1966
Pieter Lieftinck	*External Debt and Debt-Bearing Capacity of Developing Countries*	1966
Egon Sohmen	*The Theory of Forward Exchange*	1966
Benjamin J. Cohen	*Adjustment Costs and the Distribution of New Reserves*	1966
Ronald I. McKinnon and Wallace E. Oates	*The Implications of International Economic Integration for Monetary, Fiscal, and Exchange-Rate Policy*	1966
Fritz Machlup	*The Need for Monetary Reserves* [reprinted from *Banca Nazionale del Lavoro Quarterly Review*, vol. 77, September 1966]	1966
Fritz Machlup	*World Monetary Debate--Bases for Agreement* [reprinted from *The Banker*, vol. 116, September 1966]	1966
Fritz Machlup	*International Monetary Systems and the Free Market Economy* [reprinted from *International Payments Problems: A Symposium*, Washington: American Enterprise Institute, 1966]	1966
E. Ray Canterbery	*Foreign Exchange, Capital Flows, and Monetary Policy*	1965
W. M. Corden	*Recent Developments in the Theory of International Trade*	1965
George N. Halm	*The Band Proposal: The Limits of Permissible Exchange-Rate Variations*	1965
John H. Williamson	*The Crawling Peg*	1965

Author	Title	Year
Tibor Scitovsky	*Requirements of an International Reserve System*	1965
Sidney Weintraub	*The Foreign-Exchange Gap of the Developing Countries*	1965
Jacques Rueff and Fred Hirsch	*The Role and the Rule of Gold: An Argument*	1965
Charles P. Kindleberger	*Balance- of-Payments Deficits and the International Market for Liquidity*	1965
Fritz Machlup	*Real Adjustment, Compensatory Corrections, and Foreign Financing of Imbalances in International Payments* [reprinted from Robert E. Baldwin et al., *Trade, Growth, and the Balance of Payments*, Chicago: Rand McNally; Amsterdam: North-Holland, 1965]	1965
Fritz Machlup	*The Cloakroom Rule of International Reserves: Reserve Creation and Resources Transfer* [reprinted from *Quarterly Journal of Economics*, vol. 79, August 1965]	1965
Robert Triffin	*The Evolution of the International Monetary System: Historical Reappraisal and Future Perspectives*	1964
Jacob Viner	*Problems of Monetary Control*	1964
Weir M. Brown	*The External Liquidity of an Advanced Country*	1964
Robert Z. Aliber	*The Management of the Dollar in International Finance*	1964
Harry G. Johnson	*Alternative Guiding Principles for the Use of Monetary Policy*	1963
Marius W. Holtrop	*Monetary Policy in an Open Economy: Its Objectives, Instruments, Limitations, and Dilemmas*	1963
Sir Dennis Robertson	*A Memorandum Submitted to the Canadian Royal Commission on Banking and Finance*	1963
Friedrich A. Lutz	*The Problem of International Liquidity and the Multiple-Currency Standard*	1963
Arthur I. Bloomfield	*Short-Term Capital Movements under the Pre-1914 Gold Standard*	1963
Peter B. Kenen	*Reserve-Asset Preferences of Central Banks and Stability of the Gold-Exchange Standard*	1963
Fritz Machlup	*Plans for Reform of the International Monetary System*	1962; rev. Mar. 1964
Samuel I. Katz	*Sterling, Speculation and European Convertibility: 1955–1958*	1961
Brian Tew	*The International Monetary Fund: Its Present Role and Future Prospects*	1961
Sir Donald MacDougall	*The Dollar Problem: A Reappraisal*	1960

Source: Princeton University. The International Economics Section (formerly the International Finance Section) published short monographs and policy essays in four series: **Essays in International Economics** (previously Essays in International Finance), **Princeton Studies in International Economics** (previously Princeton Studies in International Finance), **Special Papers in International Economics**, and **Reprints in International Finance**.

13 THE IMPACT OF THE BELLAGIO GROUP ON INTERNATIONAL TRADE AND FINANCE SCHOLARSHIP FROM THE 1960S TO THE PRESENT

Introduction

Sitting at the Bellagio Group meetings, students, teachers and colleagues were reunited – Burton Malkiel with Fritz Machlup; Peter Kenen and Harry Johnson with Gottfried Haberler and Alan C. L. Day; Alexandre Lamfalussy with Leon Dupriez and Robert Triffin; Robert Mundell with Charles Kindleberger and Harry Johnson – a tribute to the closeness of the relationships these academics had built and, if it is not going too far, the mutual pride taken in scholarship.

Recalling Machlup's criterion for membership in the Bellagio Group that economists should have achieved prominence in the field of international finance, especially those with an international reputation as writers or teachers, this chapter examines a few of the teachers and their students, protégés and close associates who were *not* members of the Bellagio Group. What distinguishes these relationships is the sheer effort invested in developing new talent and the range of subject areas – from economic growth to international finance to international business to public policy to corporate strategy – in which their students and advisees specialized, having begun their studies in economics. My own interest in Fritz Machlup originated in research into Machlup's student Edith Penrose and my interpretation of her work as economic growth strategy where firms and government are actors.

The period covered in this book, largely 1963 to 1977, was distinguished by the proliferation of new hybrid organization forms that were neither markets nor hierarchies to discuss and manage world and regional problems, and the introduction of new methodologies to explore opportunities for and limits to national economic or firm growth (Machlup 1943, Harrod 1939, Miller 1958, Penrose 1959). They were supranational organizations like the IMF, OECD and WTO as well as non-governmental organizations committed to advisement or action or both. The economist as corporate strategist and methodologist was on the ascent in companies like ExxonMobil and IBM, firms that sent representatives to the Bürgenstock conferences who then published in finance and economic journals. The economist would become an agent of change within and beyond academia for the next twenty years.

In this chapter I have chosen two scholars whose influence extended to firm theory and foreign direct investment, and two who assumed public policy roles while still contributing to the literature of finance and international monetary reform. I will talk first about Edith Penrose and her mentor Fritz Machlup, then about Stephen Hymer and his mentor Charles Kindleberger. I will speak about Andrew Crockett of the Bank for International Settlements and the Group of Thirty (now at JP Morgan Chase) and Edwin Truman of the US Treasury and Peterson Institute (now retired), both students of Robert Triffin. Finally, I will talk about the group of scholars in Europe, former students of Robert Triffin, who have reopened the debate on the Triffin Dilemma and how to solve it.

Who is a Mentor? The Literature

A broad literature has developed around what mentors do. A mentor may be a role model, advocate, sponsor, adviser, guide, developer of skills and intellect, listener, host, coach, challenger, visionary, balancer, friend, sharer, facilitator, resource provider. A mentor may be a leader through rough terrain marked by the footprints of a prior generation of scholars and practitioners. Both Laurent Daloz (1986) and Michael Galbraith (1991) established that the purposes and objectives of mentoring are tied to the goals of learning by a process in which teacher and student collaborate, exchanging information useful to both and making the learning experience mutually enriching and pivotal for mentor and protégé.[1] While recognizing the importance of learning to successful mentoring, Kurt Kraiger et al. (1993) emphasized the importance of cognitive learning, specifically how mentors help students to structure or map knowledge to represent the interrelationships among information, as well as mental activities that enhance the acquisition and application of knowledge.[2]

Introduction to the world of academic publishing, critical to colleges and universities with a research agenda as well as to the newly minted PhD, has long been part of the mentor mission, as Carol Mullen (2003) pointed out.[3] Without a mentor's guidance, most new scholars learn what Mullen called 'the gambling rules ... in the casino of academe' gradually and independently. Learning the rules from an experienced mentor may be more problematic for females than for males, as Patricia Smit (2003) argued.[4] Most senior academics and administrators are males and are therefore also the people who tend to mentor less experienced colleagues, with the result that women are often left out of the mentoring process, or the bond devolves from a colleague-to-colleague into a father-to-daughter relationship, inhibiting risk taking and independence. Gender issues may be more or less pronounced when there are also cultural differences at play that influence the form mentorship takes. Kevin Barham and Christopher Conway (1998) emphasized national cultural differences, identifying key factors that shape the mentor-protégé relationship, including the expectations and roles of mentor and protégé; the nature of the mentoring agreement; the participants' feedback style; and their attitudes towards confidentiality.[5] Whatever form mentorship takes, Kathy Kram (1983) emphasized the evolution of the mentoring relationship through four predictable, distinct and sequential phases, beginning with the conception phase and maturing until a final parting phase is achieved.[6]

Edith Penrose and Fritz Machlup

Few management scholars today are unfamiliar with the work of Edith Penrose, and yet it was only in 1984, with the publication of Birger Wernerfelt's article 'A Resource-Based Theory of the Firm', that the seminal work of this American economist came to light. Since then, Penrose has attracted enormous attention as a founding mother of resource-based theory, a view that sees firm growth as dependent upon change in firm knowledge, capability and resource use. At a time when neoclassical economists were describing the firm as a 'black box' whose inner workings were outside their sphere of interest, Penrose's *Theory of the Growth of the Firm* (1959) proposed a dynamic, knowledge-driven process theory of the growth of firms, which emerge from the mind of the entrepreneur and evolve over time into diversified large firms that continue to compete, acquire and adapt in a universe of firms, all contributing to the growth of the economy as a whole. Since the 1980s, a generation of management theorists has cited her work as fundamental to their perspective on the role of the entrepreneur, the pursuit of knowledge and the availability of managerial services to the growth of firms. Citing Robert Triffin (1940), Penrose argued that the innovating firm is, for theoretical purposes, a new creation. 'Each innovation modifies the level of profit opportunities attached to a firm or rather creates a new firm, provided with profit opportunities of its own'.[7] Nevertheless, 'economists writing about the firm as an institution have often insisted on putting some of their own discussion in terms relevant only to a theory uninterested in institutional factors but asking and answering entirely different questions. For this reason, I have always looked askance at references to "efficient markets" or even "market failure" in relation to the behaviour of firms as organizations in real markets and in relation to the firm/market dichotomy'.[8]

In her later work (1957–73), government as an economic actor in the theory of the growth would distinguish Penrose's research on multinational enterprises (MNEs) from the international business theory of Peter Buckley and Mark Casson (1976); Alan Rugman (1981); Alain Verbeke and Rugman (1998); and Jean-Francois Hennart (1982, 1989).[9] According to Christos Pitelis (2002), Penrose was among the first theorists to discuss transfer pricing and repatriation of profits.[10] Based on her case study research into chemicals, petroleum and automotive industries, I argue that Penrose's 'interstices' (areas of white space or potential opportunity ignored or abandoned by large firms) are often moderated by national governments to the advantage of domestic small firms. Her interstices argument and case study findings offer a complement to new trade theory, where governments moderate the comparative advantage of first mover large firms, thus increasing national welfare by improving the terms of trade. In the case of the Hercules Powder Company, anti-monopoly action gave this firm opportunity for profitable growth at increased size. In the case of the oil company nationals and independents, government's desire to lessen the power of the oil majors led to new opportunities for domestic industry. In the case of GM-Holden's, government might impose a heavy imports tax to encourage the plough back of profits into the host country subsidiary. All three cases described in Penrose's research required or benefited from some level of government involvement as anti-monopolist, purchaser or regulator.

Penrose's interest in government and firms as a duopoly in the growth process occurred as the world's economists were engaged in a struggle to reform the world financial system. Penrose's teacher and mentor Fritz Machlup was organizing the Bellagio Group. Robert Triffin was arguing that G10 deficits (and restrictions on raw materials purchases) had their ultimate impact on underdeveloped countries. Penrose would take the Triffin view herself, arguing that the growth of foreign indebtedness, like the growth of domestic indebtedness, need not be of particular concern in a growing economy, if the net income out of which the indebtedness can be serviced also grows accordingly. The contribution of foreign direct investment (FDI) to net domestic income must exceed the amount of profits repatriated by foreign firms. If not, Penrose argued, government would be wise to find an alternative route to new technology, skills improvement and overall productivity growth without the 'costs' of lost autonomy and control.

Charles Kindleberger, an occasional critic of Penrose, maintained that it is not the size of the profits or the issue of reinvestment versus new investment that raises difficulties for developing economies, but the fact that foreign investment encourages excessive spending and gives rise to an imbalance in the balance of payments.[11] Penrose and Kindleberger viewed the large international firm and host country government as engaged in a bilateral monopoly. However, Kindleberger took issue with Penrose's use of the term 'exploitation' in an assessment of the relation between oil companies and the countries in which they operate. It is significant that Penrose, who seldom acknowledged criticism in her published writings, rose to Kindleberger's challenge. Responding to Kindleberger's objection to her use of the word 'exploitation' in a discussion of FDI, Penrose argued that the perception of 'exploitation' as 'disproportionate gain' ought 'to be treated as one aspect of a political attitude towards foreign investment in general, for the feeling of being exploited increases an existing resentment against foreigners, and the psychological disutility of having to put up with extensive foreign influence is intensified if it is felt that the bargain is not fair or, conversely, is reduced if it is felt that the foreigner is going out of his way to be fair'.[12] It is interesting that Kindleberger's student Stephen Hymer would come to take the same view of foreign direct investment and would draw on some of the same sources, notably Maurice Bye, as discussed below.

Penrose was also influenced by the dynamic economics of Roy Harrod, another member of Machlup's group of non-governmental economists seeking reform of the world monetary system. She had read and cited Harrod's 1952 *Economic Essays* in *The Theory of the Growth of the Firm*, specifically in her discussion of the receding managerial limit, where the capacities of the firm's existing managerial personnel necessarily set a limit to the expansion of the firm in any given period. Like Penrose, Harrod was interested in the impact of entrepreneurs on growth – and in the limits to growth imposed by available entrepreneurial/managerial services.[13] One implication of the growth model developed by Harrod is that the key problem for developing countries was to increase the share of resources devoted to investment.

Among Penrose's influences at the time was the French structural economist Maurice Bye, who investigated the impact on the world economy of the interplay of flows and forces depending neither entirely on government nor on firms. Focusing on wasting assets (oil and mines), Bye warned that given the differential planning horizons of foreign investing firms and national governments, the latter cannot delay public welfare for long-term growth gains that might materialize only after the resource had been depleted, but must fund social programmes in the short term via taxes, tariffs and other action directed at what he called the 'large multi-territorial unit'.[14]

Penrose read Nicholas Kaldor (1934), whom she cited approvingly in her 1994 retrospective article 'Strategy/Organization and the Metamorphosis of the Large Firm'.[15] Kaldor's growth model is based, by his own admission, on Keynesian techniques of analysis, and follows the well-known 'dynamic' approach originally developed by Harrod. Kaldor's model differs from Harrod's in that it is assumed that in a growing economy the general level of output at any one time is limited by available resources, and not by effective demand. It does not distinguish between changes in techniques (and in productivity) that are induced by changes in the supply of capital relative to labour, and those induced by technical invention or innovation, i.e. the introduction of new knowledge. The use of more capital per worker (whether measured in terms of the value of capital at constant prices, in terms of tons of weight of the equipment, mechanical power, etc.) inevitably entails the introduction of superior techniques that require 'inventiveness' of some kind, though these need not necessarily represent the application of basically new principles or ideas. Finally, the prime mover in the process of economic growth is the readiness to absorb technical change combined with the willingness to invest capital in business ventures.[16] Edith Penrose was a theorist interested in economic growth, not in firm growth only, and she drew on the best minds of her generation to create a unique view of growth as a two-player game.

Given Machlup's Austrian background and jaundiced view of the capability of policymakers to fix or to grow the economy, what role might one expect him to play in the life of an independent scholar with a quite different view? What did Fritz Machlup bring to his role as mentor? What was the nature of the mentorship relationship, and how is Machlup's mentorship reflected in Penrose's work? We are lucky to have their publications and their personal correspondence, exchanged over a quarter century when both Machlup and Penrose were travelling or teaching abroad, to answer these questions. While this pair of renowned economists is hardly representative, their relationship evokes some of the major focus areas of contemporary literature on mentorship, including learning as an objective and purpose of mentorship, induction into the community of scholars, gender issues and cultural differences, and the phase transition of the mentorship relationship. Remarkably, an examination of their publications and personal correspondence provides a historical record of their relationship.

Under the mentorship of Fritz Machlup, Penrose completed her MA and PhD in 1951, thereafter taking on the roles of lecturer and research associate for Machlup. Over the next eight years, Penrose benefited from an extremely high level of interaction with her mentor. Communication between the two was frequent, both formally as befits the teacher/pupil relationship, and informally, as one might expect between two friends and colleagues. The way Barham and Conway's cultural factors operated at Johns Hopkins University reflected not only the peculiar character of American education in the late 1940s and 1950s, but more importantly the intent of John Hopkins' President Gilman and his successors to create a strong mentoring culture at the university.[17]

Following Daloz, Galbraith and Kraiger, it is clear that Fritz Machlup was a teacher-mentor. His modus operandi was to equip graduate students with 'frameworks' (Machlup's term) for organizing the knowledge emerging from their research, analysis and theory generation. Machlup's methodology courses and his published works on methodology, along with his documented guidance and the published work of his student Edith Penrose, support this deliberate strategy and purpose. Adopting his four-part approach to all economic analysis that included an initial definition of terms, taxonomy or classification of phenomena, history of the subject and contributions to theory, Penrose followed

Machlup's methodological framework in *The Economics of the International Patent Regime* (the basis for both her MA and PhD in political economy) as well as in *The Theory of the Growth of the Firm.*[18] Underlying *The Theory of the Growth of the Firm* was an analytical apparatus modelled after Machlup's adjustment model for interpreting, measuring and verifying adaptation to a change in knowledge from one period to another. The model was unique in that, unlike the neoclassical model, there was no final equilibrium, but a continuous series of changes as knowledge gained in one period became action in a succeeding period and so on. Like Machlup, his mentor Mises and others in the Austrian tradition, Penrose was interested in modelling a process, in this case a process by which a change in knowledge, in the entrepreneur's 'image' of productive opportunity, from one period to the next, allows the firm to grow. Over time, this growth will be limited only by the availability of managers who can harness knowledge for growth. The inputs into Penrose's process theory of the growth of firms were discussed, debated and shaped by the correspondence exchanged by Penrose and Machlup during 1955. Together, they represent the unique core of Penrose's work. They are the catalysts for growth not only of the firm, but of industries and of the national economy itself : 1) Growth is limited to a firm's productive opportunity, which is a composite of all the productive possibilities that its entrepreneurs see, choose or are able to take advantage of. 2) The capacities of the managerial personnel in the firm set a limit to the growth of the firm for a period of time, until the capacities of managerial personnel can be released for additional expansion. 3) If the power of the expanding firm is believed to be great, each of the other firms in market will be devalued and will be become a potential merger or acquisition candidate. 4) The maximum amount of expansion of any firm will be determined by the relevant managerial services available for expansion in relation to the amount of these services required per dollar of expansion. 5) As larger firms expand, their very growth opens up new opportunities for smaller firms, because of the expansion of incomes, the demand for producers' goods, and the increase and diffusion of technological knowledge.

The Machlup/Penrose relationship closely followed the phases suggested by Kram. The initial phase (1947–51) began when Machlup and Penrose took up their work on the international patent regime, determined its major issues and structure and planned the sequence of publications, joint and individual, that they would develop from the research. In this phase, Penrose worked closely with Machlup and the analysis followed very closely Machlup's methodological framework. In the second, or cultivation, phase, the positive expectations that emerged during the initiation phase are continually tested against reality. It began when Fritz Machlup and G. Heberton Evans, chairman of the Johns Hopkins' Department of Political Economy, brought Edith Penrose into their study of the growth of business firms, funded by the Merrill Lynch Foundation.

Three Johns Hopkins PhDs were involved in the research and analysis effort: Dr Gertrude Schroeder worked on 'The Growth of the Major Basic Steel Companies, 1900–1950'; Dr Edgar O. Edwards worked on 'Studies on the Growth of the Individual Firm, with Application to Firms in the Chemical Industry'; and Dr Edith Penrose worked on a general study of business growth under the title 'On the Theory of the Growth of the Firm'. This phase extended beyond the Merrill research to 1955, during which Machlup and Penrose met regularly and corresponded every ten days or more frequently if either was travelling, as documented by their copious letters, when Penrose was deeply involved in writing *The Theory of the Growth of the Firm*.

The third, or separation, phase was one marked by significant changes in the relationship, e.g. new independence and autonomy on the part of Penrose, as well as the inner feelings of turmoil, anxiety and loss that often follow a widening distance – whether physical or caused by the passage of time – between two human beings who have long had a close relationship of any kind. It began when Edith and her husband left Johns Hopkins on sabbatical for Canberra's Australian National University. Here Edith's letters reveal a considerable amount of anxiety and well-articulated feelings of loss, as entirely on her own and far from her mentor, she is deep into the writing of *The Theory of the Growth of the Firm*. The feelings were exacerbated when the Penroses moved on to the University College of Arts and Sciences in Baghdad, 1957–9. Here Edith was engaged in studying the international oil majors and continued to seek Machlup's counsel on her papers. The nature of her theory – the government firm duopoly in economic growth – was a major contribution, but it was also evidence of a growing autonomy.

The fourth or final phase is redefinition, during which the relationship takes on a different character, as mentor and protégé recognize that a shift in developmental tasks has occurred and that the prior mentorship process is no longer needed or desired. Increasingly, it was Penrose who was – if not the mentor – a fully fledged knowledgeable partner in a position to dispense learning from her own viewpoint. In this role, she was to read and comment on Machlup's papers before they were presented and/or published. Her former mentor undoubtedly took pride in his realization that he could now rely firmly on the judgement of the erstwhile protégé. As Carol Mullen would argue, there is always a need for new scholars to be able to call on a 'trusted other', an individual who knows the intended audience and venue, to read and comment on papers. The need, stated Mullen, is especially important in the early years, but she emphasized that it is a need that never really gets *less* important. In the substance of the Machlup/Penrose correspondence, that need is fully reflected – first on the part of Penrose and, in the relationship's later stages, on the part of Machlup.

Describing his own experience with Machlup as a mentor, Jacob Dreyer, a student of Machlup's at New York University in the early 1970s, said of Machlup: 'he would create the ambiance of a joint enterprise, of a partnership set up to investigate a certain problem, of an intellectual voyage in which his student and himself are fellow sailors on equal footing, even though they are assigned different tasks'.[19]

Edith Penrose was still seeking Fritz Machlup's career advice in 1978: she was sixty-four; he was seventy-eight.

Stephen Hymer and Charles Kindleberger

There are a few similarities between Penrose and Stephen Hymer. Both students were taught by powerful teachers at the apex of their academic careers, engaged in publishing widely and acting as advisers to government and non-governmental committees on issues important to economic growth. Both would focus on developing countries. Both would put a unique stamp on the role of firms and government. Both would spend significant time in their careers working in developing countries.

The story of Stephen Hymer's contribution to a theory of foreign direct investment has been told by many writers. A special issue of *Contributions to Political Economy* was dedicated to Hymer in 2002. Perhaps none have done so much to promote Hymer's reputation as John Dunning and Christos Pitelis.[20] Hymer, who was born in 1934 and died in a car accident forty years later, made a lasting contribution to the theory of the MNE and FDI, and to international political economy (IPE). He was one of the first economists to explore the nature and determinants of the internationalization of production ('globalization') and its relationship to international development, MNE-host country relationships and global governance. Hymer first articulated his views fifty years ago in his doctoral thesis (completed in 1960), *The International Operations of National Firms: A Study of Foreign Direct Investment*, and later in around forty articles in economics and political economy journals. While foreign direct investment would frequently benefit recipient economies, he argued (like Prebisch) that more often than not this was not the case in underdeveloped countries, where investment resulted in dependence, uneven development, the erosion of power in host country governments, and the creation of an international capital market based on lowest interest cost where the amount of investment is dwarfed by the interest losses of local lenders.[21]

Besides Dunning and Pitelis, no one did more to establish the posthumous reputation of Stephen Hymer as the father of FDI than his mentor and teacher Charles Kindleberger. Hymer had come to MIT to study industrial relations, but found himself drawn like Penrose to economic theory, industrial organization and international trade. Kindleberger supervised Hymer's dissertation from 1958 to 1960. In the year that his dissertation was completed, MIT had begun to publish dissertations of outstanding merit. Kindleberger submitted Hymer's dissertation, but it was rejected by the selection committee. As Kindleberger explained, 'It was stated by one member of the selection committee that the argument was too simple and straightforward. My reply did not move the committee: that to make clear a field in which theory had long been confused was a first-class contribution to scholarship'.[22] Kindleberger himself used Hymer's approach and cited the thesis is the second and third editions of his textbook *International Economics*. While it appears a major university press asked to publish the thesis on the tenth anniversary of its completion, Hymer agreed but said he wanted to make changes. By the time of his death, three or so years later, he had not changed the work beyond a few edits. Hymer's dissertation was published in 1976 because of the concerted efforts of his mentor Charles Kindleberger. From 1963 to 1967, Kindleberger would discuss (as well as cite) Stephen Hymer's work in his own publications. In 'The Pros and Cons of an International Capital Market' (1967), Kindleberger used Hymer's international capital market contribution in his discussion of recent calls by the IMF, BIS and EEC for an international or regional capital market.[23] Kindleberger's *Multinational Excursions* (1984) would devote nearly an entire chapter to putting Hymer's theory in context as a disruptive innovation in the literature of foreign direct investment, while simultaneously assessing Penrose, Bye, Dunning and others as 'not quite grasping it'.[24]

James Tobin, Andrew Crockett, Edwin Truman, the International Triffin Foundation and Robert Triffin

Not every mentor is a teacher or thesis adviser. In *Essays in Economics: National and International*, James Tobin acknowledged Robert Triffin as a mentor, a generation ahead of him at Harvard. 'His generation was a spectacular group, making new economics while teaching both old and new'. Their close and long-standing relationship really began not at Harvard but at Yale in 1951. 'Robert founded and fostered a programme to train economists sent by foreign governments for a year or two of graduate work, oriented towards economic development and international economic relations. The programme continues, and its alumni – many of them personally taught and inspired by Robert, occupy position of importance in central banks, ministries and international organizations all over the world'.[25] Triffin's protégés included Jacque van Ypersele de Strihou, whom he met in Washington when he offered Ypersele a job at the IMF, as well as Sir Andrew Crockett, Edwin Truman, former Federal Reserve Banker Ralph C. Bryant, now at Brookings, and Herbert Grubel, a professor of economics at Simon Fraser University.

Sir Andrew Crockett captured some of Triffin's teaching style in a paper published in *Fragility of the International Financial System* (2001): 'Students were asked to undertake high-level role-play, in which we would act as members of the IMF Executive Board, in the Group of 10, Working Party 3, or some other body dealing with international monetary issues'.[26] Crockett was exceptional, but he was also one of many of Triffin's students who went on to play a public finance or public policy role.

Crockett became President of JPMorgan Chase International and a member of the Executive Committee of JPMorgan Chase & Co. in 2003. Prior to joining Chase, he had been general manager (CEO) of the Bank for International Settlements, serving two five-year terms. He also served from 1999 to 2003 as the first chairman of the Financial Stability Forum, a group of senior financial officials from the major economies that monitors the health of the International Financial System. Earlier in his career, Crockett held senior positions at the Bank of England and the International Monetary Fund. Crockett was also chairman of Working Party 3 of the OECD, an alternate governor of the IMF for the United Kingdom, a member of the Monetary Committee of the European Union and a Trustee of the International Accounting Standards Committee Foundation. He was a member of the Group of Thirty, chairman of the Per Jacobsson Foundation, member of the International Council of the China Banking Regulatory Commission, member of the International Council of the China Development Bank, director of the International Centre for Leadership in Finance (Malaysia), and a trustee of the American University of Beirut.

Crockett has published on the Eurocurrency market (1976) and stabilization policy (1981). His 1976 paper with Morris Goldstein, 'Inflation under Fixed and Flexible Exchange Rates', found that the type of exchange rate system has relatively little influence on the average rate of world inflation, but from the viewpoint of an individual country, the exchange rate regime may well influence how much inflation it generates, transmits or receives.[27] His paper 'Control Over International Reserves' (1978) discussed the reasons why control over liquidity (in the form of international reserves) is important to the stability of the system, but risks concentrating on the economic instrument (the control of the stock of liquidity) at the expense of the economic objective (the adoption of appropriate adjustment policies).[28]

Crockett's work on financial stability has been published in academic journals as well as in the publications of the Group of Thirty, BIS and International Triffin Foundation. In *The Theory and Practice of Financial Stability* (1997), Crockett explained that monetary and financial stability are of central importance to the effective functioning of a market economy, providing the basis for rational decision making about the allocation of real resources through time and improving the climate for saving and investment. Instability creates damaging uncertainties that can lead to resource misallocation and unwillingness to enter into intertemporal contracts. In extreme cases, disruptions in the financial sector can have severe adverse effects on economic activity and even on political structures. Maintaining stability is thus a key objective of financial authorities, with the emphasis on the ex ante potential for economic disruption, not waiting to clean up the damage ex post.[29]

In a 1998 paper for the Group of Thirty entitled 'Banking Supervision and Financial Stability', written during the Asian financial crisis, 'the most severe financial crisis of the post-war era', Crockett acknowledged that even in countries that have escaped a full-scale financial crisis, market turbulence has placed strains on financial intermediaries and resulted in serious volatility in asset prices, and this calls for a new financial architecture. Crockett argued that the banks are part of the picture, and if the crisis has taught us anything, it is that in an integrated world financial system the stability of markets and financial intermediaries, wherever they are located, are increasingly interdependent. Measures to strengthen the system need to be mutually consistent and reinforcing.[30]

Until his death in 2012, Crockett had also been active with the International Triffin Foundation and contributed to its 2000 conference 'Fragility of the International Financial System: How Can We Prevent New Crisis in Emerging Markets?' with a discussion of the contribution of volatile capital flows to destabilization. He painted a picture of a 'malign cycle' of confidence, growth, capital inflow, increased credit availability and rising domestic asset values, intensification of capital inflows, exchange rate intervention (holding it fixed) and reserve accumulation, leading to more foreign investment attracted by an interest rate spread between local and international claims. The counterpart of strong capital flows is often a rising current account deficit. At some stage, often for political rather than economic reasons, the process goes into reverse and investors bolt, leaving the authorities unable to persuade investors they can manage the situation, and a disorderly devaluation can ensue.

From 2000 to 2003, he spoke on financial stability and banking supervision at BIS conferences, and returned on 24–5 June 2010 for the BIS Ninth Annual Conference on 'The Future of Central Banking under Post-Crisis Mandates' in Lucerne, Switzerland.

Edwin M. Truman has been a senior fellow at the Peterson Institute since 2001. Triffin was Truman's thesis adviser at Yale. Truman remembered Triffin's practical advice for getting started (and finishing up): 'For a year I worked away and felt I had made little resulting progress. After twelve months, very much discouraged, I went in to see Professor Triffin. He said: "Go away and come back to see me in two weeks and summarize for me by then all that you have learned". I went away, worked very hard over the next two weeks, returned to Triffin, and made by presentation. He said: "Fine, start writing it up". This blessing of my work – and I was right it was not profound – is something for which I have always been grateful.'[31]

Truman served as assistant secretary of the US Treasury for International Affairs from December 1998 to January 2001, and returned as counsellor to the secretary from March to May 2009. He directed the Division of International Finance of the Board of Governors of the Federal Reserve System from 1977 to 1998. From 1983 to 1998, he was one of three economists on the staff of the Federal Open Market Committee.

Truman has been a member of numerous international groups working on economic and financial issues, including the Financial Stability Forum's Working Group on Highly Leveraged Institutions (1999–2000), the G22 Working Party on Transparency and Accountability (1998), the G10-sponsored Working Party on Financial Stability in Emerging Market Economies (1996–7), the G10 Working Group on the Resolution of Sovereign Liquidity Crises (1995–6), and the G7 Working Group on Exchange Market Intervention (1982–3).

He has published on international monetary economics, international debt problems, economic development and European economic integration. His studies include *Sovereign Wealth Funds: Threat or Salvation?* (2010), *Reforming the IMF for the 21st Century* (2006), *A Strategy for IMF Reform* (2006), *Chasing Dirty Money: The Fight Against Money Laundering* (2004) and *Inflation Targeting in the World Economy* (2003).

Like Crockett, Truman too has been active with the International Triffin Foundation and has written on international capital flows for the organization's conference on financial fragility. Truman urged a greater sense of shared responsibility for the management of the international financial system. He articulated his hope for the Group of Twenty, a group of finance ministers and central bank governors from twenty major economies (nineteen countries plus the European Union), formally established at the G7 finance ministers' meeting on 26 September 1999. During the global financial crisis, collective action by the G20 was critical for avoiding a catastrophic financial meltdown and a possible depression. In a study of 'The G-20 and International Financial Institution Governance' (2010), Truman argued for an expansion of the role of the IMF as lender of last resort, a larger surveillance role for the IMF as a prerequisite for IMF assistance, and a substantial increase in IMF resources.[32] In a 2006 paper 'The International Monetary Fund and Regulatory Challenges', comparing the strong controls of the WTO with the weak controls of the IMF, Truman called for a stronger peer review process for IMF member states and a balanced adjustment process that would impose discipline equally on surplus as well as deficit countries. While he did not believe that payments imbalances played a major causal role in the financial crisis of 2007–9, he saw both the imbalances and the financial crisis as 'jointly caused by failures of macroeconomic policies in the United States and many other countries compounded by regulatory and supervisory failures that contributed to an orgy of excess in the financial sector'. Further, he believed that disagreement on the diagnosis of the causes of the crisis has complicated the cure.[33]

The International Triffin Foundation has become a virtual movement of active scholars pursuing work on the international monetary system and more general work in the fields of economics, finance and social sciences through education, research and conferences, and a greater attention to the lessons of history. The membership of the International Triffin Foundation includes many scholars researching and writing on financial system reform and linked by the feeling that they owe Triffin a debt of gratitude. The organization is chaired by Alexandre Lamfalussy, a former member of the Bellagio Group and one of the leading central bankers of his time, who has become one of the main proponents for a single capital market within the European Union. He was a member of the Delors Committee for the Study of European Economic and Monetary Union, the general manager of the Bank for International Settlements and the first president of the European Monetary Institute (in charge of preparing the third stage of EMU).

Conclusions

Whether they were members of the Bellagio Group or not, the students and colleagues of Machlup, Kindleberger and Triffin seemed to have immersed themselves in the issues important their mentors. Penrose, Hymer, Tobin, Crockett and Truman perceived a role for government in relieving market failures and opportunism. In this regard, Penrose and Hymer went far afield of Machlup and Kindleberger, while Tobin, Crockett and Truman aligned closely with Triffin.

In all cases presented here, the failure of monetary system reform was a catalyst for their research, publication and civic involvement. This failure of collective will is inversely proportional to scholarly output. The continued work of the International Triffin Foundation and its close association with the Bank for International Settlements puts contributing scholars in the right place to effect reform, in that they can address, as the Bellagio Group did, the institutional and operational mechanisms necessary to monitor and control it.

CONCLUSIONS

This final chapter of the book first summarizes the conclusions drawn from each chapter, before returning to the initial questions and hypotheses raised in the Introduction. The chapter ends with a few overarching conclusions.

Chapter 1 argued that the Great Depression and World War II – both problems and goals for the future – influenced how economists thought about policy, inflation, interest rates, deficits and government intervention. Policymakers had a complicated relationship with their former allies and enemies as their world became more interdependent and appeared to require some kind of collective action. The Bretton-Woods Agreement, which had created the current monetary system as well as supranational institutions like the IMF, the OEEC (now OECD) and the World Bank, continued to play an important role in the development of solutions to payments imbalance and liquidity issues. Tensions began to build as US policies jeopardized confidence in the dollar, the primary medium of international trade, even as Europe and Japan were experiencing rapid economic growth. Economists in Europe and the USA were exploring solutions that included wholesale system change. An announcement by US Treasury Secretary Douglas Dillon set a series of monetary system studies in motion by the IMF and Group of Ten – and also by Machlup, Triffin and Fellner, leaders of the Bellagio Group.

Chapter 2 introduced Fritz Machlup, who would lead the Bellagio Group conferences from 1963 to 1977. The chapter examined Machlup's early experience in Austria and his writings leading up to the conferences to understand both his general research interests and his thinking about the balance of payments adjustment problems. Machlup's partial equilibrium adjustment model proved invaluable to an exploration of the effect of monetary policy on outcomes, as Machlup acknowledged in his biographical essays for *Banca Nazionale del Lavoro Quarterly Review*. Machlup was the first economist to introduce the language of liquidity, adjustment and confidence into the discussion of policy objectives.

Like his Bellagio Group co-leader William Fellner, Machlup had broad interests in aspects of national competitiveness, on which he continued to publish even as he immersed himself in monetary reform. These issues are not separate and distinct from monetary reform, but are heavily influenced by issues like capital flows, availability of talent and investment. Like Robert Triffin, Machlup published on every aspect of monetary reform. Triffin would later identify Machlup's methodology as key to his achievements and to his particular strength as an organizer.

Chapter 3 introduced the second of the triumvirate of Bellagio Group leaders, Robert Triffin, who was as deeply involved in European integration as he was in international monetary reform. Both Triffin and Machlup believed that confidence played a critical role in the monetary system. Triffin was single-mindedly committed to monetary system issues both European and international during the period covered by this book. While Triffin believed that his impact was limited to European integration, his plans for a European Reserve Fund and his active campaign for an international reserve unit led to the creation of the special reserve unit or special drawing rights (SDRs) in the IMF. Triffin saw the European monetary unification experience as a lesson for the world, and so it has become.

Chapter 4 examined the work of William Fellner and explored the commonalities between Fellner and Machlup. Both wrote on a range of issues related to competitiveness, innovation, productivity, oligopoly and monopoly – issues all related to economic growth. Like Machlup, Fellner continued to write on these issues even as he played a co-leader role in the Bellagio Group conferences and began writing on balance of payments issues. While Fellner's work on balance of payments problems is perhaps not as well known as Machlup's, is it clear that he deeply immersed himself in these issues from the beginning of the 1960s. Both economists were committed to freely floating exchange rates, but in their own writing and in the Bellagio Group conferences explored myriad possible solutions, given the ultimate decision would be made by the national governments of IMF member nations. Both economists shared a belief that government intervention in market mechanisms was to be avoided.

Chapter 5 introduced Machlup's grand experiment – to unlock the assumptions that were the sources of disagreement among economists – through a series of conferences. Machlup framed the problem in terms of adjustment, liquidity and confidence, forcing participants to focus on outcomes and the institutions necessary to achieve them, as well as to consider the opportunity cost of a focus on one outcome versus another. The economists invited to participate in the conferences were drawn from Group of Ten countries and had prior public policy experience. This enhanced their credibility and influence with the deputies of the Group of Ten, who were engaged in their own study and who would come to think of the Bellagio Group as a think tank.

Machlup took another approach familiar to contemporary strategy consulting, with its focus on cross-functional teams. He engaged every participant in every effort, so that all work belonged to every member of the group. It was essential to the Bellagio Group's approach and, when depicted in the final conference report, very appealing to the international bodies – the deputies of Group of Ten and the IMF – that were pursuing official studies and struggling with issues of group cohesion and the need to focus on outcomes rather than on blame.

Fritz Machlup and the Bellagio Group would do much, through conferences and print media, popular as well as academic, to expose audiences of academics, bankers, business leaders and policymakers to exchange rate solutions to payments adjustment problems and, ultimately, to the logic of managed flexibility of exchange rates and credit reserves under the International Monetary Fund as a preferred, hybrid solution.

Meanwhile, discussion of the options available to solve the adjustment, liquidity and confidence problems identified by Machlup and the Bellagio Group continued outside the conferences. Discussion and publication of alternative plans for solving the confidence and liquidity problems continued during and after the meetings. Chapter 6 explored a variety of multiple reserve currency plans. Perhaps the most popular solution for a time, and the purpose of all of these multiple reserve currency plans (with the exception of the European unit of account), was to avoid the problems associated with a single key currency.

Chapter 7 added another element important to the story of payments adjustment and liquidity – the importance of national discretion in macroeconomic policymaking. Both fixed and flexible rates had their advocates before and throughout the period covered in this book, many as early as the 1930s. Through the 1960s, the drive to maintain full employment while balancing international payments resulted in many innovations in economics. Some economists trusted an automatic mechanism; others sought to use interdependence to advantage. It is clear they were also reading each other's work, cherry-picking innovative policy and theory, and modifying or extending it.

The final report of the Bellagio Group conferences, *International Monetary Arrangements: The Problem of Choice* (1964), had attracted the attention of the Group of Ten, whose chairman Otmar Emminger asked Machlup and the Group to assist their study of adjustment policies and special drawing rights. The Group of Ten countries had signed the General Arrangements to Borrow.

In fact, the General Arrangements to Borrow created the burning platform necessary to bond European policymakers to seek a European voice in the IMF. This is the story told in Chapter 8. Machlup and the Bellagio Group would play a critical role in the development of that voice in the resolution of payments adjustment issues and in the adoption of special drawing rights through a series of conferences from 1964 to 1977.

Chapter 9 continued the story of the Joint Meetings of Officials and Academics. These meetings played an important role in the history of adjustment policy recommendations and special reserve assets (or SDRs as they came to be called). While the SDR was originally envisaged as a means of alleviating a shortage of international reserves, the suspension of gold convertibility, elimination of par values and development of international credit markets during the 1970s eliminated the role of the SDR in helping to maintain gold convertibility. Nevertheless, other aspects of the SDR became more salient, including reserve supplementation, reserve refinancing, and an alternative to international financial markets when the creditworthiness of individual countries or confidence in the system as a whole is in crisis.

The Joint Meetings of Officials and Academics reflected the decision of the deputies of the Group of Ten to pursue a separate identity from the IMF as a whole. They also met separately from the executive directors of the Fund to formulate their own platform on issues of balance of payments adjustment, SDRs and the inclusion of developing countries in the allocation of SDRs. The Joint Conferences of Officials and Academics preceded the required submission of major reports promised by the deputies to the ministers and governors of the Group of Ten. The research presented here supports the argument made by James and others that the move to separate meetings reflects the increasing Europeanization of the deputies of the Group of Ten, and demonstrates where these separate meetings took place, who organized them, what was on the agenda, and – for the first time – who attended these meetings. The data suggests as well that the deputies were often far from ready to reach the agreement on issues necessary to satisfy the IMF executive directors. Meeting together, the executive directors doubtless sought to reach faster closure on key issues and to identify next steps. At the Joint Meetings of Officials and Academics, there was far more open-ended discussion and seldom a neatly packaged set of recommendations and conclusions.

Chapter 10 focused on Machlup's expansion of the Bellagio Group approach to an audience of business leaders and bankers. Machlup would later attribute the extension of the conferences to a corporate audience to a suggestion made by Otmar Emminger. Nevertheless, the strategy of enlarging the audience for an examination of greater exchange rate flexibility and using publication, including the academic and trade media outreach of Bürgenstock members, was a dissemination approach associated with Machlup since *Financing American Prosperity* in 1945 and *Maintaining Balance in International Payments* in 1966.

The absence of an adjustment mechanism and the failure to control international liquidity seemed to rule out multiple currencies and the semi-automatic gold standard for the Bellagio Group conferees, just as unlimited, unmanaged flexibility of exchange rates was effectively ruled out by the Bürgenstock conferees. Nevertheless, the dramatic reversal of thinking among the corporate executives at the Bürgenstock conferences – after rigorous discussion and commitment to research, write, present and re-edit for publication – is telling: 100 per cent against any change to the existing exchange rate regime at the start of the conference, and more than 75 per cent for flexible rates at its conclusion.

The disciplined exploration of alternative scenarios and their consequences for policy, management and institutional decisions prepared conferees for a range of contingencies and ensured the diffusion of the scenario approach to audiences in academia, public policy and management.

Chapter 11 focused on the Group of Thirty as a successor to the Joint Meetings of Officials and Academics, although operating with a formal structure and a larger budget. Unlike the Joint Meetings of Officials and Academics, where the focus was on the Group of Ten countries, the intention of the Consultative Group was to draw developing countries into the membership. Members of the Group of Thirty included central bankers and public officials, corporate executives and academics. A number of the founding members had been members of the Bellagio Group, Bürgenstock Group or the Joint Meetings of Officials and Academics.

Chapter 12 addressed the impact the Bellagio Group had on monetary reform. Contemporaries and insiders testified to the Bellagio Group's impact, noting its focus on outcomes, specifically adjustment, liquidity and confidence; its stress on exchange rate regimes for payments adjustment; its exposure of audiences of academics, policymakers and bankers to an exploration of alternative exchange rate scenarios; its exploration of flexible exchange rates at a time when policymakers as well as bankers were against (or at least very uncomfortable with) a move to exchange rate flexibility; and most particularly its work on 'the pretty solution that was found for the liquidity problem', Machlup's words in 1968 for the SDR. Machlup's fear was that the Bellagio Group had made a mistake giving priority to the problem of liquidity and disregarding the problems of confidence and adjustment. 'Responsible governments may reflect on the possible developments and realize that a failure to negotiate collective actions solving the problems of confidence and adjustment might jeopardize the successful solution of the liquidity problem'.

Chapter 13 introduced some of the scholars who have worked and are working under the influence of the Bellagio Group. Whether or not they were members of the Bellagio Group, the students and colleagues of Machlup, Kindleberger and Triffin seem to have immersed themselves in the issues important to their mentors. Penrose, Hymer, Tobin, Crockett and Truman perceived a role for government in relieving market failures and opportunism. In this regard, Penrose and Hymer went far afield of Machlup and Kindleberger, while Tobin, Crockett and Truman aligned closely with Triffin.

In all cases presented here, the failure of monetary system reform was a catalyst for their research, publication and civic involvement. This failure of collective will is inversely proportional to scholarly output. The continued work of the International Triffin Foundation and its close association with the Bank for International Settlements placed contributing scholars in the right place to effect reform, if they can address as the Bellagio Group did the institutional and operational mechanisms necessary to monitor and control it.

Initial Questions and Hypotheses

The research plan for the book focused on four questions and four preliminary hypotheses, given in the Introduction.

The first question was: What are the payments problems that stimulated academics and policymakers to recommend changes to the existing system? What were the origins of these problems? The first question and initial hypothesis drove the research for Chapter 1. Whether or not Triffin's statement to the US Congress and the publication of *Gold and the Dollar Crisis* overstated the problem in 1959–60, he did not overstate the fears of Europeans dependent on a single reserve currency for international trade, investment and defence.

On the question of origins, contemporaries are divided along national lines. The Europeans, particularly the French, have argued that the USA used its largesse to spread its influence around the world and generate income from investment at a time when domestic long-term capital gains were scarce. Investment as an instrument of economic and social capital has been a long-term research interest of mine. I have tracked the contributions of foreign firms to GDP in host countries and found that contribution to GDP inevitably gives the foreign entity more influence on economic policy as a matter of course. This point was made by Andre de Lattre, and underlies Giscard d'Estaing's push for surveillance powers and controls to prevent the use of additional liquidity in the system to fund more influence building and more deficits.

In the early mid-1960s, four major policy areas had emerged for reform of the monetary system. Many economists and policymakers, including the Group of Ten and the IMF, had plans (sometimes more than one) to solve the system's problems. In time, because of continuous discussion and publication, and the opportunities provided by the Bellagio Group conferences, the reform policies advocated by both economists and policymakers evolved or mutated from their original positions.

This brings us to the second question: for each of the policy proposals, who were the advocates? Chapter 2 introduced the advocates and their preferred plans. Chapter 6 focused on multiple reserve currency plans. As the Group of Ten grew in importance, as Europe became stronger economically, a move to multiple reserve currencies would have been a reasonable, multilateral solution. Indeed, for a time it seemed that the USA had accepted this solution as well. The issue became more complicated when it appeared that multiple reserve currencies were also intended to increase liquidity and hence might offer countries in payments deficit an opportunity to spend far more beyond their means to pay. The moral hazard problem would stymie plans for an international reserve currency.

Chapters 7 delved more deeply into the economic theory contributions of advocates of exchange rate solutions. As the 1990s and early 2000s were to technology innovation, so too were the 1960s to theory contributions related to flexible rates and regionally fixed rates.

Again, question two asked: What were the macroeconomic effects anticipated for each proposal? Machlup's determination to frame problems in the system and potential solutions in terms of their impact on liquidity, adjustment and confidence was an attempt to focus the discussion on macroeconomic effects. The Bellagio Group examined alternative solutions to the problems confronting the monetary system from the vantage point of outcomes and the consequences of the opportunity foregone. The approach, which also ferreted out underlying assumptions, values, prejudices and the like, was a novel approach, although Machlup had used similar techniques in his work for the Twentieth Century Fund and in his teaching.

I had hypothesized that choice of exchange rate regime would have a profound influence on stability and growth. So had most of the thinkers in Chapter 7. As flexible rates gained greater acceptance in the late 1960s, concerns about instability had taken a back seat to the ability of the market to assess the wisdom of national monetary policies, the need to eliminate payments imbalances and national competitive advantage.

While wildly fluctuating rates, exacerbated by speculation, political unrest or one-off events, has proved a contributor to instability since 1973, yet there seems little proof that exchange rate fluctuation per se has had a sizable impact on trade or growth. Unilateral government action (USA goes ex-gold) did roil the markets for a period of time, and the threat of financial crises continues to do so, limiting investment and therefore growth.

Question three asked: What was the Bellagio Group's impact on policy then and now? I had hypothesized that the Bellagio Group members had been active in public policy and went on to have impact on policy change. The research yielded a major finding: Given the assignment of the Group of Ten to reports on liquidity and adjustment, the selection of Bellagio Group members who were from Group of Ten countries and who had public policy experience was important to credibility and influence. Not ivory-tower intellectuals with little or no practical experience, the Bellagio Group economists knew what they were talking about, and they commanded the respect of the finance and treasury officials who were the deputies of the Group of Ten. A number of Bellagio Group members and members of the Joint Meetings of Officials and Academics were also engaged in European integration as previously noted, where some, like Otmar Emminger and Alexandre Lamfalussy, continue to be very important to the effort.

It must be emphasized that the Bellagio Group was, in the end, an NGO, not a policymaking body. Machlup, Triffin and Emminger were disappointed in the final results, not because flexible exchange rates were approved, but because adjustment itself was given little attention, and SDRs, approved for use as an international currency, were severely restricted for fear that they would be overused by the USA. Nevertheless, fear is a self-limiting emotion. There is a comparison to be made with the fears generated by the financial crisis of 2008–9 and the current European debt crisis. How have these fears influenced the search for a proper diagnosis and the exploration of possible solutions?

Question four asked: What was the legacy of the Bellagio Group members of international trade and finance scholarship? I had hypothesized that Bellagio Group members, chosen because of their reputation as scholars and teachers, would have significant impact on research going forward as well as on the research and career choices of their students. My research revealed the continuous stream of research and publication of Bellagio Group members. Chapters 2, 3 and 4 focused on the contributions of Machlup, Triffin and Fellner. Chapters 6 and 7 depicted Bellagio Group members continuously working on contributions to policy and theory. Chapter 13 focused on a few students of Machlup, Triffin and Kindleberger. This chapter sacrifices breadth for depth; the many for the few. This is a serious limitation that will be addressed my future research. Nevertheless, it appears that the students of Machlup, Kindleberger and Triffin, even though they were not members of the Bellagio Group themselves, were led in research directions that paralleled their mentors and the research trends of the 1960s.

I began this study on a very personal quest – to understand where Edith Penrose fits in the story of Machlup, her mentor, and the Bellagio Group. A simple answer would have been 'nowhere', as she was not a member. However, the examination of the research published by Bellagio Group members and their students during the 1960s and after presents a different picture, one of economists engaged in innovative work around the issues important to trade and growth. Using this frame, there is Penrose as well as Stephen Hymer, along with other innovators, treading new ground or extending existing theory.

A Few Meta-Conclusions

Are there any meta-conclusions that can be drawn from the research and analysis presented here? Are there any lessons for today's problems of deficits and unemployment, unilateralism and multilaterism? The impact of the Bellagio Group on public policy was one of approach as well as outcome. Since the approach has perennial value, I begin with that.

Modern strategy practice focuses on strategic planning by cross-functional, cross-geographic teams. The objective is a unifying decision process, to use the name of a seminal article on collaborative planning. Teams and decision makers meet to achieve agreement on goals, the work to be done, the timing and the outputs. Decisions are rendered and the team returns to its work. Essential to this collaborative view of strategy is the fact that it is not unilateral. It is a conversation as Kees van der Heijden (2005) would say. A major purpose is the elimination of silos, whether functional, geographic or ideological. The Bellagio Group, Joint Meetings and Bürgenstock conferences provided the opportunity for such collaborative planning. Here, important tools are used to help otherwise disparate groups to focus on common work (and ultimately common goals). These tools include framing. Changing the frame changes the group's perception of the alternative or scenario being explored. Machlup's use of his partial equilibrium adjustment model – the need to identify disturbing changes and adjusting changes – would lead to counter-intuitive findings. As Machlup wrote, balance of payments and dollar shortage theorists did not understand that monetary policy and misaligned exchange rates were the disturbing changes causing an adjusting change – reduced monetary reserves.

His framing of alternative scenarios in terms of outcomes with respect to liquidity, adjustment and confidence is one of a number of matrix scenario approaches in common practice today for situations where uncertainty is high. The method ensures the development of three or four stories that are as different from each other as possible within the limits of credibility to the scenario user. Pierre Wack, one of the foundational scenarists mentioned in Chapter 10, said, 'Good scenarios emerge from an intensely experienced polarity'. Recall Machlup's words in Chapter 5 about his choice of economists from divergent, even feuding points of view. Note that Machlup reduced alternative policy regimes to only four for consideration at the Bellagio Group conferences. At the Bürgenstock conferences in the late 1960s and early 1970s, he did the same, but all scenarios reflected some degree of managed or unmanaged floating, a consequence of the growing acceptability of some degree of exchange rate flexibility.

The choice of participants was as much a strategic factor as the discussion process itself. Again, it is common to strategy practice to assemble a team that is reflective of the stakeholders involved. Clearly, that was the intention of the Bellagio Group's choice of experts from Group of Ten countries and experts with prior public policy experience. Let us not forget the word 'expert' used here. The subject knowledge of experts invited to join the group ensured relevant and thoroughgoing discussion. The same experts would co-facilitate the Bürgenstock conferences, opening up the discussion, while the corporate executives and bankers introduced new perspectives. In fact, the original Bellagio Group and Bürgenstock conferences were closely facilitated to achieve these ends.

Nevertheless, all conferences between 1963 and 1977 focused on Group of Ten membership only, leaving most members of the IMF outside the strategy circle. A world trading system that is as dependent on raw materials and intermediate goods as on final goods and customer relations needs to draw all IMF members in. The creation of the Group of Thirty, after the last Joint Meeting of Officials and Academics at Basle in 1977, reflects, in my view, an attempt to open up the conferences to a more diverse membership. The fact that the Bellagio Group was resurrected in 2006 and continues under the leadership of Barry Eichengreen suggests a continuing need for the candid discussions of the Bellagio Group outside a formal institution.

The focus of the Bellagio Group economists was largely on trade and growth. That orientation is clear from their publication record before and during the conferences. Hence, understandably, the outcome of the Bellagio Group conferences was a system of flexible exchange rates that left macroeconomic policy to national governments, protected by special drawing rights of the IMF, in the event of serious payments imbalance or financial crisis. Based on their shared background in the Depression and World War II, the orientation is reasonable. Bordo and Rousseau (2011) attributed the rising importance of trade in explaining growth to major post-World War II changes in tariffs and quantity restrictions associated with the GATT, the establishment of the European Common Market, and the gradual elimination of capital controls after 1973.

In fact, the growing relationship of trade to GDP can be seen as early as 1960. Trade as a per cent of GDP hovered at 9 per cent in the USA, but at 25 per cent in France and Italy in 1960, climbing to 31 per cent in 1970. Other European countries experienced a higher trade to GDP ratio – 98 per cent for Belgium, 43 per cent for the UK in 1970. This was a golden age of growth for Europe. If the nation is trading and growing, any problem is soluble. The Bellagio Group economists rightly put the emphasis on trade and growth first.

Is growth no longer our primary concern? Yes, growth remains an underlying concern. Given slow or negative growth, unemployment rates are persistently very high. Like the Group of Ten in 1962, the Group of Twenty stepped in to support their banking systems through the financial crisis of 2008–9. In the words of the World Economic Forum report *Outlook on the Global Agenda*

2012, 'they brought the problem onto their own balance sheets'. The world's largest economies are now facing sovereign debt crises, while at the same time the system lacks a globally accepted financial regulatory system. Lack of confidence and speculation are rife. Leadership is also weak. At a time when debt is obviously a foremost issue and solutions call for austerity, the world needs to focus on trade and growth as well as on greater coordination of policy and regulation. The world needs a bigger safety net – perhaps an extended SDR programme – and perhaps renewed Bellagio Group effort to focus the discussion on desired outcomes and the cost of opportunities foregone.

NOTES

1 A Crisis in Confidence

1. R. Triffin, *Gold and the Dollar Crisis: The Future of Convertibility* (New Haven, CT: Yale University Press, 1960).
2. R. Triffin, 'An Economist's Career: What? Why? How?', *Banca Nazionale del Lavoro Quarterly Review*, 138 (1981), pp. 239–60, on p. 245.
3. C. F. Bergsten, 'Exchange Rate Policy', in M. Feldstein (ed.), *American Economics Policy in the 1980s* (Chicago, IL: University of Chicago Press, 1994), p. 44.
4. Triffin, *Gold and the Dollar Crisis: The Future of Convertibility*, p. 8.
5. M. De Vries, *Balance of Payments Adjustment* (Washington, DC: International Monetary Fund, 1987), p. 80.
6. B. Eichengreen, *Globalizing Capital* (Princeton, NJ: Princeton University Press, 2008), pp. 91–2.
7. G. Toniolo, *Central Bank Cooperation at the Bank for International Settlements, 1930–1973* (Cambridge: Cambridge University Press, 2005), pp. 460–1.
8. Ibid., pp. 351–2.
9. Ibid., p. 353.
10. F. Gavin, *Gold, Dollars and Power: The Politics of International Monetary Relations, 1958–1971* (Chapel Hill, NC: University of North Carolina Press, 2004).
11. Eichengreen, *Globalizing Capital*, p. 115.
12. K. Dyson and K. Featherstone, *The Road to Maastricht* (Oxford: Oxford University Press, 1999), p. 83.
13. B. Eichengreen and H. James, 'Monetary and Financial Reform in the Two Eras of Globalization', in M. Bordo, A. Taylor and J. Williamson (eds), *Globalization in Historical Perspective* (Chicago, IL: University of Chicago Press, 2003), pp. 515–48, on p. 515.
14. I. Maes, 'The Ascent of the European Commission as an Actor in the Monetary Integration Process in the 1960s', European Union Studies Association Biennial Conference, conference paper (2 November 2004), p. 1–26, on p. 6, at http://aei.pitt.edu/3009/1/MMTEC60art.pdf [accessed 24 August 2012].
15. C. Hefeker, 'The Political Choice and Collapse of Fixed Exchange Rates', *Journal of Institutional and Theoretical Economics*, 152 (1996), pp. 360–79; J. Frieden, 'The Impact of Goods and Capital Market Integration on European Monetary Politics', *Comparative Political Studies*, 29 (1996), pp.193–222.
16. I. Maes and L. Quaglia, 'France's and Italy's Policies on European Monetary Integration: A Comparison of Strong and Weak States', Robert Schumann Centre for Advanced

Studies, EIU Working Papers, 10 (2003), pp. 1–33, on p. 10, at http://www.eui.eu/RSCAS/WP-Texts/03_10.pdf [accessed 24 August 2012].

17. F. Machlup, 'Summary and Analysis', in P. Homan and F. Machlup (eds), *Financing American Prosperity: A Symposium of Economists* (New York: Twentieth Century Fund, 1945), pp. 394–496, on p. 397.

18. P. Homan, 'Introduction', in P. Homan and F. Machlup (eds), *Financing American Prosperity: A Symposium of Economists* (New York: Twentieth Century Fund, 1945), pp. 1–8, on p. 3.

19. US Treasury, 'Major Foreign Holders of US Securities (through April 2012)', US Treasury Data and Charts Center (2012), at http://www.treasury.gov/resource-center/data-chart-center/tic/Documents/mfh.txt [accessed 24 August 2012].

20. M. Obstfeld and K. Rogoff, 'Global Imbalances and Financial Crisis: Products of Common Causes', Federal Reserve Bank of San Francisco Asia Economic Policy Conference, conference paper (2009) pp. 1–63.

21. Homan, 'Introduction', pp. 1–3.

22. A. Hansen, 'Stability in Expansion', in P. Homan and F. Machlup (eds), *Financing American Prosperity: A Symposium of Economists* (New York: Twentieth Century Fund, 1945), pp. 199–265.

23. Ibid., p. 200.

24. P. Kenen, 'Nature, Capital and Trade', *Journal of Political Economy*, 73:5 (1965), pp. 437–60.

25. H. Johnson, 'The Theory of Tariff Structure, with Special Reference to World Trade and Development' in H. Johnson and P. Kenen, *Trade and Development* (Geneva: Librarie Droz, 1965), pp. 9–29.

26. J. Vanek, *General Equilibrium of International Discrimination: The Case of Customs Unions* (Cambridge, MA: Harvard University Press, 1965).

27. Johnson, 'Theory of Tariff Structure', pp. 9–29; M. Corden, 'The Tructure of a Tariff System and the Effective Protective Rate', *Journal of Political Economy* (June 1966), pp. 221–37.

28. H. Johnson, *Economic Policies Towards Less Developed Countries* (Washington, DC: Brookings Institution, 1965), pp. 163–211; B. Belassa, 'The Impact of the Industrial Countries' Structure on their Imports of Manufactures from Less-Developed Areas', *Economica* (November 1967), pp. 372–83.

29. M. Bordo, E. Simard and E. White, 'France and the Bretton Woods International Monetary System: 1960 to 1968', NBER Working Paper, 4642 (1994), pp. 1–42, at http://www.nber.org/papers/w4642 [accessed 24 August 2012].

30. P. Einzig, *Behind the Scenes of International Finance* (New York: Arrno Press, 1978), p.vii.

31. L. Wray, 'Keynes's Approach to Money: An Assessment after Seventy Years', *Atlantic Economic Journal*, 34 (2006), pp. 183–93.

32. L. von Mises, 'The Gold Problem', *The Freeman*, 15:6 (1965), para. 1, at http://www.thefreemanonline.org/featured/the-gold-problem/ [accessed 24 August 2012].

33. R. Cooper, 'Exchange Rate Choices', in J. Little and G. Olivei (eds), *Rethinking the International Monetary System*, Conference Series 43 (Boston, MA: Federal Reserve Bank, 1999), pp. 99–123, at http://www.bos.frb.org/economic/conf/conf43/99p.pdf [accessed 24 August 2012].

34. M. Friedman, 'The Case for Flexible Exchange Rates', in M. Friedman, *Essays in Positive Economics* (Chicago, IL: University of Chicago Press, 1953), pp. 157–203, on p. 199.

35. R. Triffin, 'The Impact of the Bellagio Group on World Monetary Reform', in J. Dreyer (ed.), *Breadth and Depth in Economics: Fritz Machlup—The Man and His Ideas* (Lexington, MA: Lexington Books, 1978), pp. 145–58, on p. 147.
36. F. Machlup, *International Monetary Arrangements: The Problem of Choice; Report on the Deliberations of an International Study Group of 32 Economists* (Princeton, NJ: International Finance Section, Princeton University, 1964), p. 8.
37. R. Roosa, *Monetary Reform for the World Economy* (New York: Harper & Row, 1965), p. vii.
38. Ibid.
39. Ibid., p. 40.
40. O. Emminger, 'The D-Mark in the Conflict between Internal and External Equilibrium, 1948–75', Essays in International Finance, 122 (Princeton, NJ: International Finance Section, Princeton University, 1977), pp. 1–54, on p. 47.
41. A. de Lattre, *Politique économique de la France depuis 1945* (Patis: Editions Sirey, 1966), pp. 329, 336.

2 Fritz Machlup, his Research and Methodology

1. F. Machlup, 'My Early Work on International Monetary Problems', *Banca Nazionale del Lavoro Quarterly Review*, 133 (1980) pp. 115–46, on p. 114.
2. F. Machlup, *International Payments, Debts and Gold* (New York: Charles Scribner's Sons, 1964). See also note 9 below.
3. F. Machlup, *International Monetary Systems and the Free Market Economy*, Reprints in International Finance (Princeton, NJ: International Finance Section, Princeton University, 1966).
4. J. Williamson, 'Machlup and International Monetary Reform', in J. Dreyer (ed.), *Breadth and Depth in Economics: Fritz Machlup—The Man and His Ideas* (Toronto: Lexington Books, 1978), pp.159–72, p. 167.
5. Machlup, 'My Early Work', p. 119.
6. Ibid.
7. Ibid., pp. 136–7.
8. Ibid., p. 137.
9. F. Machlup, 'Theory of Foreign Exchanges', in F. Machlup, *International Monetary Economics* (London: Routledge, 2003), pp. 7–50, on p. 11. This book was published by Charles Scribner's Sons in 1964 under the title *International Payments, Debts and Gold*.
10. Machlup, 'Theory of Foreign Exchanges', p. 10.
11. F. Machlup, 'Elasticity Pessimism in International Trade', in F. Machlup, *International Monetary Economics* (London: Routledge, 2003), pp. 51–68, on p. 55.
12. F. Machlup, 'Interview with Fritz Machlup', *The Austrian Economics Newsletter*, 3:1 (1980), para. 15, at http://mises.org/journals/aen/aen3_1_1.asp [accessed 24 August 2012].
13. L. von Mises, *Human Action: A Treatise on Economics* (London: William Hodge, 1949), pp. 97, 393.
14. J. Schumpeter, *History of Economic Analysis* (Oxford: Oxford University Press, 1954).
15. D. Bernhofen, 'Gottfried Haberler's 1930 Reformulation of Comparative Advantage in Retrospect', SSRN Working Paper (2005), pp. 1–5, at http://papers.ssrn.com/sol3/papers.cfm?abstract_id=863924 [accessed 24 August 2012].
16. 'Interview with Fritz Machlup', para. 10–11.

17. J. Proops and P. Safonov (eds), *Modelling in Ecological Economics* (London: Edward Elgar Publishing, 2005).
18. J. Buchanan, *Cost and Choice: An Enquiry in Economic Theory* (Chicago, IL: Markham, 1969).
19. F. Machlup, 'Eight Questions on Gold', in F. Machlup, *International Monetary Economics* (London: Routledge, 2003), pp. 228–38, on p. 231.
20. Ibid., p. 232.
21. Ibid., p. 233.
22. See Chapter 5 for the use of adjustment, liquidity and confidence in the Bellagio Group conferences, and Chapter 12 for an acknowledgement of his contribution by contemporaries.
23. F. Machlup, 'My Work on International Monetary Problems, 1940–1964', *Banca Nazionale del Lavoro Quarterly Review*, 140 (1982), pp. 3–36, on p. 22.
24. F. Machlup, *Methodology of Economics and Other Social Sciences* (New York: Academic Press, 1978), p. 143.
25. R. Langlois and R. Koppl, 'Fritz Machlup and Marginalism', *Methodus*, 3 (1991), pp. 86–102, on p. 88.
26. R. Koppl, 'Invisible Hand Explanations and Neoclassical Economics: Toward a Post Marginalist Economics', *Journal of Institutional and Theoretical Economics*, 148 (1992), pp. 292–313, on p. 295.
27. Machlup, *Methodology of Economics*, p. 148.
28. Koppl, 'Invisible Hand', p. 303.
29. F. Machlup, 'Equilibrium and Disequilibrium: Misplaced Concreteness and Disguised Politics', *Economic Journal*, 68 (1958), pp. 1–24. Quoted in Machlup, 'My Work on International Monetary Problems', p. 20.
30. Machlup, 'My Work on International Monetary Problems', p. 22.
31. Williamson, 'Machlup and International Monetary Reform', p. 167.
32. F. Machlup, *World Monetary Debate: Bases for Agreement*, Reprints in International Finance (Princeton, NJ: International Finance Section, Princeton University, 1966), p. 2.
33. Ibid.
34. Ibid.
35. Ibid., p. 3.
36. Ibid., pp. 4–5.
37. Ibid., p. 5.
38. Ibid., p. 6.
39. F. Machlup, *The Need for Monetary Reserves*, Reprints in International Finance (Princeton, NJ: International Finance Section, Princeton University, 1966), p. 27.
40. Ibid., p. 29.
41. Ibid., p. 30.
42. Ibid., p. 31.
43. F. Machlup, 'Plans for Reform of the International Monetary System', *International Monetary Economics* (London: Routledge, 2003), pp. 282–366, on p. 278.
44. Ibid., p. 366.
45. F. Machlup and E. Penrose, 'The Patent Controversy in the Nineteenth Century', *Journal of Economic History*, 10:1 (1950), pp. 1–29; E. Penrose, *The Economics of the International Patent System* (Baltimore, MD: John Hopkins University Press, 1951); F. Machlup, 'The Optimum Lag of Imitation behind Innovation', in Nationaløkonomisk

Forening, *Festskrift til Frederik Zeuthen* (Copenhagen: Nationaløkonomisk Forening, 1958), pp. 239–46.

46. F. Machlup, 'Patents and Inventive Effort', *Science*, new ser., 133:3,463 (1961), pp. 1463–6.
47. W. Baumol and D. Fischer, 'Optimal Lags in a Schumpeterian Innovation Process', C. V. Starr Working Papers, RR77–17 (1977), at http://www.econ.nyu.edu/cvstarr/working/1977/RR77-17.pdf, pp. 1–40 [accessed 24 August 2012].
48. F. Machlup, 'The Supply of Inventors and Inventions', *Weltwirtschaftliches Archiv*, 85:2 (1960), pp. 210–54, on p. 241.
49. R. Nelson, 'Introduction', in National Bureau Committee for Economic Research, *The Rate and Direction of Inventive Activity: Economic and Social Factors* (Washington, DC: NBER Books, 1962), pp. 3–16, on p. 3.
50. F. Machlup, *The Production and Distribution of Knowledge in the United States* (Princeton, NJ: Princeton University Press, 1962), p. 3–4.
51. Ibid., p. 5.
52. Ibid., p. 7.

3 Robert Triffin and the Triffin Plan

1. C. Ferrant, J. Sloover, M. Dumoulin and O. Lefebvre, *Robert Triffin, conseiller des princes : souvenirs et documents* (Brussels: PIE-Peter Lang, 2010), p. 23.
2. Triffin, 'An Economist's Career'.
3. A. Endres, *Great Architects of International Finance* (London: Routledge, 2005).
4. E. Helleiner, 'Dollarization Diplomacy: US Policy Toward Latin America Coming Full Circle', *Review of International Political Economy*, 10:3 (2003), pp. 406–29; M. Flandreau, *Money Doctors: The Experience of International Financial Advising 1850–2000* (London: Routledge, 2003).
5. M. Blaug, *Great Economists since Keynes: An Introduction to the Lives and Works of One Hundred Modern Economists* (Totowa, NJ: Barnes & Noble, 1985), pp. 250–1.
6. B. Lambert, 'Willard L. Thorp, 92, Economist Who Helped Draft Marshall Plan', *New York Times*, 11 May 1992, para. 1 and 9, at http://www.nytimes.com/1992/05/11/us/willard-l-thorp-92-economist-who-helped-draft-marshall-plan.html [accessed 24 August 2012].
7. Triffin, 'The Impact of the Bellagio Group', p. 145.
8. Ibid., p. 146.
9. Ibid.
10. R. Triffin, 'National Central Banking and the International Economy', *Review of Economic Studies*, 14:2 (1947), pp. 53–75, on p. 53.
11. Ibid., p. 60.
12. R. Triffin, *Europe and the Money Muddle: From Bilateralism to Near Convertibility, 1947–1956* (London: Oxford University Press, 1957), pp. 296–7.
13. R. Triffin, 'Updating the Triffin Plan', in R. Triffin, *The World Money Maze* (New Haven, CT: Yale University Press, 1965), pp. 346–73, on pp. 349–50.
14. Triffin, *Europe and the Money Muddle*, p. 303.
15. I. Maes, 'Macroeconomic and Monetary Policy-Making at the EC, from the Rome Treaties to the Hague Summit', National Bank of Belgium Working Paper, 58 (2004), pp. 1–28, on p. 9, at http://ssrn.com/abstract=1691479 [accessed 24 August 2012].
16. Triffin, *Europe and the Money Muddle*, p. 289.
17. Ibid., p. 290.

18. Ibid., p. 288.
19. See Chapter 1 for a definition and brief discussion of the 'Triffin Dilemma'.
20. R. Triffin, *Gold and the Dollar Crisis: Yesterday and Tomorrow*, Essays in International Finance, 132 (Princeton, NJ: International Finance Section, Princeton University, 1978), p. 3.
21. Ibid., p. 3.
22. Ibid., p. 5.
23. Triffin, *Gold and the Dollar Crisis: The Future of Convertibility*, p. 106.
24. Triffin, *Gold and the Dollar Crisis: Yesterday and Tomorrow*, p. 6.
25. Triffin, *Gold and the Dollar Crisis: The Future of Convertibility*, p. 114.
26. Ibid.
27. B. Malkiel, 'Why the Triffin Plan was Rejected and the Alternative Accepted', *Journal of Finance*, 18:3 (1963), pp. 511–36, on p. 515.
28. C. Kindleberger, *Power and Money: The Economics of International Politics and the Politics of International Economics* (New York: Basic Books, 1970), p. 216.
29. Ibid.
30. O. Altman, 'Professor Triffin on International Liquidity and the Role of the Fund', *IMF Staff Papers*, 8:2 (1961), pp. 151–91, on p. 187.
31. L. Yeager, 'The Triffin Plan: Diagnosis, Remedy and Alternatives', *Kyklos*, 14:3 (1961), pp. 285–314, on p. 312.
32. J. Furth, 'Professor Triffin and the Problem of International Monetary Reform', *Journal of Economics*, 21:3–4 (1962), pp. 415–25, on p. 424.
33. R. Triffin, Robert Triffin Papers, 1934–1978. Sterling Memorial Library, Yale University, New Haven, CT. MS 874, box 1, folder 10, copyright Yale University.
34. R. Triffin, 'A Brief for the Defense', *IMF Staff Papers*, 8:2 (1961), pp. 192–4, on p. 192.
35. R. Triffin, *The Balance of Payments and the Foreign Investment Position of the United States*, Essays in International Finance, 55 (Princeton, NJ: International Finance Section, Princeton University, 1966), pp. 9–14.
36. Robert Triffin Papers. MS 874, box 12, folder 10, copyright Yale University.
37. R. Triffin, 'After the Gold Exchange Standard', *Weltwirtschaftliches Archiv*, 87 (1961), pp. 188–207, on p. 199.
38. Robert Triffin Papers. MS 874, box 1, folder 1, 'The International Monetary Crisis', pp. 7–8, copyright Yale University.
39. Robert Triffin Papers. MS 874, box 1 folder 1, copyright Yale University.
40. Triffin, 'An Economist's Career', p. 245.
41. Ibid.
42. R. Triffin, 'The Trade Expansion Act of 1962', *Proceedings of the Annual Meeting*, American Society of International Law, 56 (1962), pp. 139–58, on p. 139.
43. Ibid., p. 141.
44. Bureau of Labor Statistics, 'Unemployment in the G7 Countries: 1960–1973' (September 2002), at http://www.bls.gov/opub/ted/2002/sept/wk1/art03.htm [accessed 24 August 2012].
45. L. Crafts, 'Fifty Years of Economic Growth in Western Europe: No Longer Catching Up But Falling Behind', Stanford Institute for Public Policy Research, SIEPR Discussion Paper, 03–21 (2004), pp. 1–14, on p. 11.
46. K. Kliesen, 'An Oasis of Prosperity: Soley an American Phenomenon', *The Regional Economist*, Federal Reserve Bank of St Louis, 3 (1999), Table 1, at http://www.stlouis-fed.org/publications/re/articles/?id=1745 [accessed 24 August 2012].

47. Triffin, 'The Trade Expansion Act', p. 141.
48. Ibid., p. 142.
49. Ibid.
50. Ibid., p. 143.
51. Triffin, 'The Impact of the Bellagio Group', p. 154.
52. Ibid.
53. R. Triffin, 'The IMS (International Monetary System ... or Scandal?) and the EMS (European Monetary System ... or Success?)', *Banca Nazionale del Lavoro Quarterly Review*, 179 (1991), pp. 399–436, on p. 406–7.
54. F. Ritzmann, 'Money, a Substitute for Confidence?', *American Journal of Economics and Sociology*, 58:2 (1999), pp. 167–92, on pp. 176–7.
55. D. Dequech, 'Expectations and Confidence under Uncertainty', *Journal of Post Keynesian Economics*, 21:3 (1999), pp. 415–30, on p. 419.
56. J. Keynes, *The General Theory of Employment, Interest and Money* (Cambridge: Cambridge University Press, 1936), p. 148.
57. S. Dow, 'Mainstream Methodology, Financial Markets and Global Political Economy', *Contributions to Political Economy*, 27:1 (2009), pp. 13–29, on p. 2.
58. T. Nelson, Z. Oxley and R. Clawson, 'Toward a Psychology of Framing Effects', *Political Behavior*, 19:3 (1997), pp. 221–46.
59. A. Mintz and S. Redd, 'Framing Effects in International Relations', *Synthese*, 135:1 (2003), pp. 193–213, on p. 195.

4 William Fellner and the Intersection of Macro and Microeconomics

1. J. Marshall, *William J. Fellner: A Bio-Bibliography* (Westport, CT: Greenwood Press, 1992), pp. xiii–xiv.
2. F. Machlup, Register of the Fritz Machlup Papers, 1911–1983. Hoover Institution Archives, Stanford University, CA. Box 37, folders 1–2, copyright Stanford University.
3. B. Belassa and R. Nelson, *Economic Progress, Private Values and Public Policy: Essays in Honor of William Fellner* (Amsterdam: North-Holland Publishing Co., 1977), p. v.
4. Machlup, 'Summary and Analysis', p. 396.
5. W. Fellner, 'War Finance and Inflation', *American Economic Review* 32:2 (1942), pp. 235–54, on p.
6. W. Fellner, 'Postscript on War Inflation: A Lesson from World War II', *American Economic Review*, 37:1 (1947), pp. 76–91, on p. 91.
7. Ibid.
8. W. Fellner, M. Gilbert, B. Hansen, R. Kahn, F. Lutz and P. deWolff, *The Problem of Rising Prices* (Paris: Organisation for European Economic Co-operation, 1961).
9. Ibid., p. 73.
10. Ibid., p. 74.
11. Ibid.
12. W. Fellner, 'Hansen on Full-Employment Policies', *Journal of Political Economy*, 55 (June 1947), pp. 254–6, on p. 255.
13. W. Fellner, *Trends and Cycles in Economic Activity: An Introduction to Problems of Economic Growth* (New York: Holt, 1956), pp. 98, 304.

14. W. Fellner, 'Rapid Growth as an Objective of Economic Policy', *American Economic Review*, 50 (May 1960), pp. 93–105, on p. 93.

15. W. Fellner, *Competition among the Few: Oligopoly and Similar Market Structures* (New York: A. A. Knopf, 1949).

16. W. Fellner, *Towards a Reconstruction of Macroeconomics: Problems of Theory and Policy* (Washington, DC: American Enterprise Institute, 1976), p. 2.

17. W. Fellner, 'Budget Deficits and their Consequences', *Proceedings of the Academy of Political Science*, 27:3 (1963), pp. 29–38, on p. 30.

18. Ibid., p. 32.

19. Ibid.

20. W. Fellner, 'Rules of the Game', in W. Fellner, F. Machlup and R. Triffin (eds), *Maintaining and Restoring Balance in International Payments* (Princeton, NJ: Princeton University Press, 1966), pp. 11–31, on p. 11.

21. Ibid., p. 12.

22. Ibid., p. 20.

23. Ibid., p. 27.

24. W. Fellner, 'On Limited Exchange-rate Flexibility', in W. Fellner, F. Machlup and R. Triffin (eds), *Maintaining and Restoring Balance in International Payments* (Princeton, NJ: Princeton University Press, 1966), pp. 111–22, on pp. 118–19.

25. W. Fellner, 'Specific Proposal for Limited Exchange-Rate Flexibility', *Weltwirtschaftliches Archiv*, 104:1 (March 1970), pp. 20–35.

26. W. Fellner, 'A "Realistic" Note on Threefold Limited Flexibility of Exchange Rates', in G. Halm (ed.), *Approaches to Greater Flexibility of Exchange Rates: The Bürgenstock Papers* (Princeton, NJ: Princeton University Press, 1970), pp. 237–44.

27. W. Fellner, 'The Dollar's Place in the International System: Suggested Criteria for the Appraisal of Emerging Views', *Journal of Economic Literature*, 10:3 (1972), pp. 735–56.

28. W. Fellner, 'Controlled Floating and the Confused Issue of Money Illusion', *Banca Nazionale del Lavoro Quarterly Review*, 106 (1973), pp. 206–34, on p. 206.

29. Ibid., p. 214.

30. W. Fellner, 'Schools of Thought in the Mainstream of American Economics', *Acta Oeconomica*, 18:3–4 (1977), pp. 247–61, on p. 247.

31. Fellner, 'Controlled Floating', p. 207.

32. W. Fellner, 'The Credibility Effect and Rational Expectations: Implications of the Gramlich Study', *Brookings Papers on Economic Activity*, 1 (1979), pp. 167–89, on p. 168.

33. W. Fellner, 'The Valid Core of Rationality Hypotheses in the Theory of Expectation', *Journal of Money, Credit and Banking*, 12:4 (1980), pp. 763–87, on p. 766.

34. E. Le Heron and E. Carré, 'Credibility Versus Confidence in Monetary Policy', Institute of Political Studies, Bordeaux, Working Paper, pp. 1–38, on pp. 1–2.

5 Why Economists Disagree: The Role of Framing in Consensus Building

1. F. Machlup, 'Why Economists Disagree', *Proceedings of the American Philosophical Society*, 109 (1965), pp. 1–7.

2. Ibid., p. 7.

3. D. Snow and R. Benford, 'Master Frames and Cycles of Protest', in A. Morris and C. Muller (eds), *Frontiers in Social Movement Theory* (New Haven, CT: Yale University Press), pp. 133–55, on p. 137.

4. Ibid., p. 136.

5. R. Entman, 'Framing: Toward Clarification of a Fractured Paradigm', *Journal of Communication*, 43:4 (1993), pp. 51–8, on p. 52.

6. A. Tversky and D. Kahneman, 'The Framing of Decisions and the Psychology of Choice', *Science*, new ser., 211:4,481 (1981), pp. 453–8, on p. 457.

7. P. Nutt, 'Framing Strategic Decisions', *Organization Science*, 9:2 (1998), pp. 195–216, on p. 212.

8. A. Huff, *Mapping Strategic Thought* (Chichester: John Wiley & Sons, 1990); J. Porac and H. Thomas, 'Managing Cognition and Strategy: Issues, Trends and Future Directions', in A. Pettigrew, H. Thomas and R. Whittington (eds), *Handbook of Strategy and Management* (London: Sage, 2002), pp. 165–81; P. Barr, J. Stimpert and A. Huff, 'Cognitive Change, Strategic Action, and Organizational Renewal', *Strategic Management Journal*, 13 (1992), pp. 15–36.

9. D. Hambrick and P. Mason, 'Upper Echelons: The Organization as a Reflection of its Top Managers', *Academy of Management Review*, 9 (1984), pp. 193–206.

10. G. Hodgkinson, N. Bown, A. Maule, K. Glaister and A. Pearman, 'Breaking the Frame: An Analysis of Strategic Cognition and Decision Making under Uncertainty', *Strategic Management Journal*, 20:10 (1999), pp. 977–85.

11. Fritz Machlup Papers. Box 43, folder 10. Letter of invitation to the first Bellagio Group conference, copyright Stanford University.

12. Robert Triffin Papers. MS 874, box 12, folder 1, copyright Yale University.

13. Machlup, *International Monetary Arrangements*, pp. 8–9.

14. M. Alacevich and P. Asso, 'Money Doctoring after World War II: Arthur I. Bloomfield and the Federal Reserve Missions to South Korea,, *History of Political Economy Journal*, 41:2 (2009), pp. 249–70, on p. 251–2.

15. L. Chandler, 'Federal Reserve Policy and the Federal Debt', *American Economic Review*, 39:2 (1949), pp. 405–29, on p. 405.

16. J. Salerno, 'Biography of Gottfried Haberler (1901–1995)', Ludwig von Mises Institute, at http://mises.org/page/1452/Biography-of-Gottfried-Haberler-19011995 [accessed 24 August 2012].

17. J.-O. Hesse, 'Some Relationships between a Scholar's and an Entrepreneur's Life: The Biography of L. Albert Hahn', *History of Political Economy*, 39:1 (2007), pp. 215–33, on p. 215.

18. J. Williamson, 'In Memoriam: Fred Hirsch 1931–*1978*', *Journal of International Economics*, 8:4 (1978), pp. *579*–80.

19. P. McNelis and R. Driskill, 'In Memoriam: Jurg Niehans 1919–2007', *Journal of International Money and Finance*, 28:5 (2009), pp. 739–41.

20. Triffin, 'The Impact of the Bellagio Group', p. 148.

21. Ibid., p. 149.

22. Robert Triffin Papers. MS 874, box 12, folder 1, copyright Yale University.

23. Ibid.

24. Ibid.

25. Ibid.

26. Machlup, *International Monetary Arrangements*, pp. 101–2.

27. Machlup, *Methodology of Economics*, p. 148.

6 'Assuring the Free World's Liquidity' through Multiple Reserve Currencies

1. International Monetary Fund, 'Articles of Agreement', I.iv, at http://www.imf.org/external/pubs/ft/aa/index.htm [accessed 24 August 2012].
2. 'The Adequacy of Monetary Reserves', *IMF Staff Papers*, 3:3 (1954), pp. 181–227, on p. 181.
3. Ibid., pp. 217–18.
4. J. Horsefield, *The International Monetary Fund, 1945–1965, Vol III: Documents* (Washington, DC: International Monetary Fund, 1969), p. 355.
5. Ibid., p. 410.
6. H. James, *International Monetary Cooperation since Bretton Woods* (New York: Oxford University Press, 1996), p. 166.
7. J. Dunning, 'Explaining Changing Patterns of International Production: In Defense of the Eclectic Theory', *Oxford Bulletin of Economics and Statistics*, 41:4 (1979), pp. 269–95.
8. J. Dunning, J. Cantwell and T. Corley, 'The Theory of International Production: Some Historical Antecedents', in P. Hertner and G. Jones (eds), *Multinationals, Theory and History* (Aldershot: Gower, 1986), pp. 19–41.
9. P. Dicken, *Global Shift: Reshaping the Global Economic Map in the 21st Century* (Thousand Oaks, CA: Sage Publications, 2003).
10. Horsefield, *Vol. III: Documents*, p. 3.
11. Ibid., p. 20.
12. Ibid., p. 20–1.
13. J. Blondeel, 'A New Form of International Financing: Loans in European Units of Account', *Columbia Law Review*, 64:6 (1964), pp. 995–1,011, on p. 996.
14. Official Journal of the European Communities, Decision 3–59 (21 January 1959), at http://eur-lex.europa.eu/LexUriServ/LexUriServ.do?uri=DD:I:1959-1962:31959S0003:EN:PDF [accessed 24 August 2012].
15. Blondeel, 'A New Form of International Financing', p. 996.
16. Ibid.
17. J. Van Der Mensbrugghe, 'Bond Issues in European Units of Account', *IMF Staff Papers*, 11:3 (1964), pp. 446–56, on p. 447.
18. X. Zolotas, 'Towards a Reinforced Gold Exchange Standard', Bank of Greece Papers and Lectures, 7 (1961), p. 11; reprinted in H. Grubel (ed.), *World Monetary Reform* (CA: Stanford University Press, 1963), pp. 292–8.
19. F. Lutz, *The Problem of International Economic Equilibrium*, Professor Dr F. de Vries Lectures (Amsterdam: North-Holland Publishing Co., 1962), p. 63.
20. Ibid., p. 73.
21. Ibid., p. 66.
22. R. Roosa, 'Assuring the Free World's Liquidity', *Business Review Supplement*, Federal Reserve Bank of Philadelphia (1962), pp. 261–74, on pp. 5–7.
23. Ibid., pp. 11–12.
24. Machlup, 'Plans for Reform', p. 307.
25. Ibid., p. 308.
26. Ibid., p. 310.
27. S. Posthuma, 'The International Monetary System', *Banca Nazionale del Lavoro Quarterly Review*, 66 (1963), pp. 239–61, on p. 261.

28. E. Bernstein, 'A Practical Proposal for International Monetary Reserves', *Quarterly Review and Investment Survey*, Model, Roland & Co. (First Quarter 1963), pp. 1–8, on p. 6.
29. Ibid.
30. Ibid., p. 7.
31. Machlup, 'Plans for Reform', p. 316.
32. James, *International Monetary Cooperation*, p. 170.
33. Ibid., p. 165.
34. K. Flexner, 'The Creation of a European Payments Union: An Example of International Compromise', *Political Science Quarterly*, 72:2 (1957), pp. 241–60.
35. D. Jones, 'The European Monetary Agreement, the European Payments Union and Convertibility', *Journal of Finance*, 12:3 (1957), pp. 333–47, on p. 347.

7 Milton Friedman and the Arguments for Flexible versus Fixed Exchange Rates

1. P. Einzig, *The Case Against Floating Exchange Rates* (London: Macmillan, 1970), p. 41.
2. M. Bordo, 'Exchange Rate Regime Choice in Historical Perspective', NBER Working Paper, 9653 (2003), pp. 1–40, at http://www.nber.org/papers/w9654 [accessed 24 August 2012].
3. Ibid., p. 14.
4. M. Bordo and L. Jonung, 'A Return to the Convertibility Principle? Monetary and Fiscal Regimes in Historical Perspective', in A. Leijonhufvud (ed.), *Monetary Theory as a Basis for Monetary Policy* (New York: Palgrave MacMillan, 2001), p. 20.
5. B. Eichengreen and R. Hausmann, 'Exchange Rates and Financial Fragility', NBER Working Paper, 7418 (1999), pp. 1–56, at http://www.nber.org/papers/w7418 [accessed 24 August 2012].
6. J. Frankel, 'No Single Currency is Right for All Countries or at All Times', Essays in International Finance, 215 (Princeton, NJ: Princeton Finance Section, Princeton University, 1999), pp. 1–33.
7. Endres, *Great Architects of International Finance*.
8. F. Graham, 'Exchange Rates: Bound or Free?', *Journal of Finance*, 4:1 (1949), pp. 13–27, on p. 27.
9. F. Graham and C. Whittlesey, 'Fluctuating Exchange Rates, Foreign Trade and the Price Level', *American Economic Review*, 24:3 (1934), pp. 401–16, on p. 411.
10. G. Haberler, *Prosperity and Depression: A Theoretical Analysis of Cyclical Movements* (Geneva: League of Nations, 1937).
11. M. Bordo and H. James, 'Haberler versus Nurkse: The Case for Floating Exchange Rates as an Alternative to Bretton Woods', University of St Gallen, Department of Economics, Working Paper, 2001–08 (2001), pp. 1–33, at http://dx.doi.org/10.2139/ssrn.286132 [accessed 24 August 2012].
12. G. Haberler, 'The Choice of Exchange Rates after the War', *American Economic Review*, 35:3 (1945), pp. 308–18, on p. 310.
13. G. Haberler, *Currency Convertibility* (Washington, DC: American Enterprise Association, 1954).
14. Bordo and James, 'Haberler versus Nurkse', p. 24.
15. J. Meade, *Planning and the Price Mechanism: The Liberal-Socialist Solution* (London: George Allen and Unwin, 1948), p. 110.

16. L. Mints, *Monetary Policy for a Competitive Society* (New York: McGraw-Hill, 1950).

17. R. Dehem, 'International Payments and Economic Policy', *The Canadian Journal of Economics and Political Science / Revue canadienne d'Economique et de Science politique, 18:2 (1952)*, pp. 212–15, on p. 214.

18. Mints, *Monetary Policy*, p. 93.

19. J. Williams, *International Trade under Flexible Exchange Rates* (Amsterdam: North-Holland Publishing Co., 1954), p. 27.

20. F. Lutz, 'The Case for Flexible Exchange Rates', *Banca Nazionale del Lavoro Quarterly Review*, 7:31 (1954), pp. 175–85, on p. 180.

21. Ibid., p. 185.

22. E. Sohmen, *International Monetary Problems and the Foreign Exchanges*, Special Papers in International Economics (Princeton, NJ: International Finance Section, Princeton University, 1963), p. 6.

23. R. Caves, 'Flexible Exchange Rates', *American Economic Review*, 53:2 (1963), pp. 120–9, on p. 124.

24. A. Bloomfield, 'Recent Trends in International Economics', *Annals of the American Academy of Political and Social Sciences*, 386 (1969), pp. 148–67, on p. 161.

25. G. Halm, 'The "Band" Proposal: The Limits of Permissible Exchange Rate Variations', Special Papers in International Economics, 6 (Princeton, NJ: International Finance Section, Princeton University, 1965), p. 47.

26. Ibid., p. 49.

27. R. Mundell, 'A Theory of Optimum Currency Areas', *American Economic Review*, 51 (1961), pp. 657–65, on p. 657.

28. B. Eichengreen, *European Monetary Unification: Theory, Practice, and Analysis* (Cambridge, MA: MIT Press, 1997), pp. 1–2.

29. H. Johnson, 'The Case for Flexible Exchange Rates, 1969', Hobart Papers, 46 (1960), pp. 12–24, on p. 12.

30. Ibid., p. 13.

31. R. Cooper, 'Macroeconomic Policy Adjustment in Interdependent Economies', *Quarterly Journal of Economics*, 83:1 (1969), pp. 1–24, on p. 3.

32. J. Niehans, 'Monetary and Fiscal Policies in Open Economies under Fixed Exchange Rates: An Optimizing Approach', *Journal of Political Economy* (1968), pp. 893–920, on p. 912.

33. T. Scitovsky, 'The Theory of Balance of Payments Adjustment', *Journal of Political Economy*, 75:4 (1967), pp. 523–31, on p. 530.

34. Einzig, *The Case Against Floating Exchange Rates*, p. 187.

35. R. Harrod, 'Imbalance of International Payments', *IMF Staff Papers*, 3:1 (1953), pp. 1–46, on p. 4.

36. R. Harrod, 'World Recession and the United States', *International Affairs*, 34:4 (1958), pp. 444–53, on p. 453.

37. J. Rueff, 'The West is Risking a Credit Collapse', *Fortune*, 64 (1961), pp. 126–7, 262, 267–8.

38. J. Rueff, *The Monetary Sin of the West* (New York: MacMillan, 1972).

39. M. Heilperin, *International Monetary Economics* (New York: Longmans, Green & Co., 1939), p. 15.

40. Ibid., p. 188.

41. Ibid., p. 221.

42. Ibid., p. 223.

43. L. A. Hahn, 'Anachronism of the Gold Price Controversy', *Commercial and Financial Chronicle*, 7 March 1963.

44. O. Dahlberg, *Reduce the Price of Gold and Make Money Move* (New York: John de Graff, Inc., 1962).

45. W. Salant, 'The Demand for Money and the Concept of Income Velocity', *Journal of Political Economy*, 49:3 (1941), pp. 395–421, on p. 421.

46. Machlup, *International Monetary Systems*, p. 140.

47. A. Laffer, 'The US Balance of Payments: A Financial Center View', *Law and Contemporary Problems*, 34 (1969), pp. 33–46, on p. 34, at http://scholarship.law.duke.edu/lcp/vol34/iss1/4/ [accessed 24 August 2012].

48. E. Despres, W. Salant and C. Kindleberger, 'The Dollar and World Liquidity: A Minority View', *The Economist*, 218 (1966), pp. 526–9.

49. W. Salant, 'Financial Intermediation as an Explanation of Enduring "Deficits" in the Balance of Payments', in F. Machlup, W. Salant and L. Tarshis (eds), *International Mobility and Movement of Capital* (Washington, DC: NBER Books, 1972), pp. 607–60, on pp. 610–11, at http://www.nber.org/chapters/c3473.pdf [accessed 24 August 2012].

50. F. Modigliani, 'Comment on Arthur Laffer', in F. Machlup, W. Salant and L. Tarshis (eds), *International Mobility and Movement of Capital* (Washington, DC: NBER Books, 1972), p. 684, at http://www.nber.org/chapters/c4140.pdf [accessed 24 August 2012].

8 Collaboration with the Group of Ten

1. H. James, 'The Historical Development of the Principle of Surveillance', *IMF Staff Papers*, 42 (1995), pp. 762–91, on p. 766.

2. Ibid.

3. Ibid., p. 767.

4. Ibid.

5. R. Solomon, *The International Monetary System, 1945–1976: An Insider's View* (New York: Harper & Row, 1977), p. 138.

6. M. De Vries, *The International Monetary Fund 1966–1971. The System under Stress, Volume I: Narrative* (Washington, DC: International Monetary Fund, 1976), p. 31.

7. Ibid., p. 30.

8. Ibid.

9. Robert Triffin Papers. MS 874, box 12, folder 2, copyright Yale University.

10. De Vries, *The System under Stress*, p. 38.

11. Ibid., p. 39.

12. J. Gold, 'The Amendments', in J. Horsefield (ed.), *The International Monetary Fund 1945–1965* (Washington, DC: International Monetary Fund, 1969), pp. 595–608, on p. 600.

13. Ibid., p. 602.

14. Machlup, *International Monetary Arrangements*, p. 6.

15. D. Daane, 'The Report of the Group of Ten', *American Economic Review*, 55:1–2 (1965), pp. 150–7, on pp. 150–1.

16. J. Polak, 'The Report of the International Monetary Fund', *American Economic Review*, 55:1–2 (1965), pp. 158–65, on p. 158.

17. F. Machlup, 'The Report of the Nongovernmental Economists' Study Group', *American Economic Review*, 55 (1965), pp. 166–77, on p. 168.

18. Machlup, *International Monetary Arrangements*, p. 107.

19. Fritz Machlup Papers. Box 68, folder 2. Letter of 4 October 1964 from Robert Triffin to Fritz Machlup, quoted with the permission of the Triffin family.
20. Ibid.
21. Robert Triffin Papers. MS 874, box 12, folder 2, copyright Yale University.
22. Fritz Machlup Papers. Box 68, folder 2. Letter of 30 October 1964, from Fritz Machlup to Robert Triffin, copyright Stanford University.
23. Ibid. Box 37, folder 2. Letter of 19 October 1965, from William Fellner to Fritz Machlup, copyright Stanford University.
24. Ibid. Box 283, folder 45. Copyright Stanford University.
25. De Vries, *The System under Stress*, p. 75.
26. Fritz Machlup Papers. Box 283, folder 45. Notes of William Fellner shared with Fritz Machlup, copyright Stanford University.
27. W. Fellner, R. Triffin and F. Machlup (eds), *Maintaining and Restoring Balance in International Payments* (Princeton, NJ: Princeton University Press, 1966), pp. v–vi.
28. F. Machlup, 'In Search of Guides for Policy', in W. Fellner, R. Triffin and F. Machlup (eds), *Maintaining and Restoring Balance in International Payments* (Princeton, NJ: Princeton University Press, 1966), pp. 33–84, on p. 84.
29. R. Triffin, 'The Balance of Payments Seesaw', in W. Fellner, R. Triffin and F. Machlup (eds), *Maintaining and Restoring Balance in International Payments* (Princeton, NJ: Princeton University Press, 1966), pp. 85–110, especially pp. 102–8.
30. J. Tobin, 'Adjustment Responsibilities of Surplus and Deficit Countries', in W. Fellner, R. Triffin and F. Machlup (eds), *Maintaining and Restoring Balance in International Payments* (Princeton, NJ: Princeton University Press, 1966), pp. 201–12.
31. W. Salant, 'Capital Markets and the Balance of Payments of a Financial Center', in W. Fellner, R. Triffin and F. Machlup (eds), *Maintaining and Restoring Balance in International Payments* (Princeton, NJ: Princeton University Press, 1966), pp. 177–96.
32. A. Lamfalussy, 'Limitations of Monetary and Fiscal Policy', in W. Fellner, R. Triffin and F. Machlup (eds), *Maintaining and Restoring Balance in International Payments* (Princeton, NJ: Princeton University Press, 1966), pp. 157–60.

9 Adjustment Policies and Special Drawing Rights: Joint Meetings of Officials and Academics

1. A. Vakil, 'Confronting the Classification Problem: Toward a Taxonomy of NGOs', *World Development*, 25 (1997), pp. 2,057–70, on p. 2068.
2. H. Teegen, J. Doh and S. Vachani, 'The Importance of Nongovernmental Organizations (NGOs) in Global Governance and Value Creation: An International Business Agenda', *Journal of International Business Studies*, 35 (2004), pp. 463–83, on p. 466.
3. Ibid.; also M. Barnett and M. Finnemore, 'The Politics, Power and Pathologies of International Organizations', *International Organization*, 53 (1999), pp. 699–732.
4. Teegen et al., 'The Importance on Non-Governmental Organizations', p. 471.
5. Fritz Machlup Papers. Box 283, folder 51, copyright Stanford University.
6. Barnett and Finnemore, 'The Politics, Power and Pathologies of International Organizations', p. 721.
7. Ibid., p. 722.

8. N. Woods, 'The Challenge of Good Governance for the IMF and the World Bank Themselves', *World Development*, 28 (2000), pp. 823–41, on p. 833.
9. Ibid.; J. Gold, *Voting Majorities in the Fund: Effect of Second Amendment of the Articles* (Washington, DC: International Monetary Fund, 1977).
10. E. Eriksen, and J. Fossum, 'Europe in Search of Legitimacy: Strategies of Legitimation Assessed', *International Political Science Review*, 25 (2004), pp. 435–59, on p. 439.
11. Ibid., p. 441.
12. Robert Triffin Papers. MS 874, box 1, folder 1, copyright Yale University.
13. Fritz Machlup Papers. Box 283, folder 55, copyright Stanford University.
14. De Vries, *The System under Stress*, p. 144.
15. Ibid., p. 153.
16. Fritz Machlup Papers. Box 283, folder 48, copyright Stanford University.
17. De Vries, *The System under Stress*, p. 156.
18. Ibid., p. 160.
19. Ibid., p. 170.
20. Ibid.
21. Ibid., p. 175.
22. Fritz Machlup Papers. Box 283, folder 50, copyright Stanford University.
23. Ibid. Box 283, folder 55, copyright Stanford University.
24. Ibid. Box 284, folder 7. Letter from Fritz Machlup to Emile van Lennep, copyright Stanford University.
25. P. Clark and J. Polak, 'International Liquidity and the Role of the SDR in the International Monetary System', *IMF Staff Papers*, 51 (2004), pp. 49–71.
26. P. Alessandrini and M. Fratianni, 'International Monies, Special Drawing Rights and Supranational Money', SSRN Working Paper (2009), at http://ssrn.com/abstract=1429482 [accessed 24 August 2012].

10 From the Bellagio Group to the Bürgenstock Conferences

1. H. Kahn and A. Wiener, *The Year 2000: A Framework for Speculation on the Next Thirty-Three Years* (New York: Macmillan, 1967), pp. 262–4.
2. R. Jacobson, 'Unobservable Effects and Business Performance', *Marketing Science*, 9 (1990), pp. 74–85; R. Jacobson, 'The Austrian School of Strategy', *Academy of Management Review*, 17:17 (1992), pp. 782–807; J. Salerno, 'Ludwig von Mises's Monetary Theory in the Light of Modern Monetary Thought', *Review of Austrian Economics*, 8:1 (1994), pp. 71–115; B. Loasby, 'The Evolution of Knowledge: Beyond the Biological Model', *Research Policy*, 31 (2002), pp. 1,227–39; N. Foss, 'Strategic Belief Management', *Strategic Organization*, 5:3 (2007), pp. 249–58; P. Klein, 'The Mundane Economics of the Austrian School', *Quarterly Journal of Austrian Economics*, 11:3–4 (2008), pp. 165–87.
3. P. Aligica, 'Uncertainty, Human Action and Scenarios: An Austrian Theory-Based Decision Support Tool for Business Strategy and Public Policy', *Review of Austrian Economics*, 20 (2007), pp. 293–312, on p. 298.
4. Proops and Safonov (eds), *Modelling in Ecological Economics*, p. 59.
5. Fritz Machlup Papers. Box 285, folder 14, copyright Stanford University.
6. F. Machlup, 'On Terms, Concepts, Theories and Strategies in the Discussion of Greater Flexibility of Exchange Rates', in G. Halm (ed.), *Approaches to Greater Flexibility of*

Exchange Rates: The Bürgenstock Papers (Princeton, NJ: Princeton University Press, 1970), pp. 31–48, on p. 31.

7. Ibid., p. 33.
8. Ibid., p. 40.
9. G. Halm, 'Preface', in G. Halm (ed.), *Approaches to Greater Flexibility of Exchange Rates: The Bürgenstock Papers* (Princeton, NJ: Princeton University Press, 1970), pp. vii–viii.
10. G. Halm, 'Toward Limited Flexibility of Exchange Rates', in G. Halm (ed.), *Approaches to Greater Flexibility of Exchange Rates: The Bürgenstock Papers* (Princeton, NJ: Princeton University Press, 1970), pp. 3–26, on p. 24–5.
11. R. Roosa, 'Currency Parities in the Second Decade of Convertibility', in G. Halm (ed.), *Approaches to Greater Flexibility of Exchange Rates: The Bürgenstock Papers* (Princeton, NJ: Princeton University Press, 1970), pp. 49–56, on p. 50.
12. Ibid., p. 51.
13. Ibid., p. 56.
14. C. F. Bergsten, 'The United States and Greater Flexibility of Exchange Rates', in G. Halm (ed.), *Approaches to Greater Flexibility of Exchange Rates: The Bürgenstock Papers* (Princeton, NJ: Princeton University Press, 1970), on p. 73.
15. S. Marris, 'Decision-Making on Exchange Rates', in G. Halm (ed.), *Approaches to Greater Flexibility of Exchange Rates: The Bürgenstock Pa*pers (Princeton, NJ: Princeton University Press, 1970), pp. 77–88, on pp. 77, 80.
16. S. Marris, *The Bürgenstock Communique: A Critical Examination of the Case for Limited Flexibility*, Princeton Essays in International Finance, 80 (Princeton, NJ: International Finance Section, Princeton University, 1970).
17. D. Grove, 'The Wider Band and Foreign Direct Investment', in G. Halm (ed.), *Approaches to Greater Flexibility of Exchange Rates: The Bürgenstock Papers* (Princeton, NJ: Princeton University Press, 1970), pp. 151–166, on p. 166.
18. Ibid., p. 160.
19. Ibid.
20. A. Mosconi, 'Notes for the Bürgenstock Conference', in G. Halm (ed.), *Approaches to Greater Flexibility of Exchange Rates: The Bürgenstock Papers* (Princeton, NJ: Princeton University Press, 1970), pp. 199–202, on pp. 199–200.
21. Ibid., p. 200.
22. A. Mosconi and A. Iozzo, 'The Foundation of a Cooperative Global Financial System', The EU, the US and Global Disorder: The Need for a New Bretton Woods, conference paper (18–9 April 2008), at http://www.astrid-online.it/rassegna/Rassegna-25/30-04-2008/Iozzo_Mosconi_Aspen_18_19_4_08.pdf [accessed 24 August 2012].; A. Mosconi, 'A World Currency for a World New Deal', *Perspectives on Federalism*, 2:2 (2010), pp. 239–64.
23. P. Rogers, 'Multinational Corporations: A European Review', *Annual of the American Academy of Political and Social Sciences*, 403 (1972), pp. 58–66.
24. Fritz Machlup Papers. Box 285, folder 17, copyright Stanford University.
25. De Vries, *The System under Stress*, p. 513.
26. Ibid., p. 514.
27. Ibid., p. 515.

11 From the Bellagio Group and Joint Conferences of Officials and Academics to the Group of Thirty

1. P. Kenen, 'The G30 at Thirty', Group of Thirty, Occasional Paper, 78 (1008), pp. 1–48, on p. 12.
2. Ibid., p. 16.
3. Ibid.
4. Fritz Machlup Papers. Box 284, folder 7, copyright Stanford University.
5. Kenen, 'The G30 at Thirty', p. 19.
6. Ibid.

12 Reassessing the Bellagio Group's Impact on International Monetary Reform

1. Dyson and Featherstone, *The Road to Maastricht*, p. 83.
2. H. Dupriez, *Monetary Reconstruction in Belgium* (New York: King's Crown Press, 1947); P. Dieterlen and C. Rist, *The Monetary Problem of France* (New York: King's Crown Press, 1948).
3. Triffin, *Gold and the Dollar Crisis: The Future of Convertibility*, p. 8.
4. De Vries, *Balance of Payments Adjustment*, pp. 80–1.
5. O. Emminger, 'International Monetary Reform – Design and Reality', in J. Dreyer (ed.), *Breadth and Depth in Economics: Fritz Machlup—The Man and His Ideas* (Lexington, MA: Lexington Books, 1978), pp. 173–80, on p. 175.
6. Cooper, 'Exchange Rate Choices', p. 104.
7. Solomon, *The International Monetary System*, p. 71.
8. P. Kenen, 'Chapter 12: Peter Kenen', in R. Backhouse and R. Middleton (eds), *Exemplary Economists: North America* (London: Edward Elgar Publishing, 2000), pp. 257–77, on p. 266.
9. Triffin, 'The Impact of the Bellagio Group', p. 149.
10. Ibid.
11. F. Machlup, *Remaking the International Monetary System: The Rio Agreement and Beyond*, Committee for Economic Development (Baltimore: Johns Hopkins Press, 1968).
12. Ibid., p. 122.
13. Emminger, 'International Monetary Reform', p. 176.
14. H. Reuss, *When Government was Good* (Madison, WI: University of Wisconsin Press, 1999), pp. 97–8.
15. Ibid., p. 97.
16. M. Bordo and B. Eichengreen, 'The Rise and Fall of a Barbarous Relic: The Role of Gold in the International Monetary System', NBER Working Paper, 6436 (1998), pp. 1–87, on p. 24.
17. J. Wilson, 'Le Groupe de Bellagio: origines et premiers pas (1960–1964)', in M. Dumoulin (ed.) *Economic Networks and European Integration* (Brussels: PIE-Peter Lang, 2004), pp. 391–410.
18. Machlup, *Remaking the International Monetary System*, p. 121.

19. R. Triffin, 'Jamaica: "Major Revision" or Fiasco?', in E. Bernstein et al., *Reflections on Jamaica*, Essays in International Finance, 115 (Princeton, NJ: International Finance Section, Princeton University, 1976), pp. 45–53, on p. 45.
20. Triffin, 'The Impact of the Bellagio Group', p. 153.
21. F. Machlup, 'Between Outline and Outcome the Reform was Lost', in E. Bernstein et al., *Reflections on Jamaica*, Essays in International Finance, 115 (Princeton, NJ: International Finance Section, Princeton University, 1976), pp. 30–8, on p. 31.
22. Ibid., p. 34.
23. Ibid., p. 38.
24. E. Bernstein, 'The New International Monetary System', in E. Bernstein et al., *Reflections on Jamaica*, Essays in International Finance, 115 (Princeton, NJ: International Finance Section, Princeton University, 1976), pp. 1–8, on p. 3.
25. C. Kindleberger, 'The Exchange-Stability Issue at Rambouillet and Jamaica', in E. Bernstein et al., *Reflections on Jamaica*, Essays in International Finance, 115 (Princeton, NJ: International Finance Section, Princeton University, 1976), pp. 25–9, on p. 25.
26. J. Williamson, 'The Benefits and Costs of an International Monetary System', in E. Bernstein et al., *Reflections on Jamaica*, Essays in International Finance, 115 (Princeton, NJ: International Finance Section, Princeton University, 1976), pp. 54–9, on p. 55.
27. R. Triffin, 'The Thrust of History in International Monetary Reform', *Foreign Affairs*, 47:3 (1969), pp. 477–92, on p. 477.
28. F. Saccomanni, 'How to Deal with a Global Triffin Dilemma', Conference on the International Monetary System: Sustainability and Reform Proposals, Triffin International Foundation, keynote address (3 October 2011), pp. 1–7, on p. 6, at http://www.bis.org/review/r111007b.pdf [accessed 24 August 2012].
29. L. Bini Smaghi, 'The Triffin Dilemma Revisited', Triffin International Foundation, Brussels (October 2011), at http://www.bis.org/review/r111005a.pdf, pp. 1–8, on p. 5 [accessed 24 August 2012].
30. C. F. Bergsten, 'The Dollar and the Deficits: How Washington Can Prevent the Next Crisis', *Foreign Affairs*, 88:6 (2009), pp. 20–38.
31. R. Cooper, 'Does the SDR Have a Future?', WCFIA, Harvard University Working Paper, 2010–0006 (March 2010), pp. 1–13, on p. 3.
32. Saccomanni, 'How to Deal with a Global Triffin Dilemma', p. 4.
33. Ibid.
34. Machlup, *Remaking the International Monetary System*, pp. 121–2.

13 The Impact of the Bellagio Group on International Trade and Finance Scholarship from the 1960s to the Present

1. L. Daloz, *Mentor: Guiding the Journey of Adult Learners* (San Francisco, CA: Jossey Bass, 1999); M. Galbraith, *Facilitating Adult Learning: A Transactional Process* (Malabar, FL: Krieger, 1991.
2. K. Kraiger, J. Ford and E. Salas, 'Application of Cognitive, Skill-based, and Affective Theories of Learning Outcomes to New Methods of Training Evaluation', *Journal of Applied Psychology*, 78 (1993) pp. 311–28.
3. C. Mullen, 'Shifting the Odds in the Casino of Academic Publishing through Mentorship', in F. Kochan, and J. Pascarelli (eds), *Mentoring: Transforming Contexts, Communities, and Cultures* (Greenwich, CT: Greenwood/Praeger, 2003).

4. P. Smit, 'Women, Mentoring and Opportunity in Higher Education: A South African Experience', in F. Kochan and J. Pascarelli (eds), *Mentoring: Transforming Contexts, Communities, and Cultures* (Greenwich, CT: Greenwood/Praeger, 2003), pp. 129–48.

5. K. Barham and C. Conway, *Developing Business and People Internationally: A Mentoring Approach* (Berkhamsted: Ashridge Research, 1998).

6. K. Kram, 'Phases of the Mentor Relationship', *Academy of Management Journal*, 26 (1983), pp. 608–26.

7. R. Triffin, *Monopolistic Competition and General Equilibrium Theory* (Cambridge, MA: Harvard University Press, 1940), pp. 169–71.

8. E. Penrose, 'Strategy/Organization and the Metamorphosis of the Large Firm', *Organization Studies*, 29 (1994), p. 1,117–34, on p. 1,123.

9. P. Buckley and M. Casson, The *Future of the Multinational Enterprise* (London: Macmillan, 1976); A. Rugman, *Inside the Multinationals* (New York: Columbia University Press, 1981); A. Verbeke and A. Rugman, 'Environmental Regulations and Multinational Enterprise Strategy', *Academy of Management Review*, 23 (1998), pp. 653–5; J.-F. Hennart, *A Theory of Multinational Enterprise* (Ann Arbor, MI: University of Michigan Press, 1982); J.-F. Hennart, 'A Transaction Costs Theory of Equity Joint Ventures', *Strategic Management Journal*, 9:4 (1988), pp. 361–74.

10. C. Pitelis, 'On the Garden of Edith', in C. Pitelis (ed.), *The Growth of the Firm: The Legacy of Edith Penrose* (Oxford: Oxford University Press, 2002), pp. 1–15.

11. C. Kindleberger, *Economic Development* (New York: McGraw-Hill, 1965), pp. 270–1.

12. E. Penrose, 'International Economic Relations and the Large Industrial Firm', in E. Penrose, P. Lyon and E. Penrose, *New Orientations: Essays in International Relations* (London: Frank Cass, 1970), pp. 107–36, on p. 119.

13. R. Harrod, *Economic Essays* (London: Macmillan, 1952), pp. 184–5.

14. M. Bye, 'Self-Financed Multiterritorial Units and their Time Horizons', *International Economic Papers*, 18 (1958), p. 147–78, on p. 178.

15. N. Kaldor, *Essays on Value and Distribution* (London: Duckworth, [1934] 1960), p. 69.

16. N. Kaldor, 'A Model of Economic Growth', *Economic Journal*, 67 (1957), pp. 591–624, on pp. 593–9.

17. M. White and P. Khakpour, 'The Advent of Academic Advising in America at the Johns Hopkins University', *The Mentor: An Academic Advising Journal*, 8:4 (2006), at http://dus.psu.edu/mentor/old/articles/061025mw.htm [accessed 24 August 2012].

18. Penrose, *The Economics of the International Patent System*; E. Penrose, *The Theory of the Growth of the Firm*, 3rd edn (Oxford: Basil Blackwell, 1995).

19. J. Dreyer (ed.), *Breadth and Depth of Economics: Fritz Machlup––The Man and His Ideas* (Lexington, MA: Lexington Books), p. ix.

20. J. Dunning and C. Pitelis, 'The Political Economy of Globalization – Revisiting Stephen Hymer 50 Years On', SSRN Working Paper (2009), at http://dx.doi.org/10.2139/ssrn.1505450 [accessed 24 August 2012]; J. Dunning and C. Pitelis, 'Stephen Hymer's Contribution to International Business Scholarship: An Assessment and Extension', *Journal of International Business Studies*, 39 (2008), pp. 167–76.

21. S. Hymer, *The International Operations of National Firms: A Study of Direct Foreign Investment* (Cambridge, MA: MIT Press, 1976), p. 212.

22. C. Kindleberger, 'Introduction', in S. Hymer, *The International Operations of National Firms: A Study of Direct Foreign Investment* (Cambridge, MA: MIT Press, 1976), p. xiii.

23. C. Kindleberger, 'The Pros and Cons of an International Capital Market', *Zeitschrift für die gesamte Staatswissenschaft / Journal of Institutional and Theoretical Economics*,

123:4 (1967), pp. 600–17, on p. 601. See also Kindleberger's discussion of Hymer in: C. Kindleberger, 'European Economic Integration and the Development of a Single Financial Center for Long-Term Capital', *Weltwirtschaftliches Archiv*, 90:2 (1963), pp. 189–210, on p. 207; C. Kindleberger, 'The International Firm and the International Capital Market', *Southern Economic Journal*, 34:2 (1967), pp. 223–30, on p. 224; C. Kindleberger, 'The "New" Multinationalization of Business', *ASEAN Economic Bulletin*, 5:2 (1988), pp. 113–24, on p. 121.

24. C. Kindleberger, 'Plus ca change – A Look at the New Literature', in C. Kindleberger (ed.), *Multinational Excursions* (New York: MIT Press, 1984), pp. 180–8, on p. 181.

25. J. Tobin, *Essays in Economics, Vol. 4: National and International* (Cambridge, MA: MIT Press, 1996), p. 744.

26. A. Crockett, 'Suggestions for Further Work in the Spirit of Robert Triffin', in A. Lamfalussy, B. Snoy and J. Wilson (eds), *Fragility of the International Financial System* (Brussels: PIE-Peter Lang, 2001), pp. 216–20, on p. 216.

27. A. Crockett and M. Goldstein, 'Inflation under Fixed and Flexible Exchange Rates', *IMF Staff Papers*, 23:3 (1978), pp. 509–44, on p. 539.

28. A. Crockett, 'Control Over International Reserves', *IMF Staff Papers*, 25:1 (1978), pp. 1–24, on p. 22.

29. A. Crockett, *The Theory and Practice of Financial Stability*, Essays in International Finance, 203 (Princeton, NJ: International Finance Section, Princeton University, 1997), pp. 1–48, on p. 25.

30. A. Crockett, 'Banking Supervision and Financial Stability', Group of Thirty William Taylor Memorial Lectures 4 (1998), pp. 1–37, on p. 7.

31. E. Truman, 'International Financial Flows: Catalyst of Change or Threat to Stability', in A. Lamfalussy, B. Snoy and J. Wilson, *Fragility of the International Financial System* (Brussels: PIE-Peter Lang, 2001), pp. 221–6, on p. 221.

32. E. Truman, 'The G-20 and International Financial Institution Governance', Peterson Institute for International Economics Working Paper Series (2010), pp. 1–36.

33. E. Truman, 'The International Monetary Fund and Regulatory Challenges', Peterson Institution for International Economics Working Paper Series (2009), pp. 1–21, on p. 17.

WORKS CITED

Alacevich, M., and P. Asso, 'Money Doctoring after World War II: Arthur I. Bloomfield and the Federal Reserve Missions to South Korea', *History of Political Economy Journal*, 41:2 (2009), pp. 249–70.

Alessandrini, P., and M. Fratianni, 'International Monies, Special Drawing Rights and Supernational Money', SSRN Working Paper (2009), at http://ssrn.com/abstract=1429482 [accessed 24 August 2012].

Aligica, P., 'Uncertainty, Human Action and Scenarios: An Austrian Theory-Based Decision Support Tool for Business Strategy and Public Policy', *Review of Austrian Economics*, 20 (2007), pp. 293–312.

Altman, O., 'Professor Triffin on International Liquidity and the Role of the Fund', *IMF Staff Papers*, 8:2 (1961), pp. 151–91.

Barham, K., and C. Conway, *Developing Business and People Internationally: A Mentoring Approach* (Berkhamsted: Ashridge Research, 1998).

Barnett, M., and M. Finnemore, 'The Politics, Power and Pathologies of International Organizations', *International Organization*, 53 (1999), pp. 699–732.

Barr, P., J. Stimpert and A. Huff, 'Cognitive Change, Strategic Action, and Organizational Renewal', *Strategic Management Journal*, 13 (1992), pp. 15–36.

Baumol, W., and D. Fischer, 'Optimal Lags in a Schumpeterian Innovation Process', C. V. Starr Working Papers, RR77–17 (1977), at http://www.econ.nyu.edu/cvstarr/working/1977/RR77-17.pdf,, pp. 1–40 [accessed 24 August 2012].

Belassa, B., and R. Nelson, *Economic Progress, Private Values, and Public Policy: Essays in Honor of William Fellner* (Amsterdam: North-Holland Publishing Co., 1977).

Bergsten, C. F., 'The United States and Greater Flexibility of Exchange Rates', in G. Halm (ed.), *Approaches to Greater Flexibility of Exchange Rates: The Bürgenstock Papers* (Princeton, NJ: Princeton University Press, 1970), pp. 61–76.

—, 'Exchange Rate Policy', in M. Feldstein (ed.), *American Economics Policy in the 1980s* (Chicago, IL: University of Chicago Press, 1994).

—, 'The Dollar and the Deficits: How Washington Can Prevent the Next Crisis', *Foreign Affairs*, 88:6 (2009), pp. 20–38.

Bernhofen, D., 'Gottfried Haberler's 1930 Reformulation of Comparative Advantage in Retrospect', SSRN Working Paper (2005), pp. 1–5, at http://papers.ssrn.com/sol3/papers.cfm?abstract_id=863924 [accessed 24 August 2012].

Bernstein, E., 'A Practical Proposal for International Monetary Reserves', *Quarterly Review and Investment Survey*, Model, Roland & Co. (First Quarter 1963), pp. 1–8.

Bernstein, E., et al., *Reflections on Jamaica*, Essays in International Finance, 115 (Princeton, NJ: International Finance Section, Princeton University, 1976).

—, 'The New International Monetary System', in E. Bernstein, et al., *Reflections on Jamaica*, Essays in International Finance, 115 (Princeton, NJ: International Finance Section, Princeton University, 1976), pp. 1–8.

Bini Smaghi, L., 'The Triffin Dilemma Revisited', Triffin International Foundation, Brussels (October 2011), at http://www.bis.org/review/r111005a.pdf, p. 1–8 [accessed 24 August 2012].

Blaug, M., *Great Economists Since Keynes: An Introduction to the Lives and Works of One Hundred Modern Economists* (Totowa, NJ: Barnes & Noble, 1985).

Bloomfield, A., 'Recent Trends in International Economics', *Annals of the American Academy of Political and Social Sciences*, 386 (1969), pp. 148–67.

Blondeel, J., 'A New Form of International Financing: Loans in European Units of Account', *Columbia Law Review*, 64:6 (1964), pp. 995–1,011.

Bordo, M., 'Exchange Rate Regime Choice in Historical Perspective', NBER Working Paper, 9654 (2003), pp. 1–40, at http://www.nber.org/papers/w9654 [accessed 24 August 2012].

Bordo, M., E. Simard and E. White, 'France and the Bretton Woods International Monetary System: 1960 to 1968', NBER Working Paper, 4642 (1994), pp. 1–42, at http://www.nber.org/papers/w4642 [accessed 24 August 2012].

Bordo, M., and B. Eichengreen, 'The Rise and Fall of a Barbarous Relic: The Role of Gold in the International Monetary System', NBER Working Paper, 6436 (1998), pp. 1–87.

Bordo, M., and H. James, 'Haberler versus Nurkse: The Case for Floating Exchange Rates as an Alternative to Bretton Woods', University of St Gallen, Department of Economics, Working Paper, 2001–08 (2001), pp. 1–33, at http://dx.doi.org/10.2139/ssrn.286132 [accessed 24 August 2012].

Bordo, M., and L. Jonung, 'A Return to the Convertibility Principle? Monetary and Fiscal Regimes in Historical Perspective', in A. Leijonhufvud (ed.), *Monetary Theory as a Basis for Monetary Policy* (New York: Palgrave MacMillan, 2001).

Buchanan, J., *Cost and Choice: An Enquiry in Economic Theory* (Chicago, IL: Markham, 1969).

Buckley, P., and M. Casson, *The Future of the Multinational Enterprise* (London: Macmillan, 1976).

Bureau of Labor Statistics, 'Unemployment in the G7 Countries: 1960–1973' (September 2002), at http://www.bls.gov/opub/ted/2002/sept/wk1/art03.htm [accessed 24 August 2012].

Bye, M., 'Self-Financed Multiterritorial Units and their Time Horizons', *International Economic Papers*, 18 (1958), p. 147–78.

Caves, R., 'Flexible Exchange Rates', *American Economic Review*, 53:2 (1963), pp. 120–9.

Chandler, L., 'Federal Reserve Policy and the Federal Debt', *American Economic Review*, 39:2 (1949), pp. 405–29.

Clark, P., and J. Polak, 'International Liquidity and the Role of the SDR in the International Monetary System', *IMF Staff Papers*, 51 (2004), pp. 49–71.

Cooper, R., 'Macroeconomic Policy Adjustment in Interdependent Economies', *Quarterly Journal of Economics*, 83:1 (1969), pp. 1–24.

—, 'Exchange Rate Choices', in J. Little and G. Olivei (eds), *Rethinking the International Monetary System*, Conference Series 43 (Boston, MA: Federal Reserve Bank, 1999), pp. 99–123, at http://www.bos.frb.org/economic/conf/conf43/99p.pdf [accessed 24 August 2012].

—, 'Does the SDR Have a Future?', WCFIA, Harvard University Working Paper, 2010–0006 (March 2010), pp. 1–13.

Crafts, L., 'Fifty Years of Economic Growth in Western Europe: No Longer Catching Up But Falling Behind', Stanford Institute for Public Policy Research, SIEPR Discussion Paper, 03–21 (2004), pp. 1–14.

Crockett, A., 'Control Over International Reserves', *IMF Staff Papers*, 25:1 (1978), pp. 1–24.

—, *The Theory and Practice of Financial Stability*, Essays in International Finance, 203 (Princeton, NJ: International Finance Section, Princeton University, 1997), pp. 1–48.

—, 'Banking Supervision and Financial Stability', Group of Thirty William Taylor Memorial Lectures 4 (1998), pp. 1–37.

—, 'Suggestions for Further Work in the Spirit of Robert Triffin', in A. Lamfalussy, B. Snoy and J. Wilson (eds), *Fragility of the International Financial System* (Brussels: PIE-Peter Lang, 2001), pp. 216–20.

Crockett, A., and M. Goldstein, 'Inflation under Fixed and Flexible Exchange Rates', *IMF Staff Papers*, 23:3 (1978), pp. 509–44.

Daane, D., 'The Report of the Group of Ten', *American Economic Review*, 55:1–2 (1965), pp. 150–7.

Dahlberg, O., *Reduce the Price of Gold and Make Money Move* (New York: John de Graff, Inc., 1962).

Daloz, L., *Mentor: Guiding the Journey of Adult Learners* (San Francisco, CA: Jossey Bass, 1999).

Dehem, R., 'International Payments and Economic Policy', *The Canadian Journal of Economics and Political Science / Revue canadienne d'Economique et de Science politique*, 18:2 (1952), pp. 212–15.

de Lattre, A., *Politique économique de la France depuis 1945* (Paris: Editions Sirey, 1966).

Despres, E., W. Salant and C. Kindleberger, 'The Dollar and World Liquidity: A Minority View', *Economist*, 218 (1966), pp. 526–9.

Dequech, D., 'Expectations and Confidence under Uncertainty', *Journal of Post Keynesian Economics*, 21:3 (1999), pp. 415–30.

De Vries, M., *The International Monetary Fund 1966–1971: The System under Stress, Volume I: Narrative* (Washington, DC: International Monetary Fund, 1976).

—, *Balance of Payments Adjustment* (Washington, DC: International Monetary Fund, 1987).

Dicken, P., *Global Shift: Reshaping the Global Economic Map in the 21st Century* (Thousand Oaks, CA: Sage Publications, 2003).

Dieterlen, P., and C. Rist, *The Monetary Problem of France* (New York: King's Crown Press, 1948).

Dow, S., 'Mainstream Methodology, Financial Markets and Global Political Economy', *Contributions to Political Economy*, 27:1 (2008), pp. 13–29.

Dreyer, J. (ed.), *Breadth and Depth in Economics: Fritz Machlup—The Man and His Ideas* (Lexington, MA: Lexington Books, 1978).

Dunning, J., 'Explaining Changing Patterns of International Production: In Defense of the Electic Theory', *Oxford Bulletin of Economics and Statistics*, 41:4 (1979), pp. 269–95.

Dunning, J., J. Cantwell and T. Corley, 'The Theory of International Production: Some Historical Antecedents', in P. Hertner and G. Jones (eds), *Multinationals, Theory and History* (Aldershot: Gower, 1986), pp. 19–41.

Dunning, J., and C. Pitelis, 'Stephen Hymer's Contribution to International Business Scholarship: An Assessment and Extension', *Journal of International Business Studies*, 39 (2008), pp. 167–76.

—, 'The Political Economy of Globalization – Revisiting Stephen Hymer 50 Years On', SSRN Working Paper (2009), at http://dx.doi.org/10.2139/ssrn.1505450 [accessed 24 August 2012].

Dupriez, H., *Monetary Reconstruction in Belgium* (New York: King's Crown Press, 1947).

Dyson, K., and K. Featherstone, *The Road to Maastricht* (Oxford: Oxford University Press, 1999).

Eichengreen, B., *European Monetary Unification: Theory, Practice, and Analysis* (Cambridge, MA: MIT Press, 1997).

—, *Globalizing Capital* (Princeton, NJ: Princeton University Press, 2008).

Eichengreen, B., and R. Hausmann, 'Exchange Rates and Financial Fragility', NBER Working Paper, 7418 (1999), pp. 1–56, at http://www.nber.org/papers/w7418 [accessed 24 August 2012].

Eichengreen, B., and H. James, 'Monetary and Financial Reform in the Two Eras of Globalization', in M. Bordo, A. Taylor and J. Williamson (eds), *Globalization in Historical Perspective* (Chicago, IL: University of Chicago Press, 2003), pp. 515–48.

Einzig, P., *The Case Against Floating Exchange Rates* (London: Macmillan, 1970).

—, *Behind the Scenes of International Finance* (New York: Arno Press, 1978).

Emminger, O., 'The D-Mark in the Conflict between Internal and External Equilibrium, 1948–75', Essays in International Finance, 122 (Princeton, NJ: International Finance Section, Princeton University, 1977), pp. 1–54.

—, 'International Monetary Reform – Design and Reality', in J. Dreyer (ed.), *Breadth and Depth in Economics: Fritz Machlup—The Man and His Ideas* (Lexington, MA: Lexington Books, 1978), pp. 173–80.

Endres, A., *Great Architects of International Finance* (London: Routledge, 2005).

Entman, R., 'Framing: Toward Clarification of a Fractured Paradigm', *Journal of Communication*, 43:4 (1993), pp. 51–8.

Eriksen, E., and J. Fossum, 'Europe in Search of Legitimacy: Strategies of Legitimation Assessed', *International Political Science Review*, 25 (2004), pp. 435–59.

Fellner, W., *A Treatise on War Inflation: Present Policies and Future Tendencies in the United States* (Berkeley, CA: University of California Press, 1942).

—, *Monetary Policies and Full Employment* (Berkeley, CA: University of California Press, 1946).

—, 'Postscript on War Inflation: A Lesson from World War II', *American Economic Review*, 37:1 (1947), pp. 76–91.

—, 'Hansen on Full-Employment Policies', *Journal of Political Economy*, 55 (June 1947), pp. 254–6.

—, *Competition among the Few: Oligopoly and Similar Market Structures* (New York: A. A. Knopf, 1949).

—, *Trends and Cycles in Economic Activity: An Introduction to Problems of Economic Growth* (New York: Holt, 1956).

—, 'Rapid Growth as an Objective of Economic Policy', *American Economic Review*, 50 (May 1960), pp. 93–105.

—, 'Budget Deficits and their Consequences', *Proceedings of the Academy of Political Science*, 27:3 (1963), pp. 29–38.

—, 'Rules of the Game', in W. Fellner, F. Machlup and R. Triffin (eds), *Maintaining and Restoring Balance in International Payments* (Princeton, NJ: Princeton University Press, 1966), pp. 11–31.

—, 'On Limited Exchange-Rate Flexibility', in W. Fellner, F. Machlup and R. Triffin (eds), *Maintaining and Restoring Balance in International Payments* (Princeton, NJ: Princeton University Press, 1966), pp. 111–22.

—, 'Specific Proposal for Limited Exchange-Rate Flexibility', *Weltwirtschaftliches Archiv*, 104:1 (1970), pp. 20–35.

—, 'A "Realistic" Note on Threefold Limited Flexibility of Exchange Rates', in G. Halm (ed.), *Approaches to Greater Flexibility of Exchange Rates: The Bürgenstock Papers* (Princeton, NJ: Princeton University Press, 1970).

—, 'The Dollar's Place in the International System: Suggested Criteria for the Appraisal of Emerging Views', *Journal of Economic Literature*, 10:3 (1972), pp. 735–56.

—, 'Controlled Floating and the Confused Issue of Money Illusion', *Banca Nazionale del Lavoro Quarterly Review*, 106 (1973), pp. 206–34.

—, *Towards a Reconstruction of Macroeconomics: Problems of Theory and Policy* (Washington, DC: American Enterprise Institute, 1976).

—, 'Schools of Thought in the Mainstream of American Economics', *Acta Oeconomica*, 18:3–4 (1977), pp. 247–61.

—, 'The Credibility Effect and Rational Expectations: Implications of the Gramlich Study', *Brookings Papers on Economic Activity*, 1 (1979), pp. 167–89.

—, 'The Valid Core of Rationality Hypotheses in the Theory of Expectation', *Journal of Money, Credit and Banking*, 12:4 (1980), pp. 763–87.

Fellner, W., M. Gilbert, B. Hansen, R. Kahn, F. Lutz and P. deWolff, *The Problem of Rising Prices* (Paris: Organisation for European Economic Co-operation, 1961).

Fellner, W., F. Machlup and R. Triffin (eds), *Maintaining and Restoring Balance in International Payments* (Princeton, NJ: Princeton University Press, 1966).

Ferrant, C., J. Sloover, M. Dumoulin and O. Lefebvre, *Robert Triffin, conseiller des princes: souvenirs et documents* (Brussels: PIE-Peter Lang, 2010).

Flandreau, M., *Money Doctors: The Experience of International Financial Advising 1850–2000* (London: Routledge, 2003).

Flexner, K., 'The Creation of a European Payments Union: An Example of International Compromise', *Political Science Quarterly*, 72:2 (1957), pp. 241–60.

Foss, N., 'Strategic Belief Management', *Strategic Organization*, 5:3 (2007), pp. 249–58.

Frankel, J., 'No Single Currency is Right for All Countries or at All Times', Essays in International Finance, 215 (Princeton, NJ: Princeton Finance Section, Princeton University, 1999), pp. 1–33.

Friedman, M., 'The Case for Flexible Exchange Rates', in M. Friedman, *Essays in Positive Economics* (Chicago, IL: University of Chicago Press, 1953), pp. 157–203.

Frieden, J., 'The Impact of Goods and Capital Market Integration on European Monetary Politics', *Comparative Political Studies*, 29 (1996), pp. 193–222.

Furth, J., 'Professor Triffin and the Problem of International Monetary Reform', *Journal of Economics*, 21:3–4 (1962), pp. 415–25.

Gavin, F., *Gold, Dollars and Power: The Politics of International Monetary Relations, 1958–1971* (Chapel Hill, NC: University of North Carolina Press, 2004).

Gold, J., 'The Amendments', in J. Horsefield (ed.), *The International Monetary Fund 1945–1965* (Washington, DC: International Monetary Fund, 1969), pp. 595–608.

—, *Voting Majorities in the Fund: Effect of Second Amendment of the Articles* (Washington, DC: International Monetary Fund, 1977).

Graham, F., 'Exchange Rates: Bound or Free?', *Journal of Finance*, 4:1 (1949), pp. 13–27.

Graham, F., and C. Whittlesey, 'Fluctuating Exchange Rates, Foreign Trade and the Price Level', *American Economic Review*, 24:3 (1934), pp. 401–16.

Grove, D., 'The Wider Band and Foreign Direct Investment', in G. Halm (ed.), *Approaches to Greater Flexibility of Exchange Rates: The Bürgenstock Papers* (Princeton, NJ: Princeton University Press, 1970), pp. 151–166.

Haberler, G., *Prosperity and Depression: A Theoretical Analysis of Cyclical Movements* (Geneva: League of Nations, 1937).

—, 'The Choice of Exchange Rates after the War', *American Economic Review*, 35:3 (1945), pp. 308–18.

—, *Currency Convertibility* (Washington, DC: American Enterprise Association, 1954).

Hahn, L. A., 'Anachronism of the Gold Price Controversy', *Commercial and Financial Chronicle*, 7 March 1963.

Halm, G., 'The "Band" Proposal: The Limits of Permissible Exchange Rate Variations', Special Papers in International Economics, 6 (Princeton, NJ: International Finance Section, Princeton University, 1965).

—, 'Preface', in G. Halm (ed.), *Approaches to Greater Flexibility of Exchange Rates: The Bürgenstock Papers* (Princeton, NJ: Princeton University Press, 1970), pp. vii–viii.

—, 'Toward Limited Flexibility of Exchange Rates', in G. Halm (ed.), *Approaches to Greater Flexibility of Exchange Rates: The Bürgenstock Papers* (Princeton, NJ: Princeton University Press, 1970), pp. 3–26.

Hambrick, D., and P. Mason, 'Upper Echelons: The Organization as a Reflection of its Top Managers', *Academy of Management Review*, 9 (1984), pp. 193–206.

Hansen, A., 'Stability in Expansion', in P. Homan and F. Machlup (eds), *Financing American Prosperity: A Symposium of Economists* (New York: Twentieth Century Fund, 1945), pp. 199–265.

Harrod, R., *Economic Essays* (London: Macmillan, 1952).

—, 'Imbalance of International Payments', *IMF Staff Papers*, 3:1 (1953), pp. 1–46.

—, 'World Recession and the United States', *International Affairs*, 34:4 (1958), pp. 444–53.

Hefeker, C., 'The Political Choice and Collapse of Fixed Exchange Rates', *Journal of Institutional and Theoretical Economics*, 152 (1996), pp. 360–79.

Helleiner, E., 'Dollarization Diplomacy: US Policy Toward Latin America Coming Full Circle', *Review of International Political Economy*, 10:3 (2003), pp. 406–29.

Heilperin, M., *International Monetary Economics* (New York: Longmans, Green & Co., 1939).

Hennart, J.-F., *A Theory of Multinational Enterprise* (Ann Arbor, MI: University of Michigan Press, 1982).

—, 'A Transaction Costs Theory of Equity Joint Ventures', *Strategic Management Journal*, 9:4 (1988), pp. 361–74.

Hesse, J.-O., 'Some Relationships between a Scholar's and an Entrepreneur's Life: The Biography of L. Albert Hahn', *History of Political Economy*, 39:1 (2007), pp. 215–33.

Hodgkinson, G., N. Bown, A. Maule, K. Glaister and A. Pearman, 'Breaking the Frame: An Analysis of Strategic Cognition and Decision Making under Uncertainty', *Strategic Management Journal*, 20:10 (1999), pp. 977–85.

Homan, P., 'Introduction', in P. Homan and F. Machlup (eds), *Financing American Prosperity: A Symposium of Economists* (New York: Twentieth Century Fund, 1945), pp. 1–8.

Horsefield, J., *The International Monetary Fund, 1945–1965, Volume III: Documents* (Washington, DC: International Monetary Fund, 1969).

Huff, A., *Mapping Strategic Thought* (Chichester: John Wiley & Sons, 1990).

Hymer, S., *The International Operations of National Firms: A Study of Direct Foreign Investment* (Cambridge, MA: MIT Press, 1976).

International Monetary Fund, 'Articles of Agreement', at http://www.imf.org/external/pubs/ft/aa/index.htm [accessed 24 August 2012].

Jacobson, R., 'Unobservable Effects and Business Performance', *Marketing Science*, 9 (1990), pp. 74–85.

—, 'The Austrian School of Strategy', *Academy of Management Review*, 17:17 (1992), pp. 782–807.

James, H., 'The Historical Development of the Principle of Surveillance', *IMF Staff Papers*, 42 (1995), pp. 762–91.

—, *International Monetary Cooperation since Bretton Woods* (New York: Oxford University Press, 1996).

Johnson, H., 'The Case for Flexible Exchange Rates, 1969', Hobart Papers, 46 (1960), pp. 12–24.

—, 'The Theory of Tariff Structure, with Special Reference to World Trade and Development', in H. Johnson and P. Kenen, *Trade and Development* (Geneva: Librarie Droz, 1965), pp. 9–29.

—, *Economic Policies Towards Less Developed Countries* (Washington, DC: Brookings Institution, 1965), pp. 163–211.

Jones, D., 'The European Monetary Agreement, the European Payments Union and Convertibility', *Journal of Finance*, 12:3 (1957), pp. 333–47.

Kahn, H., and A. Weiner, *The Year 2000: A Framework for Speculation on the Next Thirty-Three Years* (New York: Macmillan, 1967).

Kaldor, N., *Essays on Value and Distribution* (London: Duckworth, [1934] 1960).

—, 'A Model of Economic Growth', *Economic Journal*, 67 (1957), pp. 591–624.

Kenen, P., 'Nature, Capital and Trade', *Journal of Political Economy*, 73:5 (1965), pp. 437–60.

—, 'Chapter 12: Peter Kenen', in R. Backhouse and R. Middleton (eds), *Exemplary Economists: North America* (London: Edward Elgar Publishing, 2000), pp. 257–77.

—, 'The G30 at Thirty', Group of Thirty, Occasional Paper, 78 (2008), pp. 1–48.

Keynes, J., *The General Theory of Employment, Interest and Money* (Cambridge: Cambridge University Press, 1936).

Kindleberger, C., 'European Economic Integration and the Development of a Single Financial Center for Long-Term Capital', *Weltwirtschaftliches Archiv*, 90:2 (1963), pp. 189–210.

—, *Economic Development* (New York: McGraw-Hill, 1965).

—, 'The Pros and Cons of an International Capital Market', *Zeitschrift für die gesamte Staatswissenschaft / Journal of Institutional and Theoretical Economics*, 123:4 (1967), pp. 600–17.

—, 'The International Firm and the International Capital Market', *Southern Economic Journal*, 34:2 (1967), pp. 223–30.

—, *Power and Money: The Economics of International Politics and the Politics of International Economics* (New York: Basic Books, 1970).

—, 'The Exchange-Stability Issue at Rambouillet and Jamaica', in E. Bernstein et al., *Reflections on Jamaica*, Essays in International Finance, 115 (Princeton, NJ: International Finance Section, Princeton University, 1976), pp. 25–9.

—, 'Introduction', in S. Hymer, *The International Operations of National Firms: A Study of Direct Foreign Investment* (Cambridge, MA: MIT Press, 1976).

—, 'Plus ca change – A Look at the New Literature', in C. Kindleberger (ed.), *Multinational Excursions* (New York: MIT Press, 1984), pp. 180–8.

—, 'The "New" Multinationalization of Business', *ASEAN Economic Bulletin*, 5:2 (1988), pp. 113–24.

Klein, P., 'The Mundane Economics of the Austrian School', *Quarterly Journal of Austrian Economics*, 11:3–4 (2008), pp. 165–87.

Kliesen, K., 'An Oasis of Prosperity: Soley an American Phenomenon', *The Regional Economist*, Federal Reserve Bank of St Louis, 3 (1999), at http://www.stlouisfed.org/publications/re/articles/?id=1745 [accessed 24 August 2012].

Koppl, R., 'Invisible Hand Explanations and Neoclassical Economics: Toward a Post Marginalist Economics', *Journal of Institutional and Theoretical Economics*, 148 (1992), pp. 292–313.

Kraiger, K., J. Ford and E. Salas, 'Application of Cognitive, Skill-based, and Affective Theories of Learning Outcomes to New Methods of Training Evaluation', *Journal of Applied Psychology*, 78 (1993) pp. 311–28.

Kram, K., 'Phases of the Mentor Relationship', *Academy of Management Journal*, 26 (1983), pp. 608–26.

Laffer, A., 'The US Balance of Payments: A Financial Center View', *Law and Contemporary Problems*, 34 (1969), pp. 33–46, at http://scholarship.law.duke.edu/lcp/vol34/iss1/4/ [accessed 24 August 2012].

—, 'International Financial Intermediation: Interpretation and Empirical Analysis', in F. Machlup, W. Salant and L. Tarshis (eds), *International Mobility and Movement of Capital* (Washington, DC: NBER Books, 1972), at http://www.nber.org/chapters/c4140.pdf [accessed 24 August 2012].

Lambert, B., 'Willard L. Thorp, 92, Economist Who Helped Draft Marshall Plan', *New York Times*, 11 May 1992, at http://www.nytimes.com/1992/05/11/us/willard-l-thorp-92-economist-who-helped-draft-marshall-plan.html [accessed 24 August 2012].

Lamfalussy, A., 'Limitations of Monetary and Fiscal Policy', in W. Fellner, R. Triffin and F. Machlup (eds), *Maintaining and Restoring Balance in International Payments* (Princeton, NJ: Princeton University Press, 1966), pp. 157–60.

Langlois, R., and R. Koppl, 'Fritz Machlup and Marginalism', *Methodus*, 3 (1991), pp. 86–102.

Le Heron, E., and E. Carré, 'Credibility Versus Confidence in Monetary Policy', Institute of Political Studies, Bordeaux, Working Paper, pp. 1–38.

Leeson, R., *Ideology and the International Economy* (London: Palgrave Macmillan, 2003).

Loasby, B., 'The Evolution of Knowledge: Beyond the Biological Model', *Research Policy*, 31 (2002), pp. 1,227–39.

Lutz, F., 'The Case for Flexible Exchange Rates', *Banca Nazionale del Lavoro Quarterly Review*, 7:31 (1954), pp. 175–85.

—, *The Problem of International Economic Equilibrium*, Professor Dr F. de Vries Lectures (Amsterdam: North-Holland Publishing Co., 1962).

Machlup, F., Register of the Fritz Machlup Papers, 1911–1983. Hoover Institution Archives, Stanford University, CA.

—, 'Summary and Analysis', in P. Homan and F. Machlup (eds), *Financing American Prosperity: A Symposium of Economists* (New York: Twentieth Century Fund, 1945), pp. 394–496.

—, 'Equilibrium and Disequilibrium: Misplaced Concreteness and Disguised Politics', *Economic Journal*, 68 (1958), pp. 1–24.

—, 'The Optimum Lag of Imitation behind Innovation', in Nationaløkonomisk Forening, *Festskrift til Frederik Zeuthen* (Copenhagen: Nationaløkonomisk Forening, 1958), pp. 239–46.

—, 'The Supply of Inventors and Inventions', *Weltwirtschaftliches Archiv*, 85:2 (1960), pp. 210–54.

—, 'Patents and Inventive Effort', *Science*, new ser., 133:3,463 (1961), pp. 1,463–6.

—, *The Production and Distribution of Knowledge in the United States* (Princeton, NJ: Princeton University Press, 1962).

—, *International Monetary Arrangements: The Problem of Choice; Report on the Deliberations of an International Study Group of 32 Economists* (Princeton, NJ: International Finance Section, Princeton University, 1964).

—, *International Payments, Debts and Gold* (New York: Charles Scribner's Sons, 1964).

—, 'The Report of the Nongovernmental Economists' Study Group', *American Economic Review*, 55 (1965), pp. 166–77.

—, 'Why Economists Disagree', *Proceedings of the American Philosophical Society*, 109 (1965), pp. 1–7.

—, 'In Search of Guides for Policy', in W. Fellner, R. Triffin and F. Machlup (eds), *Maintaining and Restoring Balance in International Payments* (Princeton, NJ: Princeton University Press, 1966), pp. 33–84, on p. 84.

—, *International Monetary Systems and the Free Market Economy*, Reprints in International Finance (Princeton, NJ: International Finance Section, Princeton University, 1966).

—, *The Need for Monetary Reserves*, Reprints in International Finance (Princeton, NJ: International Finance Section, Princeton University, 1966).

—, *World Monetary Debate: Bases for Agreement*, Reprints in International Finance (Princeton, NJ: International Finance Section, Princeton University, 1966).

—, *Remaking the International Monetary System: The Rio Agreement and Beyond*, Committee for Economic Development (Baltimore: Johns Hopkins Press, 1968).

—, 'On Terms, Concepts, Theories and Strategies in the Discussion of Greater Flexibility of Exchange Rates', in G. Halm (ed.), *Approaches to Greater Flexibility of Exchange Rates: The Bürgenstock Papers* (Princeton, NJ: Princeton University Press, 1970), pp. 31–48.

—, 'Between Outline and Outcome the Reform was Lost', in E. Bernstein et al., *Reflections on Jamaica*, Essays in International Finance, 115 (Princeton, NJ: International Finance Section, Princeton University, 1976), pp. 30–8.

—, *Methodology of Economics and Other Social Sciences* (New York: Academic Press, 1978).

—, 'Interview with Fritz Machlup', *The Austrian Economics Newsletter*, 3:1 (1980), at http://mises.org/journals/aen/aen3_1_1.asp [accessed 24 August 2012].

—, 'My Early Work on International Monetary Problems', *Banca Nazionale del Lavoro Quarterly Review*, 133 (1980), pp. 115–46.

—, 'My Work on International Monetary Problems, 1940–1964', *Banca Nazionale del Lavoro Quarterly Review*, 140 (1982), pp. 3–36.

—, 'Eight Questions on Gold', in F. Machlup, *International Monetary Economics* (London: Routledge, 2003), pp. 228–38.

—, 'Elasticity Pessimism in International Trade', in F. Machlup, *International Monetary Economics* (London: Routledge, 2003), pp. 51–68.

—, 'Plans for Reform of the International Monetary System', in F. Machlup, *International Monetary Economics* (London: Routledge, 2003), pp. 282–366.

—, 'Theory of Foreign Exchanges', in F. Machlup, *International Monetary Economics* (London: Routledge, 2003), pp. 7–50,

Machlup, F., and E. Penrose, 'The Patent Controversy in the Nineteenth Century', *Journal of Economic History*, 10:1 (1950), pp. 1–29.

Maes, I., 'The Ascent of the European Commission as an Actor in the Monetary Integration Process in the 1960s', European Union Studies Association Biennial Conference, conference paper (2 November 2004), p. 1–26, at http://aei.pitt.edu/3009/1/MMTEC60art.pdf [accessed 24 August 2012].

—, 'Macroeconomic and Monetary Policy-Making at the EC, from the Rome Treaties to the Hague Summit', National Bank of Belgium Working Paper, 58 (2004), pp. 1–28, at http://ssrn.com/abstract=1691479 [accessed 24 August 2012].

Maes, I., and L. Quaglia, 'France's and Italy's Policies on European Monetary Integration: A Comparison of Strong and Weak States', Robert Schumann Centre for Advanced Studies, EIU Working Papers, 10 (2003), pp. 1–33, at http://www.eui.eu/RSCAS/WP-Texts/03_10.pdf [accessed 24 August 2012].

Malkiel, B., 'Why the Triffin Plan was Rejected and the Alternative Accepted', *Journal of Finance*, 18:3 (1963), pp. 511–36.

Marris, S., 'Decision-Making on Exchange Rates', in G. Halm (ed.), *Approaches to Greater Flexibility of Exchange Rates: The Bürgenstock Papers* (Princeton, NJ: Princeton University Press, 1970), pp. 77–88.

—, *The Bürgenstock Communique: A Critical Examination of the Case for Limited Flexibility*, Princeton Essays in International Finance, 80 (Princeton, NJ: International Finance Section, Princeton University, 1970).

Marshall, J., *William J. Fellner: A Bio-Bibliography* (Westport, CT: Greenwood Press, 1992).

Meade, J., *Planning and the Price Mechanism: The Liberal-Socialist Solution* (London: George Allen and Unwin, 1948).

—, *The Theory of International Economic Policy: Trade and Welfare* (London and New York: Oxford University Press, 1955).

McNelis, P., and R. Driskill, 'In Memoriam: Jurg Niehans 1919–2007', *Journal of International Money and Finance*, 28:5 (2009), pp. 739–41.

Mints, L., *Monetary Policy for a Competitive Society* (New York: McGraw-Hill, 1950).

Mintz, A., and S. Redd, 'Framing Effects in International Relations', *Synthese*, 135:1 (2003), pp. 193–213.

Mises, L. von, *Human Action: A Treatise on Economics* (London: William Hodge, 1949).

—, 'The Gold Problem', *The Freeman*, 15:6 (1965), at http://www.thefreemanonline.org/featured/the-gold-problem/ [accessed 24 August 2012].

Modigliani, F., 'Comment on Arthur Laffer', in F. Machlup, W. Salant and L. Tarshis (eds), *International Mobility and Movement of Capital* (Washington, DC: NBER Books, 1972), at http://www.nber.org/chapters/c4140.pdf [accessed 24 August 2012].

Mosconi, A., 'Notes for the Bürgenstock Conference', in G. Halm (ed.), *Approaches to Greater Flexibility of Exchange Rates: The Bürgenstock Papers* (Princeton, NJ: Princeton University Press, 1970), pp. 199–202.

—, 'A World Currency for a World New Deal', *Perspectives on Federalism*, 2:2 (2010), pp. 239–64.

Mosconi, A., and A. Iozzi, 'The Foundation of a Cooperative Global Financial System', The EU, the US and Global Disorder: The Need for a New Bretton Woods, conference paper (18–9 April 2008), at http://www.astrid-online.it/rassegna/Rassegna-25/30-04-2008/Iozzo_Mosconi_Aspen_18_19_4_08.pdf [accessed 24 August 2012].

Mullen, C., 'Shifting the Odds in the Casino of Academic Publishing through Mentorship', in F. Kochan and J. Pascarelli (eds), *Mentoring: Transforming Contexts, Communities, and Cultures* (Greenwich, CT: Greenwood/Praeger, 2003).

Mundell, R., 'A Theory of Optimum Currency Areas', *American Economic Review*, 51 (1961), pp. 657–65.

Nelson, R., 'Introduction', in National Bureau Committee for Economic Research, *The Rate and Direction of Inventive Activity: Economic and Social Factors* (Washington, DC: NBER Books, 1962), pp. 3–16.

Nelson, T., Z. Oxley and R. Clawson, 'Toward a Psychology of Framing Effects', *Political Behavior*, 19:3 (1997), pp. 221–46.

Niehans, J., 'Monetary and Fiscal Policies in Open Economies under Fixed Exchange Rates: An Optimizing Approach', *Journal of Political Economy* (1968), pp. 893–920.

Nutt, P., 'Framing Strategic Decisions', *Organization Science*, 9:2 (1998), pp. 195–216.

Official Journal of the European Communities, Decision 3–59 (21 January 1959), at http://eur-lex.europa.eu/LexUriServ/LexUriServ.do?uri=DD:I:1959-1962:31959S0003:EN:PDF [accessed 24 August 2012].

Obstfeld, M., and K. Rogoff, 'Global Imbalances and Financial Crisis: Products of Common Causes', Federal Reserve Bank of San Francisco Asia Economic Policy Conference, conference paper (2009), pp. 1–63.

Penrose, E., *The Economics of the International Patent System* (Baltimore, MD: John Hopkins University Press, 1951).

—, *The Theory of the Growth of the Firm*, 3rd edn (Oxford: Basil Blackwell, 1995).

—, 'International Economic Relations and the Large Industrial Firm', in E. Penrose, P. Lyon and E. Penrose, *New Orientations: Essays in International Relations* (London: Frank Cass, 1970), pp. 107–36.

—, 'Strategy/Organization and the Metamorphosis of the Large Firm', *Organization Studies*, 29 (1994), p. 1,117–34.

Pitelis, C., 'On the Garden of Edith', in C. Pitelis (ed.), *The Growth of the Firm: The Legacy of Edith Penrose* (Oxford: Oxford University Press, 2002), pp. 1–15.

Polak, J., 'The Report of the International Monetary Fund', *American Economic Review*, 55:1–2 (1965), pp. 158–65.

Porac, J., and H. Thomas, 'Managing Cognition and Strategy: Issues, Trends and Future Directions', in A. Pettigrew, H. Thomas and R. Whittington (eds), *Handbook of Strategy and Management* (London: Sage, 2002), pp. 165–81.

Posthuma, S., 'The International Monetary System', *Banca Nazionale del Lavoro Quarterly Review*, 66 (1963), pp. 239–61.

Proops, J., and P. Safonov (eds), *Modelling in Ecological Economics* (London: Edward Elgar Publishing, 2005).

Reuss, H., *When Government was Good* (Madison, WI: University of Wisconsin Press, 1999).

Ritzmann, F., 'Money, a Substitute for Confidence?', *American Journal of Economics and Sociology*, 58:2 (1999), pp. 167–92.

Rogers, P., 'Multinational Corporations: A European Review', *Annual of the American Academy of Political and Social Sciences*, 403 (1972), pp. 58–66.

Roosa, R., 'Assuring the Free World's Liquidity', *Business Review Supplement*, Federal Reserve Bank of Philadelphia (1962), pp. 261–74.

—, *Monetary Reform for the World Economy* (New York: Harper & Row, 1965).

—, 'Currency Parities in the Second Decade of Convertibility', in G. Halm (ed.), *Approaches to Greater Flexibility of Exchange Rates: The Bürgenstock Papers* (Princeton, NJ: Princeton University Press, 1970), pp. 49–56.

Rueff, J., 'The West is Risking a Credit Collapse', *Fortune*, 64 (1961), pp. 126–7, 262, 267–8.

—, *The Monetary Sin of the West* (New York: MacMillan, 1972).

Rugman, A., *Inside the Multinationals* (New York: Columbia University Press, 1981).

Saccomanni, F., 'How to Deal with a Global Triffin Dilemma', Conference on the International Monetary System: Sustainability and Reform Proposals, Triffin International Foundation, keynote address (3 October 2011), pp. 1–7, at http://www.bis.org/review/r111007b.pdf [accessed 24 August 2012].

Salant, W., 'The Demand for Money and the Concept of Income Velocity', *Journal of Political Economy*, 49:3 (1941), pp. 395–421.

—, 'Capital Markets and the Balance of Payments of a Financial Center', in W. Fellner, R. Triffin and F. Machlup (eds), *Maintaining and Restoring Balance in International Payments* (Princeton, NJ: Princeton University Press, 1966), pp. 177–96.

—, 'Financial Intermediation as an Explanation of Enduring "Deficits" in the Balance of Payments', in F. Machlup, W. Salant and L. Tarshis (eds), *International Mobility and Movement of Capital* (Washington, DC: NBER Books, 1972), pp. 607–60, at http://www.nber.org/chapters/c3473.pdf [accessed 24 August 2012].

Salerno, J., 'Biography of Gottfried Haberler (1901–1995)', Ludwig von Mises Institute, at http://mises.org/page/1452/Biography-of-Gottfried-Haberler-19011995 [accessed 24 August 2012].

—, 'Ludwig von Mises's Monetary Theory in the Lght of Modern Monetary Thought', *Review of Austrian Economics*, 8:1 (1994), pp. 71–115.

Scitovsky, T., 'The Theory of Balance of Payments Adjustment', *Journal of Political Economy*, 75:4 (1967), pp. 523–31.

Schumpeter, J., *History of Economic Analysis* (Oxford: Oxford University Press, 1954).

Smit, P., 'Women, Mentoring and Opportunity in Higher Education: A South African Experience', in F. Kochan and J. Pascarelli (eds), *Mentoring: Transforming Contexts, Communities, and Cultures* (Greenwich, CT: Greenwood/Praeger, 2003), pp. 129–48.

Snow, D., and R. Benford, 'Master Frames and Cycles of Protest', in A. Morris and C. Muller (eds), *Frontiers in Social Movement Theory* (New Haven, CT: Yale University Press, 1992), pp. 133–55.

Sohmen, E., *International Monetary Problems and the Foreign Exchanges*, Special Papers in International Economics (Princeton, NJ: International Finance Section, Princeton University, 1963).

Solomon, R., *The International Monetary System, 1945–1976: An Insider's View* (New York: Harper & Row, 1977).

Teegen, H., J. Doh and S. Vachani, 'The Importance of Nongovernmental Organizations (NGOs) in Global Governance and Value Creation: An International Business Agenda', *Journal of International Business Studies*, 35 (2004), pp. 463–83.

—, 'The Adequacy of Monetary Reserves', *IMF Staff Papers*, 3:3 (1954), pp. 181–227.

Tobin, J., 'Adjustment Responsibilities of Surplus and Deficit Countries', in W. Fellner, R. Triffin and F. Machlup (eds), *Maintaining and Restoring Balance in International Payments* (Princeton, NJ: Princeton University Press, 1966), pp. 201–12.

—, *Essays in Economics, Volume 4: National and International* (Cambridge, MA: MIT Press, 1996).

Toniolo, G., *Central Bank Cooperation at the Bank for International Settlements, 1930–1973* (Cambridge: Cambridge University Press, 2005).

Triffin, R., Robert Triffin Papers, 1934–1978. Sterling Memorial Library, Yale University, New Haven, CT.

—, *Monopolistic Competition and General Equilibrium Theory* (Cambridge, MA: Harvard University Press, 1940).

—, 'National Central Banking and the International Economy', *Review of Economic Studies*, 14:2 (1947), pp. 53–75.

—, *Europe and the Money Muddle: From Bilateralism to Near Convertibility, 1947–1956* (London: Oxford University Press, 1957).

—, 'Statement in Employment, Growth and Price Levels', Hearings before the Joint Economic Committee, US Congress, 86th Congress, 1st Session, Part 9A (1959), pp. 2,905–54.

—, *Gold and the Dollar Crisis: The Future of Convertibility* (New Haven, CT: Yale University Press, 1960).

—, 'After the Gold Exchange Standard', *Weltwirtschaftliches Archiv*, 87 (1961), pp. 188–207.

—, 'A Brief for the Defense', *IMF Staff Papers*, 8:2 (1961), pp. 192–4.

—, 'The Trade Expansion Act of 1962', *Proceedings of the Annual Meeting*, American Society of International Law, 56 (1962), pp. 139–58.

—, 'Updating the Triffin Plan', in R. Triffin, *The World Money Maze* (New Haven, CT: Yale University Press, 1965), pp. 346–73.

—, *The Balance of Payments and the Foreign Investment Position of the United States*, Essays in International Finance, 55 (Princeton, NJ: International Finance Section, Princeton University, 1966).

—, 'The Balance of Payments Seesaw', in W. Fellner, R. Triffin and F. Machlup (eds), *Maintaining and Restoring Balance in International Payments* (Princeton, NJ: Princeton University Press, 1966), pp. 85–110, especially pp. 102–8.

—, 'The Thrust of History in International Monetary Reform', *Foreign Affairs*, 47:3 (1969), pp. 477–92.

—, 'Jamaica: "Major Revision" or Fiasco?', in E. Bernstein et al., *Reflections on Jamaica*, Essays in International Finance, 115 (Princeton, NJ: International Finance Section, Princeton University, 1976), pp. 45–53.

—, *Gold and the Dollar Crisis: Yesterday and Tomorrow*, Essays in International Finance, 132 (Princeton, NJ: International Finance Section, Princeton University, 1978).

—, 'The Impact of the Bellagio Group on World Monetary Reform', in J. Dreyer (ed.), *Breadth and Depth in Economics: Fritz Machlup—The Man and His Ideas* (Lexington, MA: Lexington Books, 1978), pp. 145–58.

—, 'An Economist's Career: What? Why? How?', *Banca Nazionale del Lavoro Quarterly Review*, 138 (1981), pp. 239–60.

—, 'The IMS (International Monetary System ... or Scandal?) and the EMS (European Monetary System ... or Success?)', *Banca Nazionale del Lavoro Quarterly Review*, 179 (1991), pp. 399–436.

Truman, E., 'International Financial Flows: Catalyst of Change or Threat to Stability', in A. Lamfalussy, B. Snoy and J. Wilson, *Fragility of the International Financial System* (Brussels: PIE-Peter Lang, 2001), pp. 221–6.

—, 'The International Monetary Fund and Regulatory Challenges', Peterson Institution for International Economics Working Paper Series (2009), pp. 1–21.

—, 'The G-20 and International Financial Institution Governance', Peterson Institute for International Economics Working Paper Series (2010), pp. 1–36.

Tversky, A., and D. Kahneman, 'The Framing of Decisions and the Psychology of Choice', *Science*, new ser., 211:4,481 (1981), pp. 453–8.

US Treasury, 'Major Foreign Holders of US Securities (through April 2012)', US Treasury Data and Charts Center (2012), at http://www.treasury.gov/resource-center/data-chart-center/tic/Documents/mfh.txt [accessed 24 August 2012].

Vakil, A., 'Confronting the Classification Problem: Toward a Taxonomy of NGOs', *World Development*, 25 (1997), pp. 2,057–70.

Van Der Heijden, K., *Scenarios: The Art of Strategic Conversation* (Chichester: John Wiley & Sons, Ltd, 2005)

Van Der Mensbrugghe, J., 'Bond Issues in European Units of Account', *IMF Staff Papers*, 11:3 (1964), pp. 446–56.

Vanek, J., *General Equilibrium of International Discrimination: The Case of Customs Unions* (Cambridge, MA: Harvard University Press, 1965).

Verbeke, A., and A. Rugman, 'Environmental Regulations and Multinational Enterprise Strategy', *Academy of Management Review*, 23 (1998), pp. 653–5.

White, M., and P. Khakpour, 'The Advent of Academic Advising in America at the Johns Hopkins University', *The Mentor: An Academic Advising Journal*, 8:4 (2006), at http://dus.psu.edu/mentor/old/articles/061025mw.htm [accessed 24 August 2012].

Wieser, F., *Natural Value (1893)*, ed. W. Smart (New York: Augustus Kelley, 1971).

—, *Social Economics (1927)*, trans. A. Hinrichs (New York: Augustus Kelley, 1967).

Williams, J., *International Trade under Flexible Exchange Rates* (Amsterdam: North-Holland Publishing Co., 1954).

Williamson, J., 'The Benefits and Costs of an International Monetary System', in E. Bernstein et al., *Reflections on Jamaica*, Essays in International Finance, 115 (Princeton, NJ: International Finance Section, Princeton University, 1976), pp. 54–9.

—, 'Machlup and International Monetary Reform', in J. Dreyer (ed.), *Breadth and Depth in Economics: Fritz Machlup—The Man and His Ideas* (Toronto: Lexington Books, 1978), pp. 159–72.

—, 'In Memoriam: Fred Hirsch 1931–1978', *Journal of International Economics*, 8:4 (1978), pp. 579–80.

Wilson, J., 'Le Groupe de Bellagio: origines et premiers pas (1960–1964)', in M. Dumoulin (ed.), *Economic Networks and European Integration* (Brussels: PIE-Peter Lang, 2004), pp. 391–410.

Wonnacott, P., 'A Suggestion for the Revaluation of Gold', *Journal of Finance*, 18:1 (1963), pp. 49–55.

Woods, N., 'The Challenge of Good Governance for the IMF and the World Bank Themselves', *World Development*, 28 (2000), pp. 823–41.

Wray, L., 'Keynes's Approach to Money: An Assessment after Seventy Years', *Atlantic Economic Journal*, 34 (2006), pp. 183–93.

Yeager, L., 'The Triffin Plan: Diagnosis, Remedy and Alternatives', *Kyklos*, 14:3 (1961), pp. 285–314.

—, 'Towards a Reinforced Gold Exchange Standard', Bank of Greece Papers and Lectures, 7 (1961), reprinted in H. Grubel (ed.), *World Monetary Reform* (CA: Stanford University Press, 1963), pp. 292–8.

INDEX

For Product Safety Concerns and Information please contact our EU
representative GPSR@taylorandfrancis.com
Taylor & Francis Verlag GmbH, Kaufingerstraße 24, 80331 München, Germany

www.ingramcontent.com/pod-product-compliance
Ingram Content Group UK Ltd.
Pitfield, Milton Keynes, MK11 3LW, UK
UKHW021618240425
457818UK00018B/633